Bow & River Gigs

Used in the Clear Streams of the Ozarks

Bow & River Gigs

Used in the Clear Streams of the Ozarks

Ray Joe Hastings

Acclaim Press
MORLEY, MISSOURI

Acclaim Press
— Your Next Great Book —

P.O. Box 238
Morley, MO 63767
(573) 472-9800
www.acclaimpress.com

Designer: M. Frene Melton
Cover Design: M. Frene Melton

Library of Congress Cataloging-in-Publication Data

Hastings, Ray Joe, 1937-
Bow & river gigs: used in the clear streams of the Ozarks / by Ray Joe Hastings.
p. cm.
Other title: Bow and river gigs
ISBN-13: 978-1-935001-00-3 (alk. paper)
ISBN-10: 1-935001-00-0 (alk. paper)
1. Bowfishing--Missouri--Ozarks, Lake of the. 2. Spear fishing--Missouri--Ozarks, Lake of the. I. Title. II. Title: Bow and river gigs.

SH459.H36 2008
799.1'409778493--DC22

2008014370

Printed in the United States of America
First Printing: 2008
10 9 8 7 6 5 4 3 2 1

Additional copies may be purchased for $24.95 (plus $3.50 shipping) each from Acclaim Press or the author: Ray Joe Hastings
HC 6, Box 338
Doniphan, MO 63935
(573) 996-7580

Cover photo: *The author, Ray Joe Hastings, is shown standing in Buffalo Creek. The bow, shaft and 2 prong bow gig were all hand made by him.*

Contents

Acknowledgments

This book could not have been written without the help of many people, and I would like to thank each and every one for his or her contribution in helping me put the book together. The information took a long period of time to gather (16 years), came from a variety of sources and from several counties. There were many people that freely gave me the bows or spikes they had, sometimes both. Many people sold me one or both and shared the history of the items–if they knew it, or sometimes we would trade, if I had something they preferred over the bow or spike.

I would like to give a personal "Thank you," to my wife, Pauline (Polly), who worked long hours cleaning up the jumbled-up mess of words I had put down on paper. I do not, by any stretch of the imagination, claim to be a writer, but I did have a great deal of history and information on the subject, as well as the bows and spikes, and thought that this story should be told. Without Polly's help it would have been almost impossible for me to have written this book, and I appreciate everything she did.

A special thank you to Bryan and Renata Culpepper, very good friends of mine, for their help and encouragement as I attempted to write this book.

Also, I would like to thank James E. Price, Ph.D. Archeologist (National Park Service, Ozark National Scenic Riverways) who unselfishly shared his knowledge of bows and spikes with me. He was indirectly responsible for my collecting of these objects used in fishing and hunting when he piqued my interest in them by showing me a two-prong he had found. He called it a spike–I called it a bow gig–and after our discussion I began finding some of them, which began my collection.

I especially want to thank Gene Braschler, a close friend of mine, who in his younger days bow and spiked the creeks of Pratt in Ripley County, Missouri, and who wrote his story when I asked him to contribute his knowledge of that areas bow and spiking activities for me. A big "Thank you" to Nick Hatch, who is also an author, for repeatedly urging me to write this book.

I would also like to thank Bill Davis for sharing the facts on pine torches and how they were made, and for the information on the years that he used them, which were 1938-1943. Thanks to Melvin Rogers for his sharing the knowledge of the coal oil (kerosene ball), a light that was used in the early years for gigging. The story is told elsewhere in this book.

A special thanks to the Harlin Museum of West Plains, Missouri, who owns the copyright of the story of John Counts, a bow and arr (arrow) fisherman of Reynolds County, Missouri, and who let me reprint it in its entirety. I would also like to thank the Saunder's Gun Museum of Berryville, Carroll County, Arkansas for their use of the picture of the collection of both river gigs and bow spikes that are located in their museum.

In addition, thanks to the Ozark National Scenic Riverways Park Service for their use of the picture and information of the spike that was archaeologically recovered from the refuse pit near Round Springs in Shannon County, Missouri.

Last, but certainly not least, I would like to thank Doug Sikes and the Acclaim Press Publishing Company for believing in my ability to compile this information into a book and for their encouragement and willingness to publish the book for me.

Although space will not allow me to thank each person individually, I would like everyone to know that this book could never have been written without all the help that I have received, and I really appreciate everyone who helped or contributed in any manner toward its compilation.

Prologue

The terms "bow and spikin'" or "bow giggin'" are hard to trace back to when they were first used or to their beginning. Around 1931 or 1932 is the earliest I have found, and both were in use by then. The use of these terms may go back a little farther, maybe to the 1920s, and possibly earlier. But wait, a third and a fourth term were also used! In the 1940s, one man referred to the sport as "bow fishing," and this was what he called it during all the years that he bow and spiked.

L.L. Broadfoot wrote a story in 1938, about John Counts that is told in this book. Mr. Counts stated that he was a "bow and arr'" (arrow) fisherman by profession, so maybe he had not heard of the other three names by which the sport was called.

In the area where we lived, the term "bow giggin'" was used by my dad, uncle, cousins, and others. That was all I had ever heard it called, while it was called "bow and spikin'" in an area less than ten miles south and southeast of us. The term "bow fishing" and "bow and arrow fishing" never caught on like the other two names did, so they are less important except for the historical value.

Whatever it was called, it came to be a way of life and a way to help people survive in the hills. Ozark hill people did not talk much about what they were doing–especially if they thought it was illegal–so no one knew what his neighbor was up to. In the 1930s, 1940s, and 1950s, houses were few and far apart, which put some distance between families and added to the secrecy of whatever was going on.

Money and food were scarce; therefore, gigging was one way the Ozark hill people found they could help feed their families. Those who lived close enough to get together would also use it as a form of entertainment, since there was very little of that in the early days. Also, the southeastern Missouri Ozarks were in somewhat of a time-warp, or a "cultural lag," might be a better definition, since they depended very little on the industrialized outside world that others were so dependent on, choosing to make most of the tools that their types of lifestyle needed for their subsistence.

My purpose for writing this book is not only to inform the reader of some of the history of how the early settlers came to the southeastern Missouri and northeastern Arkansas Ozarks, but also how they began to use the bow and gig to procure their food in the rivers and creeks that flow through this area. I also wanted to show some of the collection of bows and gigs that I have been able to put together through the years. It is my wish that everyone reading this book will enjoy it as much as I have had the pleasure of writing it, and as much as I have enjoyed putting my collection together these past years.

Anatomy of a Gig

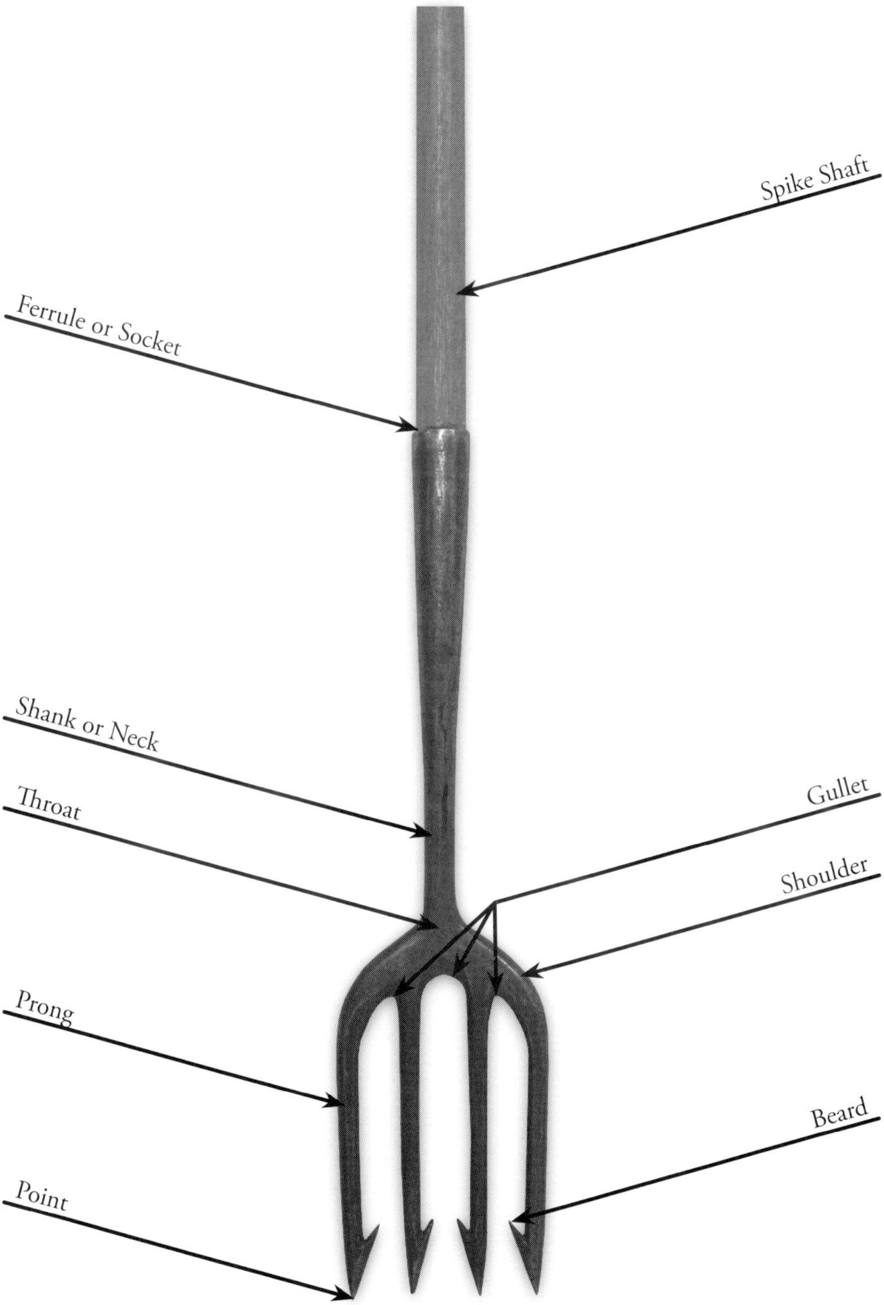

History of Bow and River Gigs

The Background

In 1803, as the United States was in the process of purchasing the vast portion of land from France that would become known as the Louisiana Purchase, the bow and arrow had already been in use for about two thousand years by the Native American Indians. Whether its invention came about as a means of protection or for the procurement of food is not known. What is known is that the early white settlers who came into the southeastern Missouri and northeastern Arkansas Ozarks, which were included in the Louisiana Purchase, knew about the bow and arrow; and some of them probably also used the primitive bow to hunt for food.

When the early settlers started migrating to this new land after 1803, the flintlock rifle was already in use. Most of the families kept one for protection and as a means of obtaining food, which was abundant and ready for the taking. Deer, bear, elk, and a few buffalo were just some of the big game that the settlers found when they entered this new land; but they also encountered many species of smaller game such as turkey, rabbit, squirrel, raccoon, and beaver.

Westward the early settlers came, slowly migrating, mostly from the Tennessee and Kentucky regions. They were undaunted by the hardships that lay ahead; and they kept coming, family after family, staking their claims. The valleys along streams were fertile land and so the settlers, who were subsistence farmers first, would stake their claims along the rivers and creeks that flowed through the new land. They supplemented their food raised on the farms with hunting, trapping and fishing. Most families had only a horse or a team of horses and a plow to break the ground, so most farms were small. Forty to one hundred acres was all that was needed, and was all that could be taken care of by a family. Keep in mind this was before the Homestead Act of 1862 granted 160 acres to any family that lived on and cultivated a farm for a period of five years.

After choosing a place for a home to be built, trees were cut down, cut to length, and then were laid in place. Sometimes the logs were hewn out, which means the logs were squared with an axe. Shingles for the roof were rived out of a block of wood, usually white oak. A fireplace that was used for cooking and warmth in the winter was put in one end of the cabin. Most homes were very small, usually one or two rooms at the most. Sometimes the loft was used for sleeping as the family grew, because in the early days it was normal for a married couple to have as many as six to ten children, and sometimes more. The practice of having large families was carried on as late as the mid 1900s.

After the cabin was built and the land cleared, the family needed to put in a patch of corn. Corn was the main staple to not only feed the chickens that produced the eggs and the hog that was butchered in the fall of the year, but it was also ground into cornmeal and used for cooking by the settlers. A place for a garden was always planned, and all of the members of the family were required to take part in planting the precious seeds that were saved from year to year; or in later years, could be ordered from mail-order catalogues.

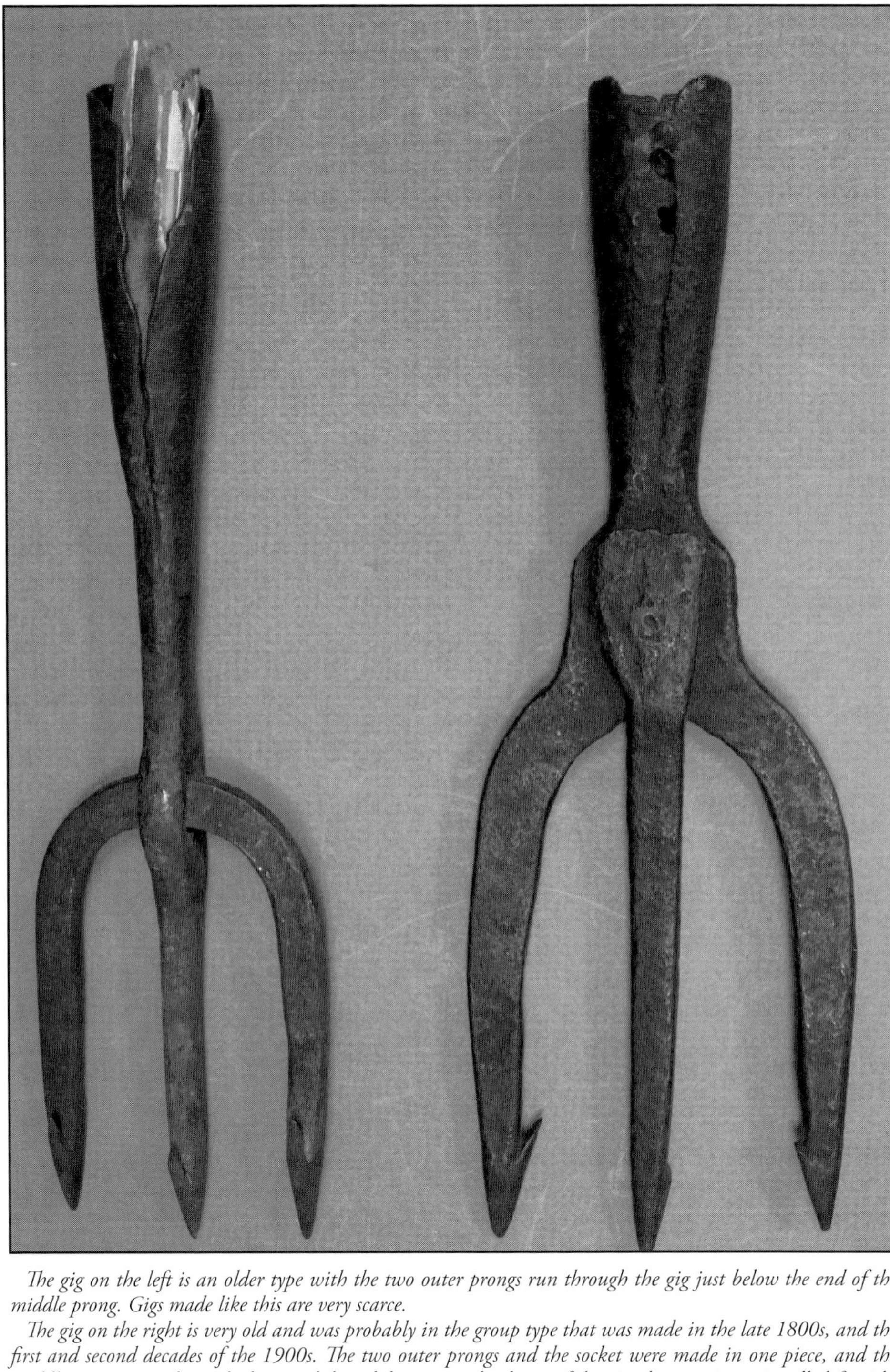

The gig on the left is an older type with the two outer prongs run through the gig just below the end of the middle prong. Gigs made like this are very scarce.

The gig on the right is very old and was probably in the group type that was made in the late 1800s, and the first and second decades of the 1900s. The two outer prongs and the socket were made in one piece, and the middle prong was split at the base and shoved down over the throat of the gig, that was intentionally left wide, and then forge-welded together. A steel brad was heated to a cherry red, and was then inserted through a hole in the prong and throat. A few blows with a hammer spread the brad on each side to further secure the prong to the rest of the gig.

Again, it was usually the entire family that tended the garden–watering and hoeing as it was needed; but the process of preserving the vegetables that had been grown would usually be left up to the women in the family. The countryside would also be diligently searched for blackberries, wild plums, grapes, and crabapples (a small and bitter wild apple). Many families would go on all-day outings, as our family did, to pick those delicious wild offerings. I am unsure of the various methods they used to preserve the foods, but in later years they would be dried, or would be canned for making pies and cobblers. They would also be "put-up" into jellies, jams, or preserves for the long winter months when no other fruit was available. During the fall months, walnuts, hickory nuts, and persimmons would also be gathered for food during the harsh winters. As such jobs were completed, the men had more time to hunt and fish. Since hunting is done mostly in the late fall and winter, this left the spare time in the summer for fishing, which was not only a pleasant pastime but was another way of putting food on the table.

The History of the First Spikes and the Counties that Used Them

The rugged hills of the southeastern Missouri and northeastern Arkansas Ozarks where the early settlers came to live were, for the most part, too rocky to farm. Also, the ground was not as fertile as that in a creek or river valley. As a result, the valleys were chosen first, leaving the rock-covered hills unsettled for many years in the early 1800s. The Ozark Hills have numerous springs that flow from their bases to "head up" the many creeks and rivers that flow through them. The gravel-bottomed, clear-flowing streams were, in fact, the perfect place for the bow and arrow to be used.

Most of the creeks were shallow enough to wade, and any hole of water that was over our heads, we bypassed by getting out on the bank and walking around it. Even the Little Black River had several holes of water in it that one could wade. It had three prongs: the south, middle, and the north prong, and at the place where each one separated, it was more shallow, and therefore more easily waded than downstream below their confluence.

The Current River was a different story because it was mostly too swift and too deep to wade. Nevertheless, it saw its share of bow and arrow fishing, which was mostly done from boats in the cutoffs and bays, or sometimes from the bank (especially when one was after bullfrogs). There were many bays up and down the river that were shallow enough to wade and use the bow and spike. One of them was Spring Bay, which is four miles above Doniphan, Missouri. I used to trap the mouth of this bay when trapping on Current River, and it was shallow enough to wade all the way to the river. Mr. Ernest Murray told me stories of past days when he and others also used to bow and spike this very bay.

A sheet-iron like point was found on a Shawnee Indian site on the Jack's Fork River, a major tributary to the Current River, in Shannon County. This point had a socket

This early spike was found in context with 1830s ceramics and other material at an archaeological site near Round Spring along the Current River within Ozark National Scenic Riverways. Shown to scale, this spike is 8 centimeters long, that is equivalent to 3.149 inches. Photograph courtesy of the National Park Service, Ozark National Scenic Riverways.

for the shaft to fit into. It is not known whether the idea of using the bow and spike was adopted from the Shawnee and Delaware Indians that lived along these rivers in the 1820s, or if it was the idea of the early settlers, or perhaps a combination of both. Sometime in just the last few years, the National Park Service in the Ozark National Scenic Riverways archaeologically recovered a tanged (bearded) spike, in context with 1830s ceramics and other material, at a site near Round Springs along the Current River in Shannon County. The spike, which is 3.149 inches long, is shown above. This early spike did not have a socket, so a hole was drilled up into the shaft, and the end of the spike was driven up and into the hole to secure it to the shaft. At barely over three inches long, there is little doubt that it was meant to be shot with a bow to take fish and possibly rabbits. The sheet-iron point may have been used mostly, if not entirely, for rabbits and other land animals. I do not want to say it could not have been used for fish, as some points similar to that one were made and used in the decades of the 1940s, the 1950s, and perhaps earlier, to bow and spike fish.

Two points, such as the one described above that has the socket and is beardless, are shown in this book. They were made by Mr. Acel Price of Ripley County for me. Mr. Price stated he sometimes used this type of point to bow and spike fish. While the finds are significant, and tell of the early use of the bow and spike, they also may be isolated cases of that use. In a somewhat lengthy discussion about the subject with James E. Price, Ph.D., Archaeologist for the National Park Service, Ozark National Scenic Riverways, we could not recall any find that either of us had made of an early spike in our many trips down through the years of walking plowed fields on Indian sites, and early white settlers homesteads along the rivers and creeks in the southeastern Missouri Ozarks. This, and the lack of any finds by others in other areas, leads me to believe that the bow and spike had very limited use in the early years from the 1820s to 1900. It does not seem to have really taken off until 1910-1920; in fact, the heyday of the use of the bow and spike was short-lived, lasting only forty or fifty years, and most of it had ended by 1960.

A chart on the following page shows the counties in which I know the bow and spike were used in Missouri and Arkansas. I live in Ripley County where most of the bows and spikes were collected and the information was gathered. Without being par-

Usage Areas in Missouri and Arkansas

Heaviest Use Area: *Ripley County, Missouri.* ***Heavy Use Area:*** *Missouri counties of Bollinger, Butler, Carter, Iron, Oregon, Reynolds, Shannon and Wayne.* ***Lighter Use Area:*** *Missouri counties of Christian, Crawford, Madison, St. Francois, Taney and Washington. Arkansas counties of Carroll, Fulton, Randolph and Sharp.*

tial to this county, this is what my research has found: Of the few counties that used the bow and spike, Ripley County seems to have been the county with the most use. At its peak in the late 1940s and early 1950s, there were probably as many as two hundred home-made bows, and other devices to shoot the arrows with; and a conservative estimate of four hundred of the one, two, three, and four-prong spikes in use, plus the other types of spikes such as those made from horse-shoe nails and heavy fence wire.

Why so many in Ripley County? Although other counties in the Ozarks used them, the number of streams seems to have been a plus with the abundance of gentle, rolling hills. There was also a fairly large population of people, which would contribute to their use. Most of the counties to the north of Ripley such as Carter, Wayne, Shannon, and Reynolds have steeper hills–some rivaling small mountains–with fewer streams crossing them. Although I cannot say the origin of taking fish with the bow and spike originated in Ripley County, it seemed to have been the hub of activity. Any direction one goes in the county, many creeks can be found.

To the west of Doniphan are Briar, Lingo, Well's, Tattle, Little Barren Creeks, and the lower stretch of Big Barren (these two creeks were, and still are, quite often pronounced "Little Barn" and "Big Barn" by the Ozark hill people). There is also the east prong of Fourche, as well as the prongs of Buffalo Creek. South of Doniphan one will find Dudley, Wolf, and Well's Creeks on the east side of the river, and on the west side there are Mulberry, Merrill, Hurricane, and Glaze Creeks, and Eagan and Everett Branches. West of South 21 Highway, one will find several prongs of Fourche Creek. The middle, south, and north prongs of Little Black River are up Highway 21, north of Doniphan, and Beaver Dam and Flat Creek, which are both tributaries to the Little Black River, plus the bays and cutoffs on Current River.

As a person travels north on Y Highway, he or she will find Bill's, Simpson, Isaac's, and Capps Creeks. Going east on Highway 142, one will cross Harris and Logan Creeks, which are both large and long creeks. One who travels eastward on Highway 160 will cross Cypress Creek, and southeast of there is Buzzard Run. Other creeks in the county are smaller but still had plenty of fish in them during that time. However, back in those days and times, a creek did not have to be very large to be filled with fish or to be a good one to bow and spike.

Counties other than Ripley that fished with the bow and spike were Carter, Wayne, Butler, Reynolds, Oregon, Shannon, Iron, and Bollinger. Counties that used them on a somewhat lesser scale were Crawford, Washington, St. Francois, and Madison. I have heard of them being used in Reynolds and Oregon Counties, but so far I have not come up with a single specimen from either county. There are also Christian and Taney Counties on the western side of the state that I was told used them. It would seem the several counties such as Ozark, Howell, Douglas, and Texas that are between the two counties of Christian and Taney, and the two counties of Shannon and Oregon, should have had at least limited use of the bow and spike. The counties of Stone, Barry and McDonald, and a few counties north of them may also have used them.

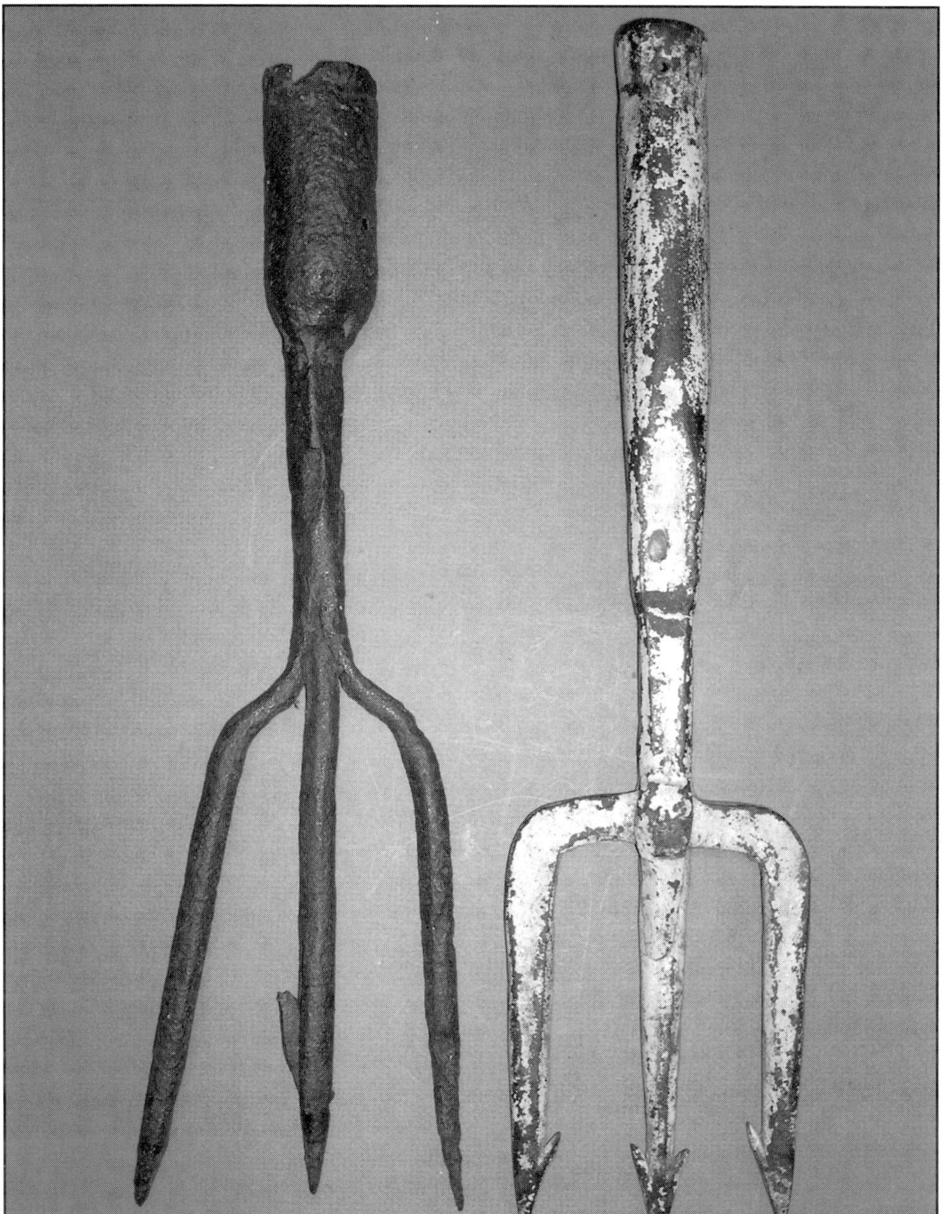

These two river gigs were probably made from the 1880s to about 1910 during the logging boom years. The one on the left is different from the others in my collection, because it has a pivotal beard on the center prong. In other words, it folds back against the prong when the gig is thrust into the fish, and then it unfolds straight out as a better way to keep the fish from getting off the gig.

I traded for the one on the right with a friend of mine, Rick Koogler, from Winona, Missouri in Carter County. In my opinion, the 1880s also saw the long, wooden johnboats come into existence, as the tie and log rafters needed a boat to push back upstream to make-up their next raft. Poling or pushing a johnboat back upstream was the only way to get back to their starting point unless they walked.

The first paddle wheel boat did not come into existence on the Current River at Doniphan, Missouri until 1902, and the professional tie or log rafter could not wait for one as they only ran periodically. The long johnboat with the rake on the front and back ends was also used in these early years for gigging.

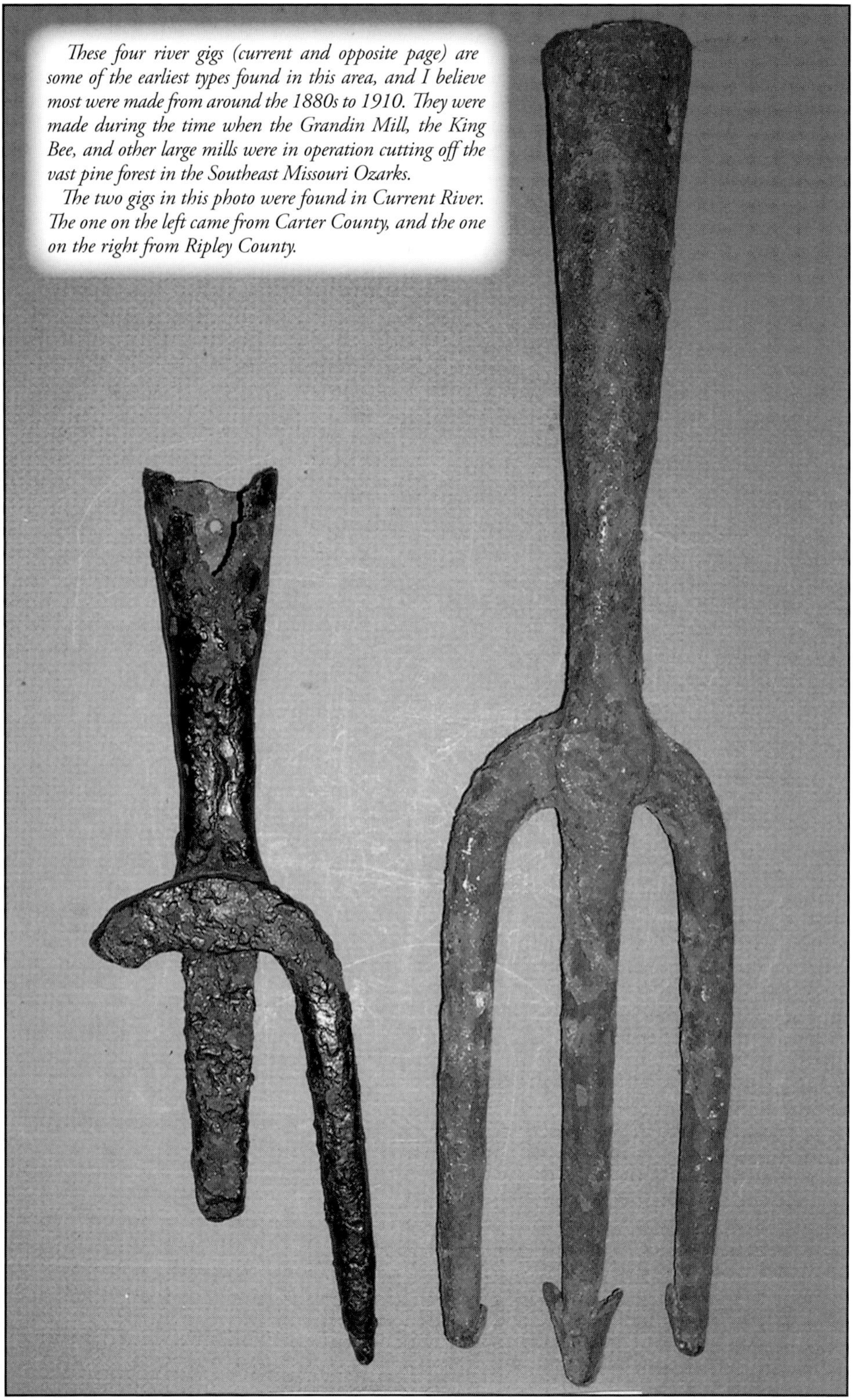

These four river gigs (current and opposite page) are some of the earliest types found in this area, and I believe most were made from around the 1880s to 1910. They were made during the time when the Grandin Mill, the King Bee, and other large mills were in operation cutting off the vast pine forest in the Southeast Missouri Ozarks.

The two gigs in this photo were found in Current River. The one on the left came from Carter County, and the one on the right from Ripley County.

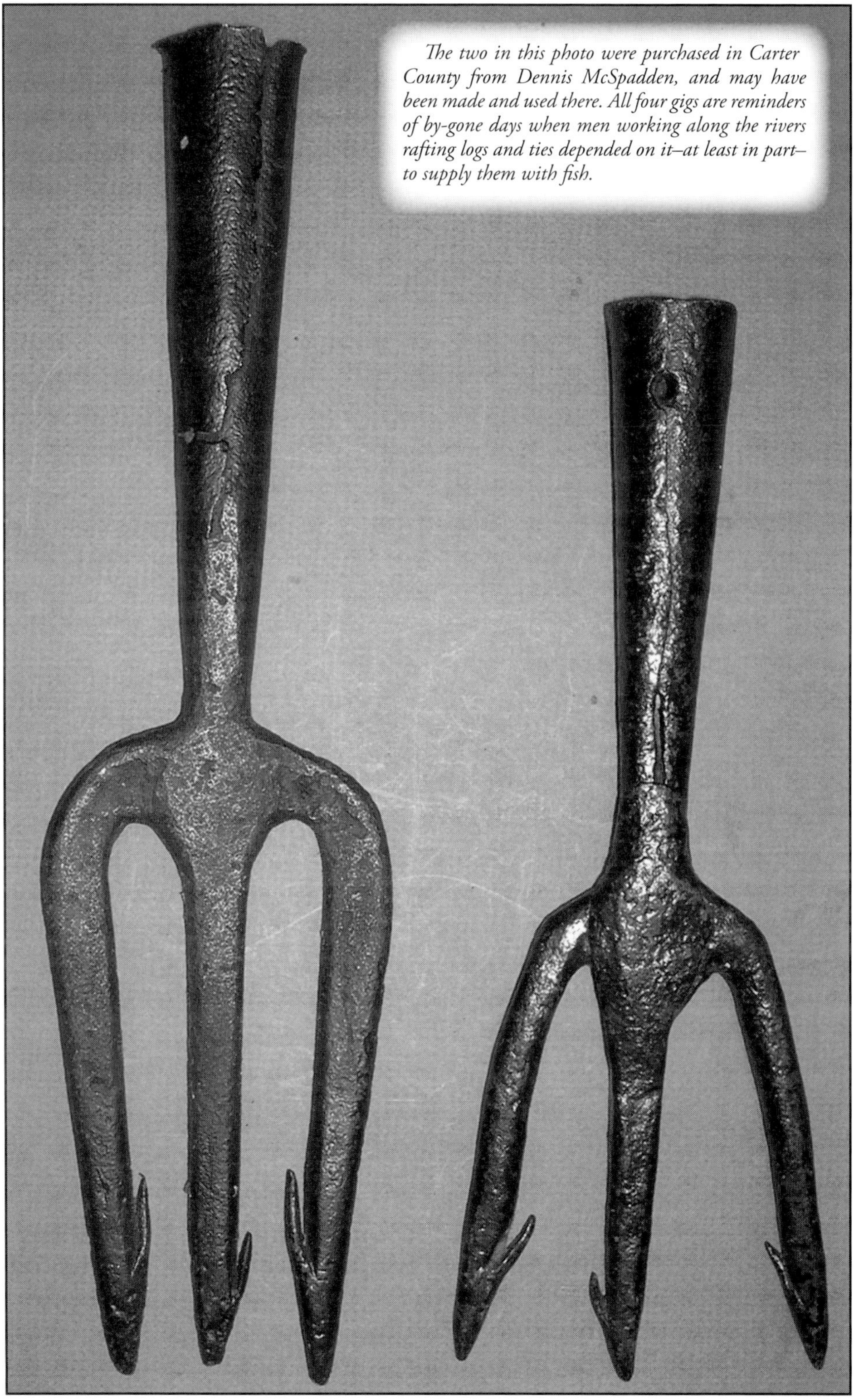

The two in this photo were purchased in Carter County from Dennis McSpadden, and may have been made and used there. All four gigs are reminders of by-gone days when men working along the rivers rafting logs and ties depended on it–at least in part–to supply them with fish.

All of the counties I have named have clear, spring-fed, gravel-bottomed streams flowing through them, which is what makes good streams to bow and spike. I also know of the four counties of Randolph, Sharp, Carroll, and Fulton in Arkansas where men bow and spiked fish because of their abundance of clear streams. There are probably more counties where they were used, but I am unaware of them at the time of the writing of this book. There is nothing in print that I have been able to find of the use of the bow and spike in other areas of the United States. If anyone who is reading this book has any information on the subject being employed elsewhere, I would appreciate a letter or photograph, if available, so the exact area of states can be better defined.

The Increase in the Use of the Bow and Spike and River Gig

"When were the earliest big-river gigs made?" is one of the unanswered, maybe unanswerable questions that bothers me. At this time, no archaeologically recovered river gig has been found that I know about. There are some clues to look for when one tries to determine their ages. Once more I turn to my friend of many years, Dr. James E. Price, who has collected and studied the home-made tools of the early settlers for many years, and is rarely fooled. Dr. Price believes that a few of the older river gigs that the two of us have collected are pre-Civil War (1860-1864), judging by the material and the way they were made. I concur that a few were made at that early time, but like the bow spikes, they were few in number until the 1880s.

Here is what I believe happened that brought about the sudden increase in the use of the bow and spike and river gig in the Ozarks: In the 1880s, timber men from Pennsylvania saw the potential for making money from the vast pine forests of the southeastern Missouri Ozarks, and they bought up several hundred thousand acres of land, mainly in Ripley, Reynolds, Carter, and Shannon Counties. They chose a place by Tolliver Pond, near what was to become known as Grandin, a town in southeast Carter County, Missouri, for the site to set their sawmills. The logging operation that followed required hundreds of men, who worked to cut and haul logs and lay tram lines, as well as those who worked at the mills. My grandfather, Mr. Lucian Hackworth, was one of those men who was employed by the Missouri Lumber and Mining company. Those men worked long, hard hours, usually ten to twelve hours for as little as a dollar to a dollar and a half per day. Before this time period, the people who lived in the southeastern Missouri Ozarks were pretty much a cashless society, i.e., when they needed help, neighbors pitched in to help each other.

In the early 1880s, two big sawmills operated on the east bank of the Current River at Doniphan. The mills were fed mostly by logs that were either rafted or free-floated down the river. Ties were also brought down the river to Doniphan and Van Buren (a town located on Current River about forty miles north of Doniphan). Rivers such as the Black, St. Francis, and the Eleven Point also had logs and ties rafted down the same way; however, the Eleven Point River was so shallow that it was very hard to bring the logs and ties down. By 1909, the virgin pine forest had been depleted and the mills at Grandin closed and moved to West Eminence, several miles northwest of Grandin. A little later a big mill known as "King Bee," located near the Little Black River in Ripley County, also closed, as well as other big mills that depended on the pine trees to keep them going.

When the big mills in Grandin (Carter County), the King Bee Mill in Ripley County, and other mills in the area shut down because of a lack of pine timber, hundreds of men who had been employed by them were suddenly out of work. For most of them, it meant going home to scratch out a meager living as best they could. Not everyone wanted to, or could, hack ties for a living, and so that appears to be when fishing with the bow and spike and river gigging really took off. Before the mills closed, only a few who farmed along the streams used the bow and spike. As I look back and weigh all the evidence, I really think the closing of the big mills had something to do with the sudden increase, which was due to the fact that men were out of work and had to hunt and fish to help feed their families.

The automobile may also have been a factor in the increase of the use of the bow and spike. Sometime during the 1920s, after the invention of the automobile and some improvement of the roads, more and more men and boys fished with the bow and spike. That was also after World War I (1914-1918) when many of the young men arrived home from the war. Although walking two

This picture came from my mom and dad's family picture album. I do not know if this is some of my immediate family, or just some friends of my parents. The picture is very old, probably in the early 1900s, and clearly shows that the bows are very short, probably less than 36 inches. Although the bows could have been used for fishing, they were probably used for land hunting rabbits, squirrels, etc. Also, the bows are shown being held perpendicularly, which is another clue that the bows were used for land animals, because all of the bows used for fishing were held horizontally–at least all that I have ever seen used.

or three miles to fish was a common thing, if one lived that far from a stream, the automobile made it easier to go farther and quicker than simply relying on "shank's mare" (legs) to get there.

However, the increase in the use of the automobile and the closing of the big mills were not the only reasons for the increase. The "Great Depression" (1929-1933) and beyond, witnessed a major increase in fishing with the bow and spike. Many people just could not find jobs, and if they did, they worked for as little as fifty cents a day, or sometimes just for their meals. Several of the bows and spikes in my collection were made in the 1920s and 1930s, a true testimonial to the hardships of that time when men relied in part on the bow and spike for food. Nor did the "hard times" stop in the thirties; the Second World War (1941-1945) inflicted more hardships on people. I was born in 1937, and remember most of the hard times, such as the government allocating ration stamps for coffee, sugar, tires, gas and other things.

Many young men had gone to war, but for those that stayed home, the traditional use of the bow and spike was carried on. By the end of the war, the winds of change had started to blow, and more importance was placed on education. The G. I. Bill made it possible for more and more high school graduates to leave home and go to college. In the late 1940s and 1950s, the big cities also beckoned, and no longer did the young men stay on the small farms to "carry on" in their father's footsteps. In the southeastern Missouri Ozarks, there was a mass migration to St. Louis, Memphis, and many other larger cities as the lure of high-paying jobs was hard to resist. Women had also begun working outside the homes during the war; therefore, more women left the smaller towns to find jobs in the metropolitan areas. This exodus brought more and more changes to the rural areas.

Progress was being made in the early 1950s, and things were really beginning to change. Electricity was being extended out into the rural areas, and televisions were brought into some of the homes. Then a different reason for get-togethers became popular: instead of "bowin' and spikin'" on Saturday nights, people watched television. Slowly but surely, the use of the bow and spike began to wind down as the economy improved and by the mid 1960s, "bow and spikin'" was almost over. A method of taking fish that had been a way of life in the Ozark hill country from at least the 1820s and 1830s to the mid 1960s–except for an isolated pocket here and there–was gone.

Planning the Fishing Trip

In the 1940s and 1950s, the families' fishing trips were sometimes planned on Saturdays when everyone was doing their shopping in the town of Doniphan, Missouri. Throngs of people filled the streets on Saturdays, and sometimes there would be so many that it was hard to walk through them. The courthouse at Doniphan still has a rock wall around it that was built in the 1930s by the WPA (Works Project Association–a government project that gave men work during the depression when many men were unemployed). It is just the right height to sit on, and back during those busy Saturdays it would be completely full. The women were usually busy doing the family shopping, but the men would be sitting there just talking to their friends, whittling, or playing checkers to pass the time, and just as many would be standing around on the courthouse lawn doing the same thing.

The youngsters would have the opportunity to go to the "picture show" at Hunt's Theatre while their parents were busy with their Saturday activities. I remember the price was ten cents for children under twelve, and thirty-five cents for those who were twelve and over. It was always a great thrill to go to the movie and see all of my favorite cowboys such as Gene Autry and Roy Rogers "whip up" on the outlaws, and once in a while I could even see a Tarzan movie, which I really enjoyed!

When the movie ended, my brother and I would search for our parents, and stay with them before returning to our homes. Somehow in that large crowd, one of my older cousins would always find my dad, and as they had a conversation, my cousin would ask in a low voice, "Want to go bow giggin' tonight, Uncle Joe?" Dad would usually answer, "I guess so." Right away, I would start asking if I could go too, and Dad's answer would always be yes. I can still recall how thrilled and excited I was to be allowed to go bow giggin', which was what my dad and cousins called it.

At that time my family lived on the east bank of Briar Creek, about four miles west of Doniphan. The starting point was about a mile and a half down the creek from our house, and we always tried to get down there about an hour before dark. It was my job, or my older brother Pal's, to lay the bows in the creek and weigh them down with a rock to keep them under water to soak for about thirty minutes to an hour prior to beginning; the soaking kept them from breaking when strung. The bow spikes were also placed in the creek to let the shaft, which was made of wood, swell so the shaft and spike would be even tighter. Even though we usually used a tack to secure the small spike to the shaft, Dad and my older cousin Junior, or Johnny Belcher, would be busy checking out our one-mantle Cole-

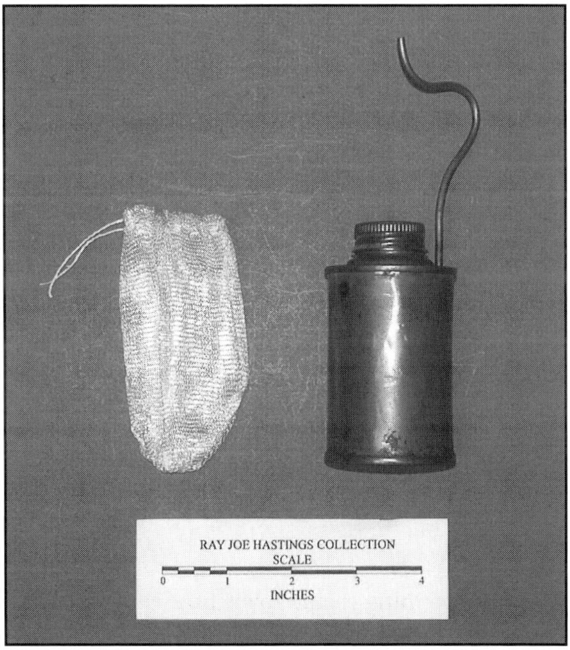

A single, long mantle like the lantern our family used, and the small metal can with the spout that was used to fill the cup or tray with alcohol inside the lantern globe. These are very hard to find, and the only one I have seen in my sixteen years of research.

The lantern on the left is a complete lantern like the one on the right that has the globe missing. Both used only one mantle and a cup that we would fill with alcohol, and then light to warm the generator before it was turned on. The alcohol was put in the cup with a special, small tin can with a bent tube about four inches long coming out of the can, and inserted up through a hole in the lantern to fill the cup or tray that held the alcohol. The lantern on the right is the one we used in the 1940s and 1950s. The globe is missing but otherwise still usable. It burned white gas or kerosene, and is still readable on the side of the lantern.

man lantern, which Dad always kept filled with white gas in readiness for our "bow and spikin'" trips. The lantern had a warm-up generator, and a small can that had about a four-inch crooked spout came with the lantern. The spout was placed through a hole in the bottom of the lantern, and a small cup inside the lantern close to the mantel was filled with alcohol. The alcohol was then lit and let burn until the generator was hot enough to light the lantern when it was time to use it.

When it was almost dark, the many varieties of frogs would begin croaking, which was Dad's signal to carefully string the bows. We pumped the lantern up once more for good measure, and lit it. Then we would ease into the cool water. At that spot on the creek we usually stopped on a good gravel bar at the upper end of a long hole of water. Although we liked to gig upstream better, we would often gig downstream through a hole of water and sometimes in the two or three holes below it. Then we would turn around and gig back upstream, usually killing more fish going back upstream.

Because I was the youngest of the three or four in the group, I carried the light first as we slowly waded along. I would be in the middle of the creek holding the lantern with Dad and my cousin on either side. Each could see his side of the creek fairly well, except when a fish would be lying beside a rock or log. I remember just like it was yesterday, Dad saying, "Shine the light over here, son, I think I see one." I would take one or two steps toward Dad, tilting the light just a little to better illuminate the fish for him, and to keep the light from shining in Dad's eyes as he lowered his bow to shoot the fish.

Left: *Some bow and spikin' at night was done with a carbide light such as this one to illuminate the fish. It was attached to a man's cap, leaving both hands free to hold the bow and spike, and allowing one man to fish by himself. With a lantern, it took two men, one to hold the lantern, and one to use the bow and spike.* ***Above:*** *Side view.*

When the fish was shot, it would thrash vigorously, causing the top of the spike shaft to churn the top of the water. We would always try to pin the fish down until it quit thrashing. Sometimes they would get off if we did not pin them down. Then we would pull the fish off the spike, and place it in a tow sack that Dad carried around his waist when we bow and spiked. The lower part of the sack would be underwater, keeping the fish wet and alive. By tying the sack around his waist in that way, Dad's hands were free to continue bow spikin'. Some men preferred to use a finger-sized tree limb with one short fork attached that was tied to the hammer loop of their overalls in order to string the fish.

We gigged fish as we made our way back upstream toward our house. The person holding the light would swap with someone else, and I would always get my turn to shoot my share of the fish. When we had enough fish, we stopped gigging and walked home. The fish were divided equally, so that everyone had a fair share, or sometimes a fish fry was set for the next day, which was always a treat for the family, and something that everyone really enjoyed.

Families Gathering on the Creek Banks

One very interesting story about how the families spent their weekends in the Ozarks was related to me by a man who used the bow and spike, and is worthy of being passed along. He lived near one of the prongs of Little Black River, and he said that a few families would get together on the weekends to camp out, fish, picnic, and visit. That was one way that many people in the hill country relaxed after a hard week of work by gathering at a well-known fishing spot on some clear stream. During this time, all of the 1940s and some of the 1950s, was before electricity had been extended out into the rural areas, so there was no staying home and watching television. All that was to come later.

The men and boys would get together to discuss which part of the stream they were going to bow and spike. Some would fish upstream, and some would walk downstream and fish back up. Sometimes on the larger streams, a slightly bigger gig that I call an intermediate size, was carried by one person to gig the bigger fish. It could also be used in deeper water, and was used like the big-river gigs today. This type of gig was only slightly bigger than the bow spike and had a six or seven-foot handle, and usually had three prongs. The planning and anticipation of the gigging trip was an exciting part of weekend camping experience.

While the men were gone, the women would visit and start preparing the meal. They would time the cooking of the food so that the fish could be included when the men and boys returned with them. After the meal was over, everyone would sit around and visit. Of course, the men would be bragging about the size of the fish they had spiked, or the big one that got away, while the women usually talked about other things. The children would be running around playing, or maybe getting into some kind of mischief, and as it began to get dark, perhaps catching fireflies. If the families were planning to spend the night, they would drag up enough firewood to feed the fire during the night. One thing was for certain: everyone had a good time during those types of "get-togethers."

Anticipation ran high as darkness approached, because that was when the bigger fish came out of hiding. Although a person could kill all the fish he needed during the day, nighttime was better. The bright light would usually hold the fish long enough to get a close shot and a "sure kill." After a few hours of fishing, the men and boys returned to camp to spend the rest of the night sleeping by the campfire under a starry sky. I have done that very thing many times as a young teenager, sometimes with my dad, my brother, and my cousins, but more often just by myself.

An Ozark tree-limb fish stringer. This type of stringer was used until the manufactured metal fish stringer came along. Some of us older Ozark fishermen sometimes use the tree limb stringer even today. Illustration by Billy Yates.

I sometimes find myself thinking about what kids today are missing. There is nothing quite like camping out on a creek bank on some clear Ozark stream with the full intention of catching a big string of bullheads after it gets dark, but then to hear a barred owl a hundred yards upstream. I remember as a young teenager when this happened to me, and my reaction the first time I heard that nine-note series of hoots they make that sounds as if they are saying, "Who cooks for you, who cooks for you all?" It was so unnerving to me that I hurried back to the safety of my camp, added some more wood to the fire, called my two dogs close to me, and that was where I spent the rest of the night!

Sometimes during the overnight stays on the creek, my dad and I would set out limb lines, or a throw line or two, and bait them with small frogs. Then early in the morning, or maybe a time or two during the night, we would run them and take the fish we had caught off the hooks and put them on a tree limb stringer. We would stick the end of the limb stringer in the bank of the creek at water level to keep the fish alive and fresh until we were ready to walk home, since Dad did the fish cleaning when we got home.

Daytime Bow and Spike Fishing by Wading in the Creek

In the daytime it was more difficult to bow and spike the fish than at night. A light was used at night and it would hold them. In other words, the fish would not swim away when the light was on them. In the daytime, however, when we walked upstream in a slow and easy manner, the fish would ofttimes stay until we were close enough to shoot the spike into them. It is good to remember that back in those days, the creeks were full of fish, and one could get all of the fish he needed in a two or three-hour period.

Most of the fish that were bow and spiked were the many different types of sunfish. Sometimes a hog sucker could also be found lying on the creek bottom. I remember the first time I saw a big hog sucker down Briar Creek. Dad and I were fishing down the creek when I saw it. I told Dad to stop because I saw a big fish. I was using a single-prong bow spike, and Dad had a two-prong. I wanted Dad to shoot the fish because I was afraid I would miss. Just about then the muddy water we had kicked up covered the fish until we could not see it, and those few moments that it took for the water to clear was all the fish needed to make its getaway. We stood there, watched it swim downstream out of sight, and we never did get that fish!

One of the reasons that everyone liked to fish upstream rather than downstream was that when wading upstream, the mud or leaves that are kicked up stay behind and do not spook the fish. Of course, a person also had to wade very slowly, which would also reduce the size of the waves, which would sometimes scare the fish away.

I have many happy memories of my younger days when I used to go "bow and spikin'" with my dad. One that I vividly remember was on a hot summer day when

Dad told me to get the bows and spikes and we would go fishing. I was always eager to go, but the creek was really low due to the heat and dry weather, and we had not been killing too many fish. About two miles up Briar Creek from our house, we came upon a long hole of water that had several big fish in it, so we began chasing them to the upper end of that long hole of water. Since they could not go up over the shoal, when we got close to them they would swim by us back downstream. We would try to shoot them, but they were swimming so fast that we would miss. Back downstream we would go after them, and after missing them on the lower end as they swam past us again, we would go back to the upper end. After four or five times of doing that, Dad got angry, and as they swam by us back downstream, he raised his bow and arched an arrow, and some thirty yards downstream from us the two-prong bow gig, as they were called, landed on one of the fish. One prong landed on one side of the fish, and the other prong landed on the other side. Although it was just a lucky shot made in desperation, it was a "moment in time" that I shared with my dad, and one I shall never forget!

The Best Shot

Each area had their best shot with a bow and spike. This was someone who could make long shots, such as my dad had made with his "lucky shot," and who could hit the fish more often than not. These legendary "shots" live on, and every once in a while, even today, someone will tell me about a certain person who was the best shot they had ever seen. They will tell stories about people who were able to shoot and hit fish from forty to fifty feet away, although most of us had to be real close in order to make a good, clean shot.

Another problem was that there was always the risk of dulling the spike if the shot was missed and it went into the gravel and rock streambed. Dad always carried a file to sharpen the points on the small gigs just in case a rock was ever hit. When we were close to the fish, we only had to pull the bow back a few inches, which would be just enough to shoot through the smaller fish, or into the bigger fish. All fish, regardless of species and if big enough were shot, including bull frogs and sometimes turtles.

The Beginning of the Heavy use of the River Gig

I once heard someone say that the fish gig was almost as old as the Ozark Mountains. This may have been just a figure of speech, but as I stated earlier, I tend to think the big river gig that is still in use today did not come into existence in large numbers in the southeastern Missouri Ozarks until the early 1880s.

On page 29 is a picture of two river gigs belonging to me and one three-prong spike belonging to Dr. James E. Price. The river gig on the right was found in Cur-

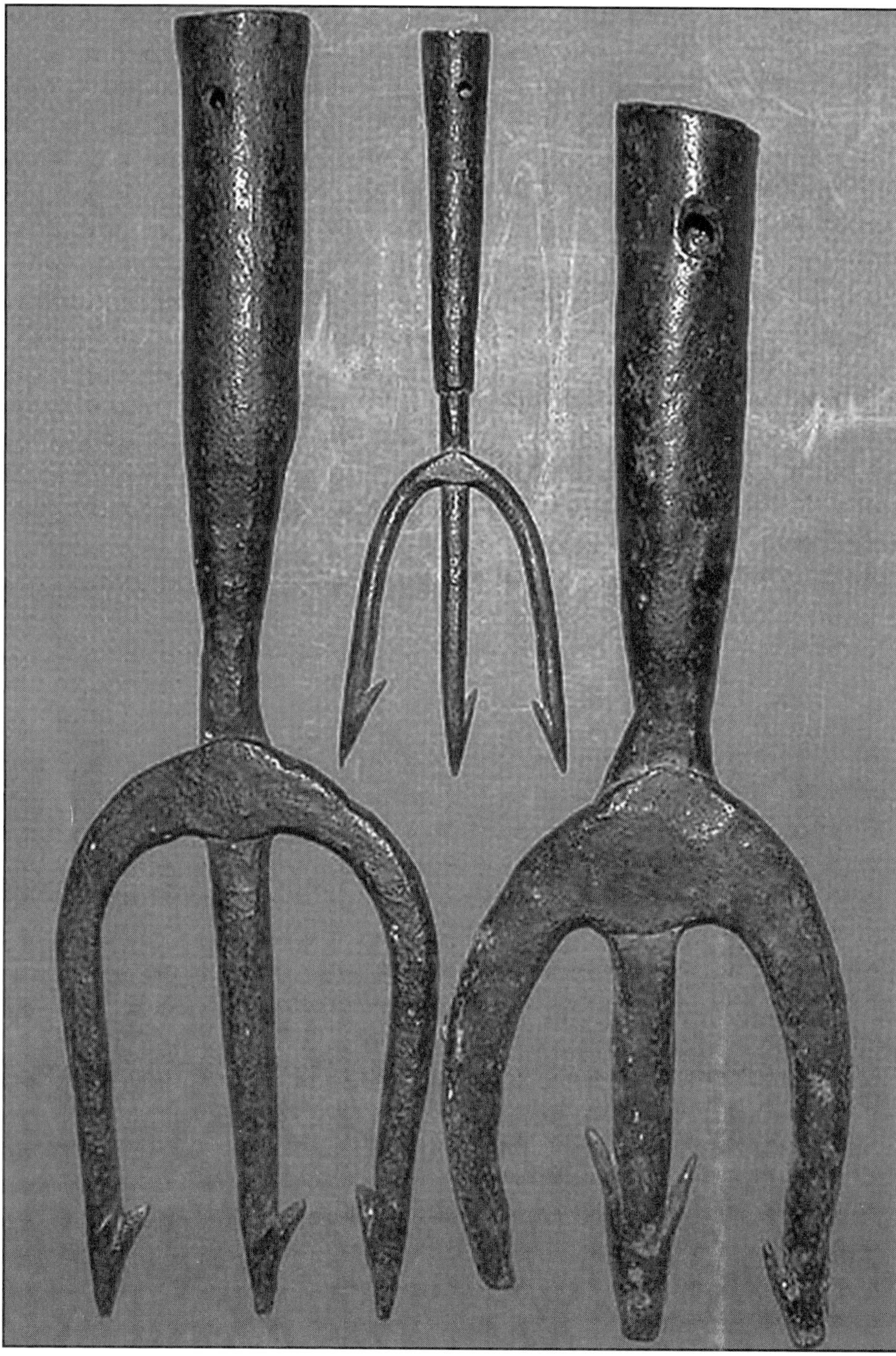

The three-prong river gigs on the left and on the right are the earliest types of gigs in my collection. The one on the right was found in Current River about five miles below Doniphan in what is known as "The Loftis Hole." The two outer prongs are made from a mule shoe. The spike in the center is very rare, and it is owned by Dr. James E. Price. It is the only one I have seen made like the two river gigs. All three were probably made in the 1880s-1910. More is written on these three early gigs in the book.

rent River a few miles down stream from Doniphan, Missouri by Mr. Rad Talbert. I purchased this gig a few years later in a Talbert yard sale. The two outer prongs were made from a mule shoe that was forge-welded to the center prong and socket, which is also made from one piece of steel. The oblong and large nail hole in the socket may be a clue to the approximate age of the gig. Although the nail is gone, it appears that a square nail was used (sometime after 1900 manufactured round nails would have been used).

The big gig on the left was made on the same pattern. The two outer prongs are forge-welded to the center prong. Although the nail hole in the socket is round, I believe they are of the same approximate age, because the patterns of the gigs are the same. One noteworthy piece of information found about these early gigs, is they are always three-pronged.

The small three-prong spike in the center is the only one I have ever seen made on the same pattern as the two big-river gigs in the picture with it. It belongs to Dr. James E. Price, and was purchased by his dad, Mr. Acel Price, in the early 1960s at an auction house in West Doniphan. This was a very significant find because it shows that the small three-prong spike was in use at the same time the other two big gigs were being used. The big question is, "Which is the oldest, the spike, or the big-river gigs?"

At one time I thought the big-river gig was the oldest, and the spikes were patterned after them; however, after further study of the tanged spike found in the refuse pit in Shannon County, and the study of the three-prong spike that Dr. Price possesses, I think it is the other way around. I believe they all had their beginnings from a single spike such as the one found in the refuse pit, and it too, may have had its origin from a flint, or iron point copied from the Indians. In my sixteen years of research, these are some of the oldest river gigs that I have found. In fact; altogether, I have only found about fifteen of these older types of gigs, and I believe most of them date after the Civil War, 1860-1864, and probably around the 1880s to 1910, and perhaps a little later.

The Appearance of Log and Tie Rafting, and Johnboats

Why did the use of the gigs suddenly increase in greater numbers in the 1880s? I think it was because of two things. The first thing was the rafting of logs and ties down the river to towns such as Van Buren and Doniphan. On September 2, 2000, six other men and I, along with the help of many others, assembled a tie raft and brought it down from Bay Mill Eddy to just above the Doniphan Bridge, which is a distance of eight miles. I noted that on the long, slow holes of water, there was not much to do on the raft but wait for the next swift shoal or sharp bend in the river where the action picked up. I realized that during the days of rafting logs and ties down the river, this would have given a gigger quite a bit of time to "gig a mess" of fish to eat, or maybe to sell when they reached their destination.

The early tie and log rafters lived, at least in part, off the land and from the streams they were around and on every day. So it was only natural that the river, which was full of fish at that time, was a source of food, and the gig was an easy and fast way to take them. There is nothing better than a "big mess" of fish that one has just caught or gigged cooked up on the gravel bar and I am sure that the men who worked long, hard days on the river thought so too.

I know that in the 1920s gigs were taken on a tie raft that was brought down to Doniphan by Mr. Howard Steen and his brother Mr. Edmond Steen. Howard Steen was a carpenter, and a brick and stone mason. I worked a few years for Mr. Steen, and he related this story to me. Keep in mind that in the 1920s, the river ran along the east side by Tunnel Bluff; it now runs on the west side that is known as Gooseneck. (These well-known named places are located at the Carter/Ripley County line on Current River.) Howard Steen explained that he and Edmond–Howard on the front of the raft and Edmond on the back–were bringing a raft of ties down to Doniphan. Howard told me that the raft bow punched a rock in the chute at Tunnel Bluff and wrecked, throwing the two river gigs that Howard was going to use out into the river, and those two gigs were never recovered. It is easy to tell from this story and others like it that rafting on the river was one thing that helped bring on the increase of gigging.

The second thing that helped bring on the increase was the appearance of the johnboat. Up until the 1880s, the boat was, for the most part, just a short simple boat, or dugout with very little rake, if any, in the front of the boat. This soon changed as the professional tie rafters had to have a way of getting back upstream to haul their oar stem and blade, plus nails or chain dogs, depending on what they were rafting (nails for ties, chain dogs for logs) plus the other gear, hammers, etc. In the early 1880s, and 1890s, the only way to get back up stream was by "poling," or pushing the boat, as the first paddlewheel boat did not come into use on Current River at Doniphan, Missouri until 1902. At least by 1898, and probably earlier, the twenty-two to twenty-six foot, and possibly longer johnboat, with the rake in the front and back, was in use for this purpose.

Mr. Ed Cox rafted ties from 1898 to 1911 on the Current River above Doniphan from as close as Spring Bay, some four miles up river; and as far as Big Springs, some thirty-five miles upriver. According to Mr. Cox, he and his partner would raft down a string of ties, load their johnboat with their rafting gear and pole or push the boat back upstream to build the next raft. One winter alone Mr. Cox and his crew had thirty thousand ties at Well's Creek, which is about five and one-half miles above the Doniphan bridge, to raft down to Doniphan. He stated that it took a day for him and his partner to push the boat upstream from Doniphan to Kelly Hollow (a distance of some twenty-three miles), and from Kelly Hollow to Big Springs, which took half a day (a distance of approximately twelve miles). That was quite a feat of strength and endurance, pushing a twenty-two to twenty-six foot johnboat upstream in the fast-moving waters of the Current River.

This type of early gigging light is almost non-existent, and I feel fortunate to have found two in my sixteen years of collecting gig paraphernalia. These became obsolete in the 1930s when gas lanterns became available. This one was found by a friend of mine, Mr. Allen Pigg, of Doniphan, Missouri in the early 1980s. He found it in Boyles Slough, a spring and river-fed stream that flows back into Current River nearly a mile below its starting point. Knowing my interest in the past history of gigging, Mr. Pigg graciously gave this old fire basket to me.

Some of the steel straps that would have held the pine knots inside are gone, but otherwise, it is intact, including the steel rod that holds the basket over the side of the boat. This would let the burning embers fall into the water. To hold the rod upright, a hole was drilled in a boat seat and the rod was run through the hole and through another drilled board just above the bottom of the boat. This method would hold the light solidly.

Although different types of boats including the dug-out had been around many years prior to the 1880s and 1890s, it is my opinion that it may have been the long johnboat that the professional log and tie rafter used that prompted the sudden use of the big-river gigs that are still in use today. The boats were sturdy and wide enough that one did not have to worry about turning the boat over, and they could be poled upstream far enough to leisurely float back down while gigging. Their light at night was a fire basket made of steel straps filled with pine knots and hung over the side of the boat by a heavy, long steel rod that was run through a hole drilled in a seat that was usually in the middle of the boat, so a gigger could stand on either side of the light. The boat was usually floated down crossways of the river so the giggers could cover a bigger area and thus gig more fish. Pictures of two of these baskets are shown here, and the original fire baskets are on display in the Current River Heritage Museum in Doniphan, Missouri.

Of the three, tie rafting, the wooden johnboat, and gigging, only one remains the same as it was years ago, and that is gigging. The last raft of ties was brought down Current River to Doniphan, Missouri in 1931 by Andrew McDowell and Howard

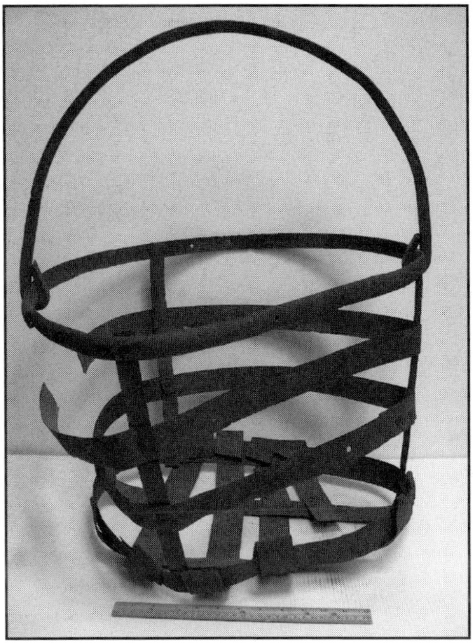 

This fire basket also burned pine knots for a light to gig with, and was found by a good friend, Mr. Ronald Steen in the 1960s, while trapping on Current River in an area known as Cedar Creek in Ripley County. This one is complete, except for the steel rod that is missing.

It took many years to track down and to acquire, as Mr. Steen had sold it to a Mr. Dennis McSpadden of Van Buren, Missouri. Mr. McSpadden has also been a friend of mine for a number of years and eventually sold it to me. Although I may never find another one, my quest still goes on for these old relics, as well as the gigs they provided a light for, and more importantly, the history that surrounds them.

Steen. In Howard's own words, "It was only a small raft of three hundred and fifty ties." Hauling ties and lumber on trucks replaced tie rafting. Today, only a handful of wooden johnboats remain on the Current River, because they have been replaced by commercially manufactured metal boats. As stated earlier, gigging is the only one of the three that is left, and the making of the old type gig is slowly being phased out as more and more gig makers pass on. Only time will tell if the gig will also be replaced by commercially manufactured ones. Luckily for the giggers, there are a few men left who still make gigs, but they too are becoming an elite minority as the years go by. Hopefully, the Missouri Folk Arts Program will be continued, and young men such as Steve Orchard will continue to be trained to carry on the art of gig making as they become masters in the tradition.

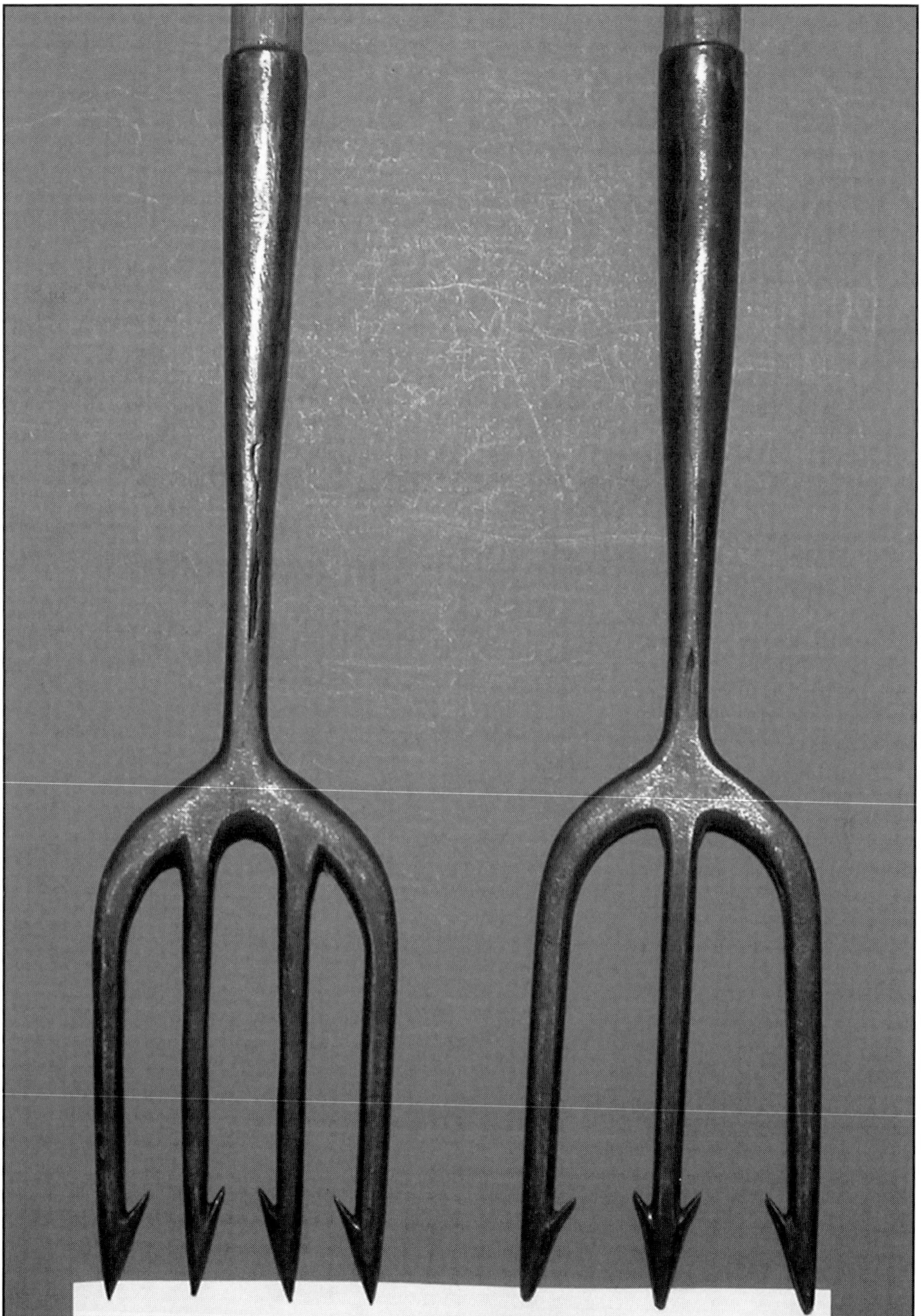

Both of these spikes were made in Ripley County, Missouri by Mr. Ernest (Punk) Murray in 1933. A matched pair, the four-prong on the left is a fine example of Mr. Murray's expertise at gig-making. The three-prong on the right is just as well made. They are both very pleasing to the eye. These three and four-prong spikes do not appear to have been used very much, because the points are still sharp. Mr. Murray probably used some of the other spikes he made more than these. He bow and spiked in Spring Bay, up river from Doniphan about four miles, and also in Simpson and Isaac's Creeks, and Little Black River near Doniphan.

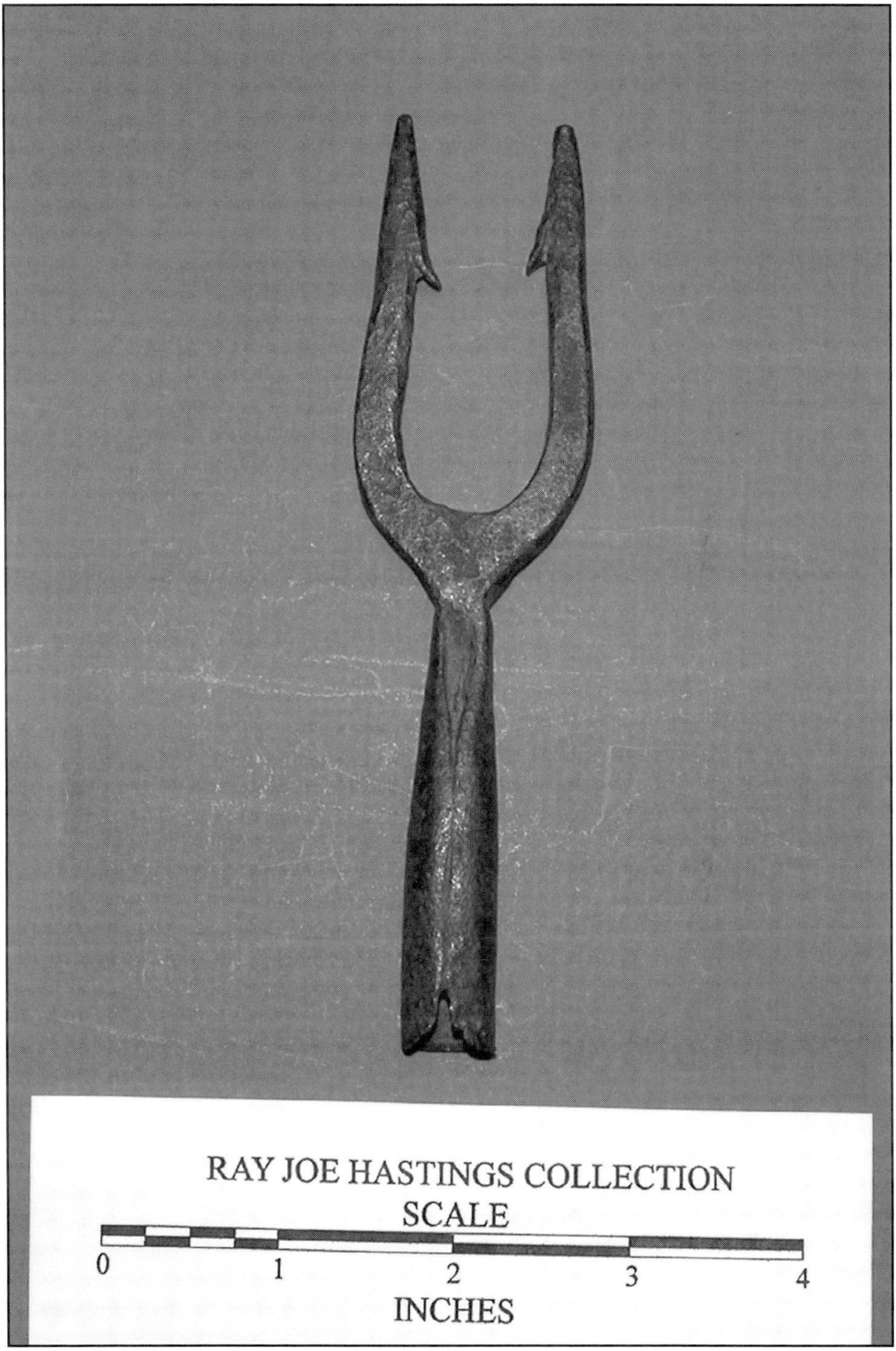

From Ripley County, Missouri. Made by Winfield Bell, a well-known blacksmith who had his shop in Doniphan, Missouri for many years before 1949. Mr. Bell made a large number of gigs, both large river gigs, and small bow spikes during his many years of blacksmithing. His gigs were very well made and durable. They are almost impossible to find today. Shown actual size.

Both of these single spikes were bought at a farm auction in Ripley County, Missouri. They belonged to Mr. John McPheeters, and were made by Mr. Winfield Bell, a blacksmith in Doniphan, Missouri, in the late 1930s. These two spikes were also used by the brothers, John and Glenn Pennington in Little Black River, Ripley County, Missouri. Nowadays, it is hard to believe that during that time period, these could be purchased for as little as fifteen cents each, or two for a quarter. Shwon actual size.

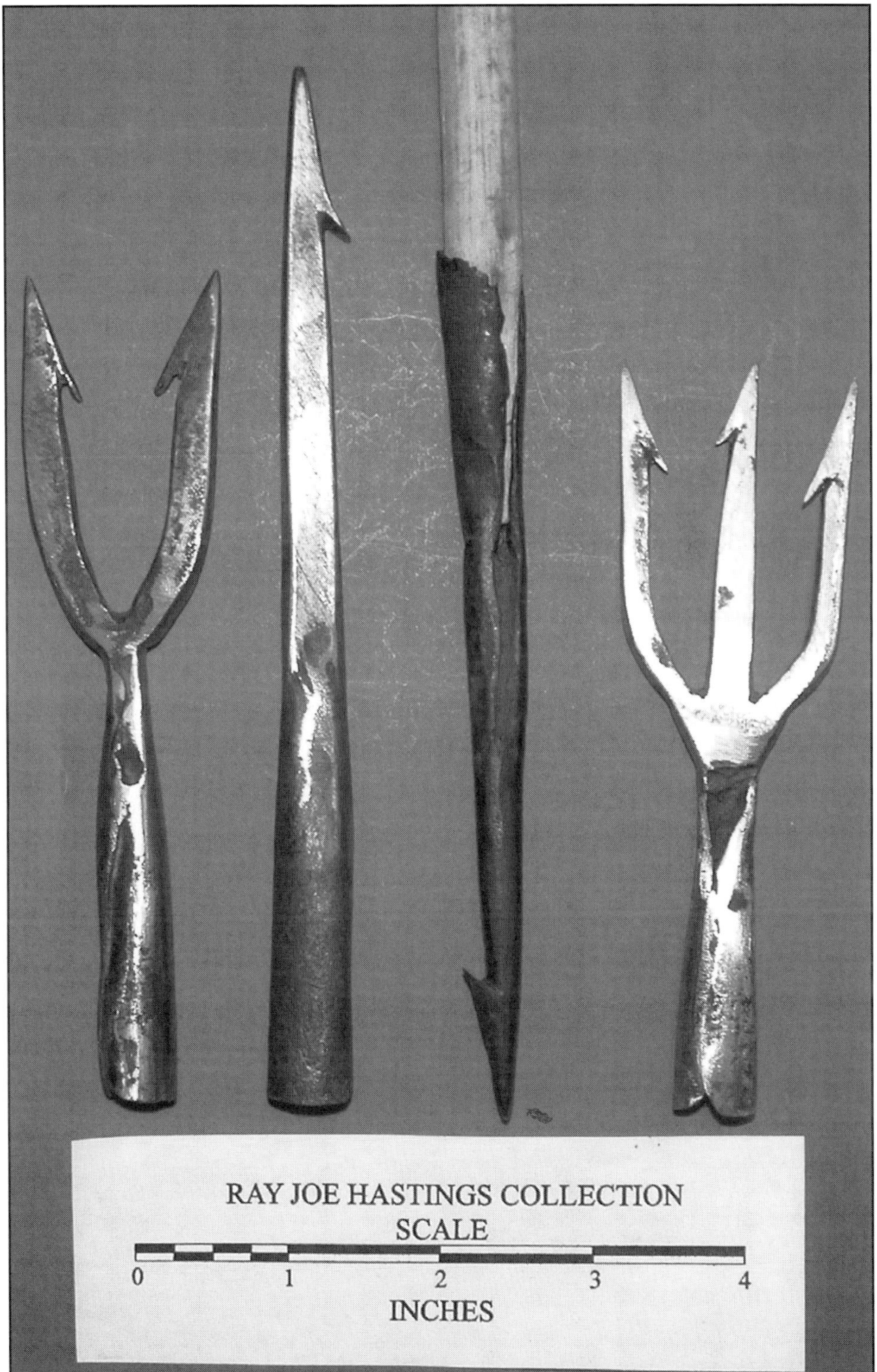

Examples of one, two, and three-prong bow spikes I made.

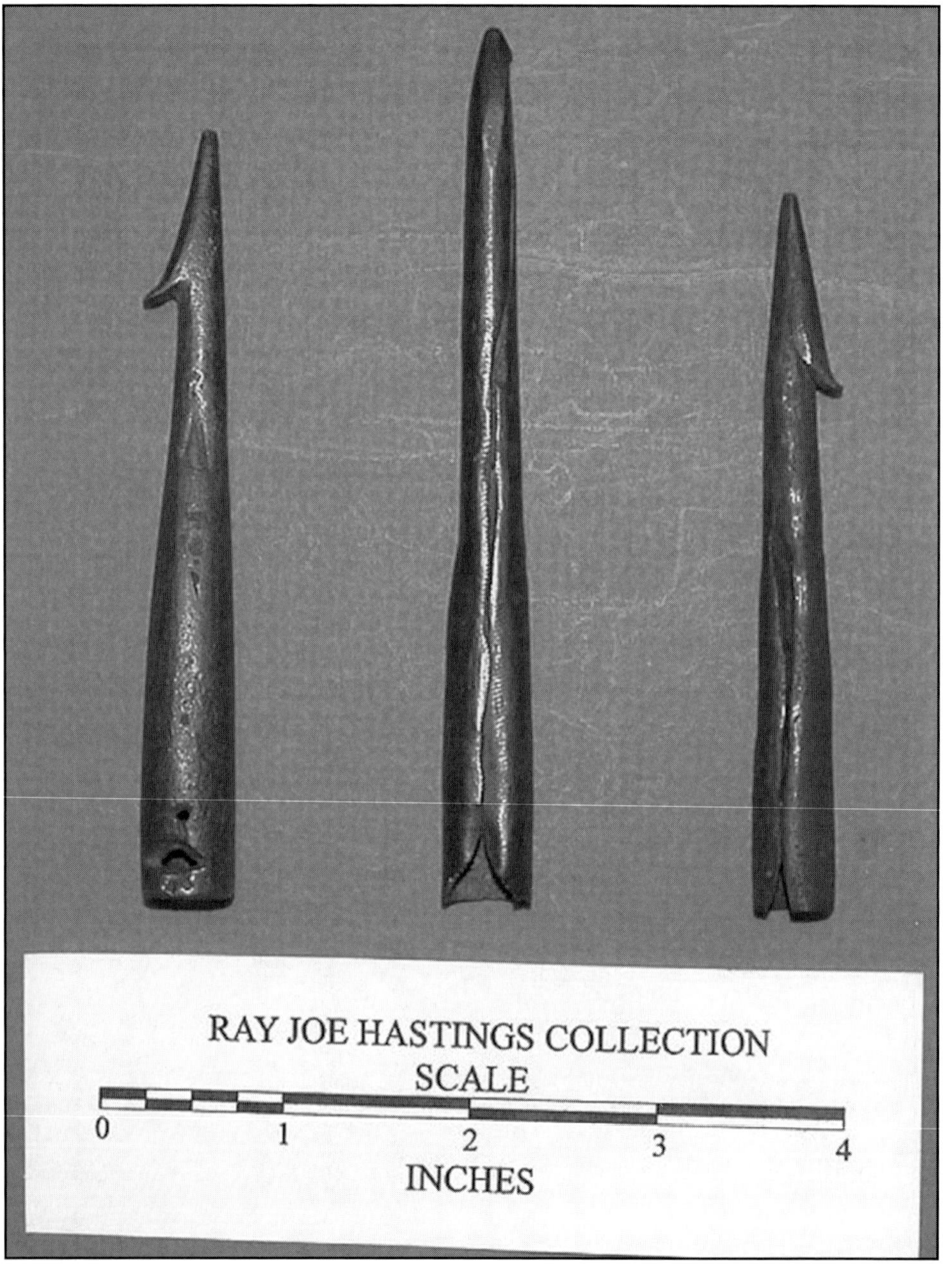

All three single spikes are from Ripley County. The single spike on the left belonged to my first cousin Junior Belcher. It looks like it was made by Mr. Oatman Tanner, a well-known gig maker of Doniphan, Missouri. Mr. Tanner made a considerable quantity of gigs and one can still find an "Oatman Tanner Gig" occasionally at a farm auction sale. The single spike in the center was made from a worn-out file by Everett Cole in 1944. I only have two spikes made from a file–a one-prong, and a two-prong. This one was used in Fourche Creek. Mr. Cole stated that he also hunted rabbits with his bow and spike. The spike on the right was made by blacksmith Winfield Bell of Doniphan in the early 1920's for Mr. Charles J. Braschler of Pratt, Missouri, Ripley County. Mr. Braschler farmed along Current River, and many times he also hunted rabbits with his bow and spike. On one hunt he killed five rabbits. So, not only did men fish with bows and spikes, but they also hunted land animals such as rabbits and sometimes other game as well. Shown actual size.

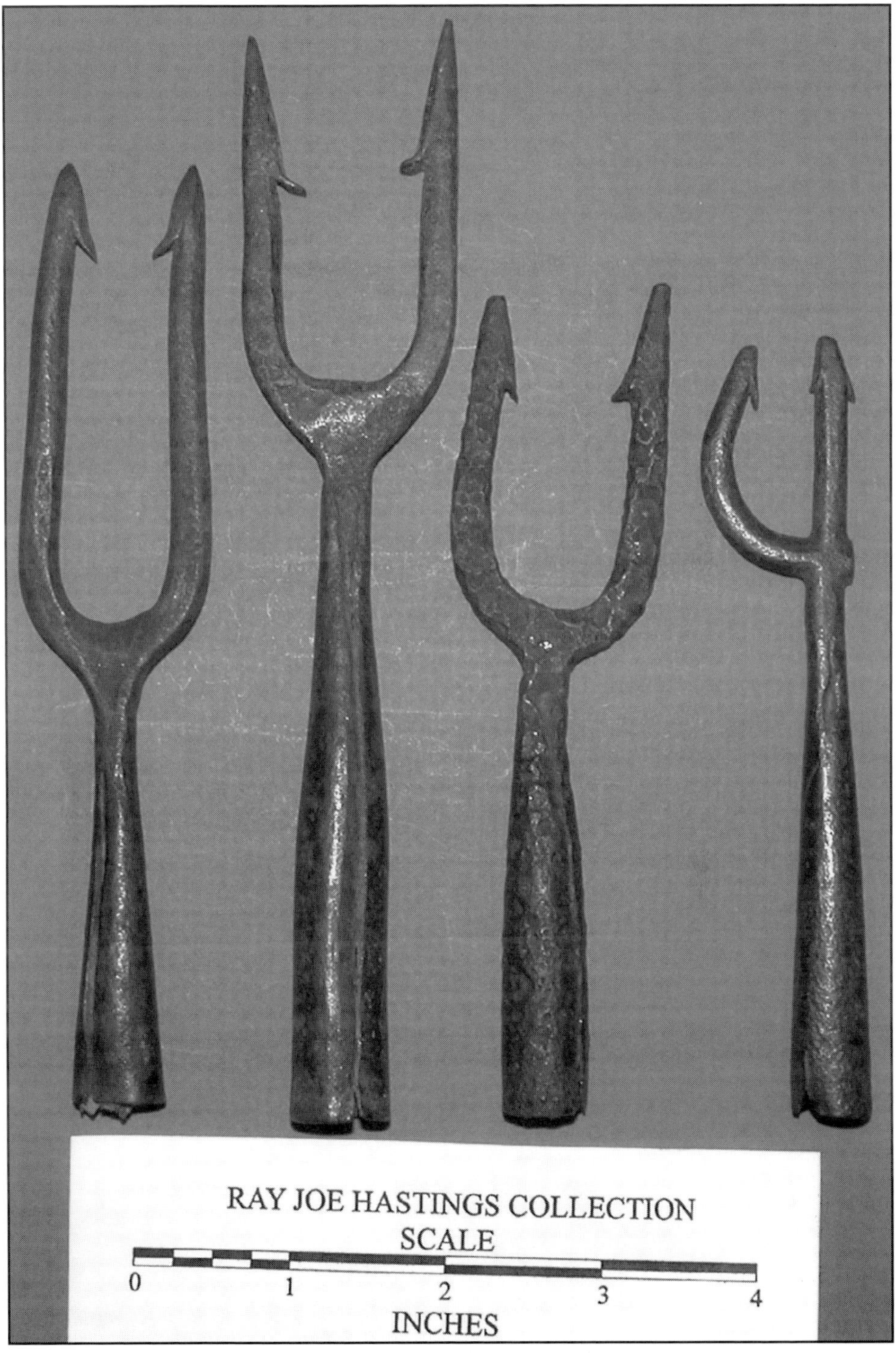

All four spikes are from Ripley County. The maker of the two-prong spike on the left is unknown. The second from the left was made by Mr. Grover Whitwell of Doniphan, Missouri. The maker of the third from the left is also unknown, and the fourth from the left was once a three-prong, but one of the outside prongs broke off. Even though this threw it off-balance, the owner probably used it as a two-prong anyway.

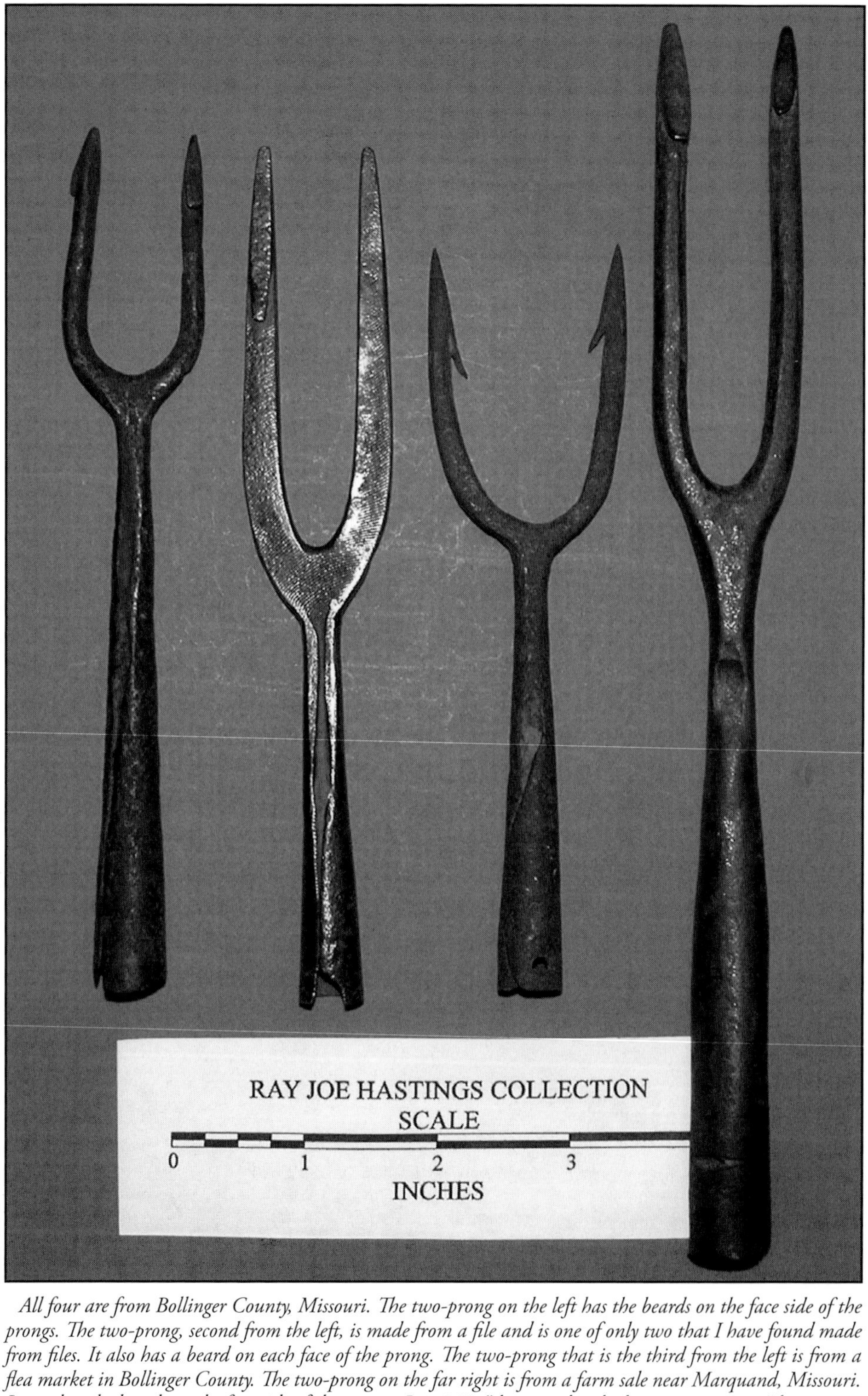

All four are from Bollinger County, Missouri. The two-prong on the left has the beards on the face side of the prongs. The two-prong, second from the left, is made from a file and is one of only two that I have found made from files. It also has a beard on each face of the prong. The two-prong that is the third from the left is from a flea market in Bollinger County. The two-prong on the far right is from a farm sale near Marquand, Missouri. It too, has the beards on the face side of the prongs. It is 9 3⁄16" long, and is the longest two-prong I have.

These three bow spikes are fine examples of the skill and workmanship that some blacksmiths possessed. The three-prong on the left was bought at a farm auction near DeSoto, Missouri, Jefferson County. The three-prong in the center looked like the work of Mr. Irving (Irv) Ellerman from Shannon County. Irv–as he was called by his friends–was one of the best gig makers around, and his gigs were, and still are, much sought after. However, after several comparisons of gigs known to have been made by Mr. Ellerman, it was determined this was not an Irv Ellerman spike. The two-prong on the right was bought at a farm sale near the Ripley/Butler County line and may have been made and used in either county.

These three spikes were made in Shannon County, Missiouri many years ago, and were probably used in the streams up there before the owner moved to Ripley County and used them here. The three-prong on the left has a piece that was broken off the socket in 1996, when the previous owner weakened the metal by heating it to drill the tack hole, and then tried to put a small gig pole that was too big in the socket.

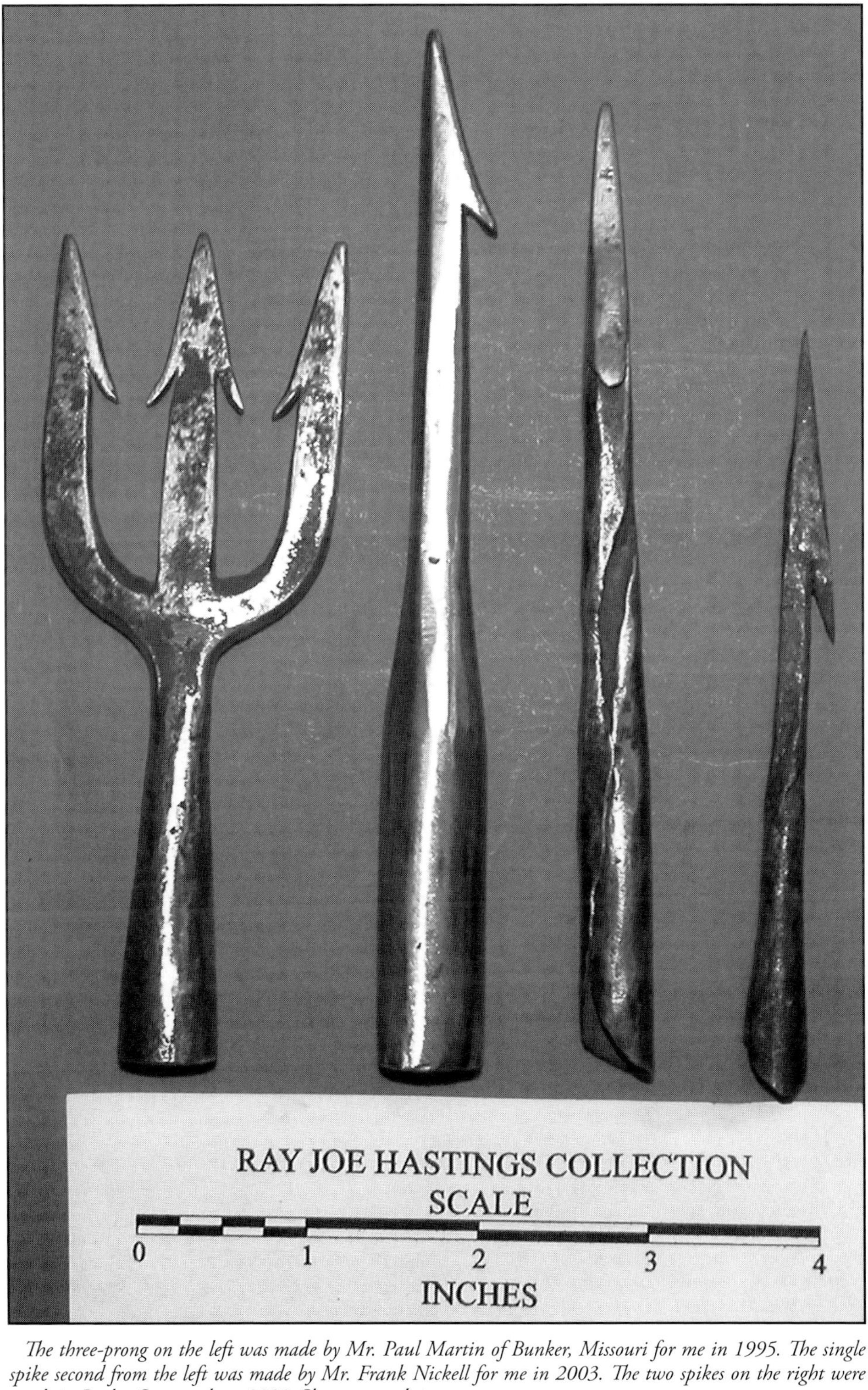

The three-prong on the left was made by Mr. Paul Martin of Bunker, Missouri for me in 1995. The single spike second from the left was made by Mr. Frank Nickell for me in 2003. The two spikes on the right were made in Butler County about 2000. Shown actual size.

The three-prong on the left was made from a small, factory-made garden tool. The prongs were straightened, and an attempt was made to cut the beards on the prongs. The two-prong was bought at an auction house in Stoddard County and could have come from another county either west or north of there. Shown actual size.

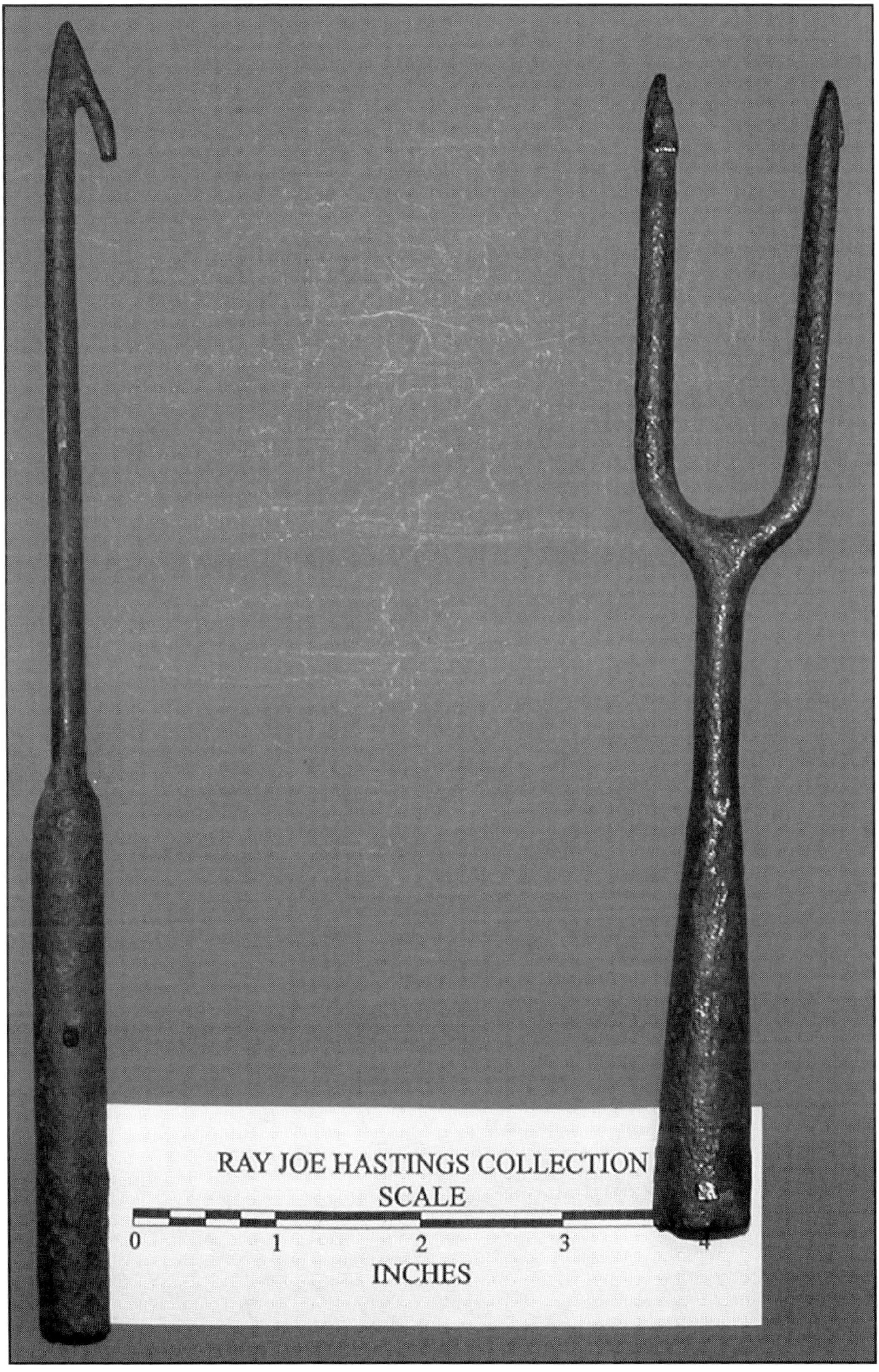

The single spike on the left is almost 9" long and came from Piedmont, Missouri, Wayne County. The two-prong came from Lodi, Missouri, Wayne County, and is 7 ⅞" long.

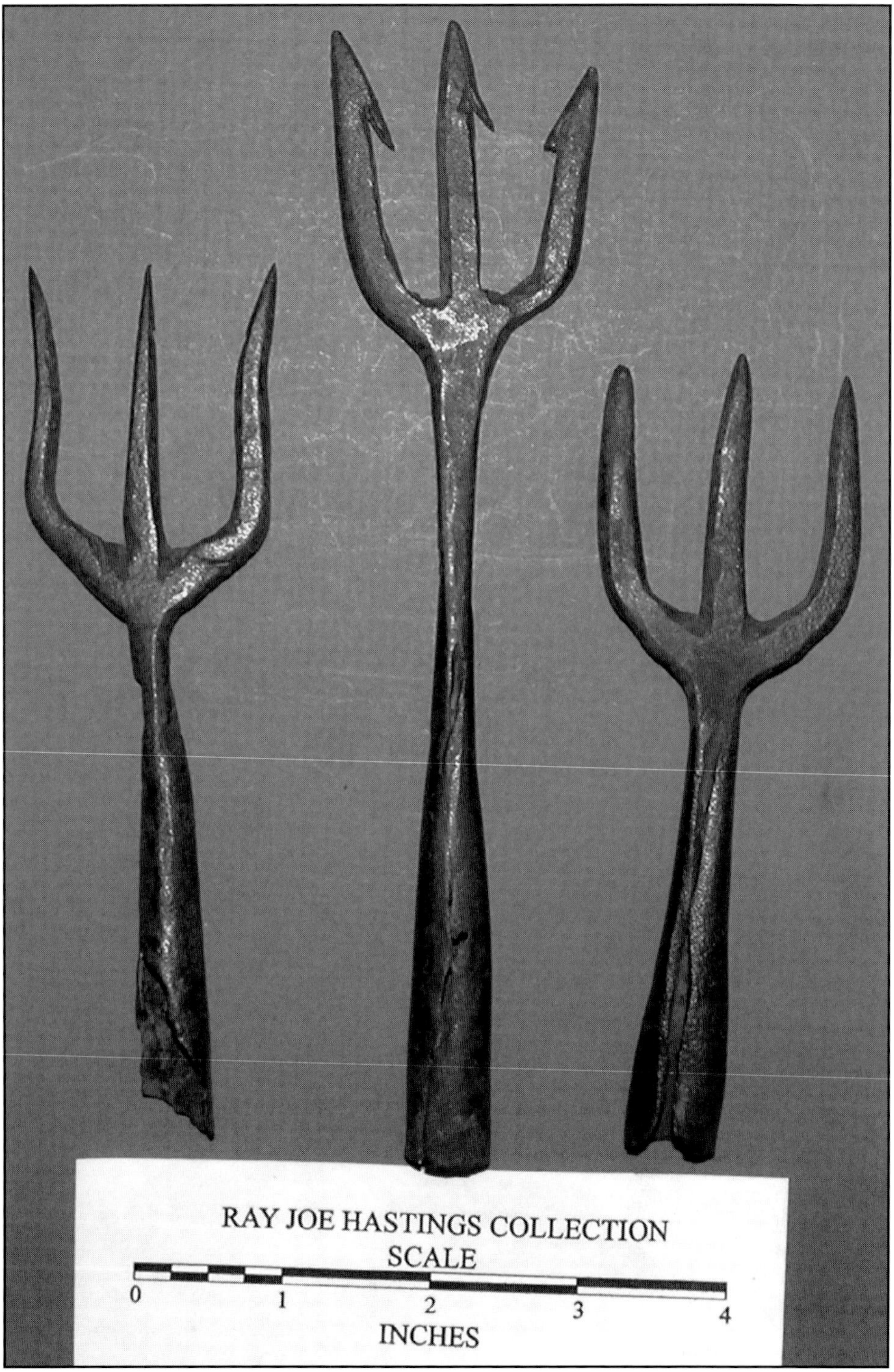

All three spikes came from Wayne County at a farm auction near Leeper, Missouri. These three were used extensively, especially the one on the left, and the one on the right, as no beards are left on the prongs. The three-prong in the center is 7 ⅜" long.

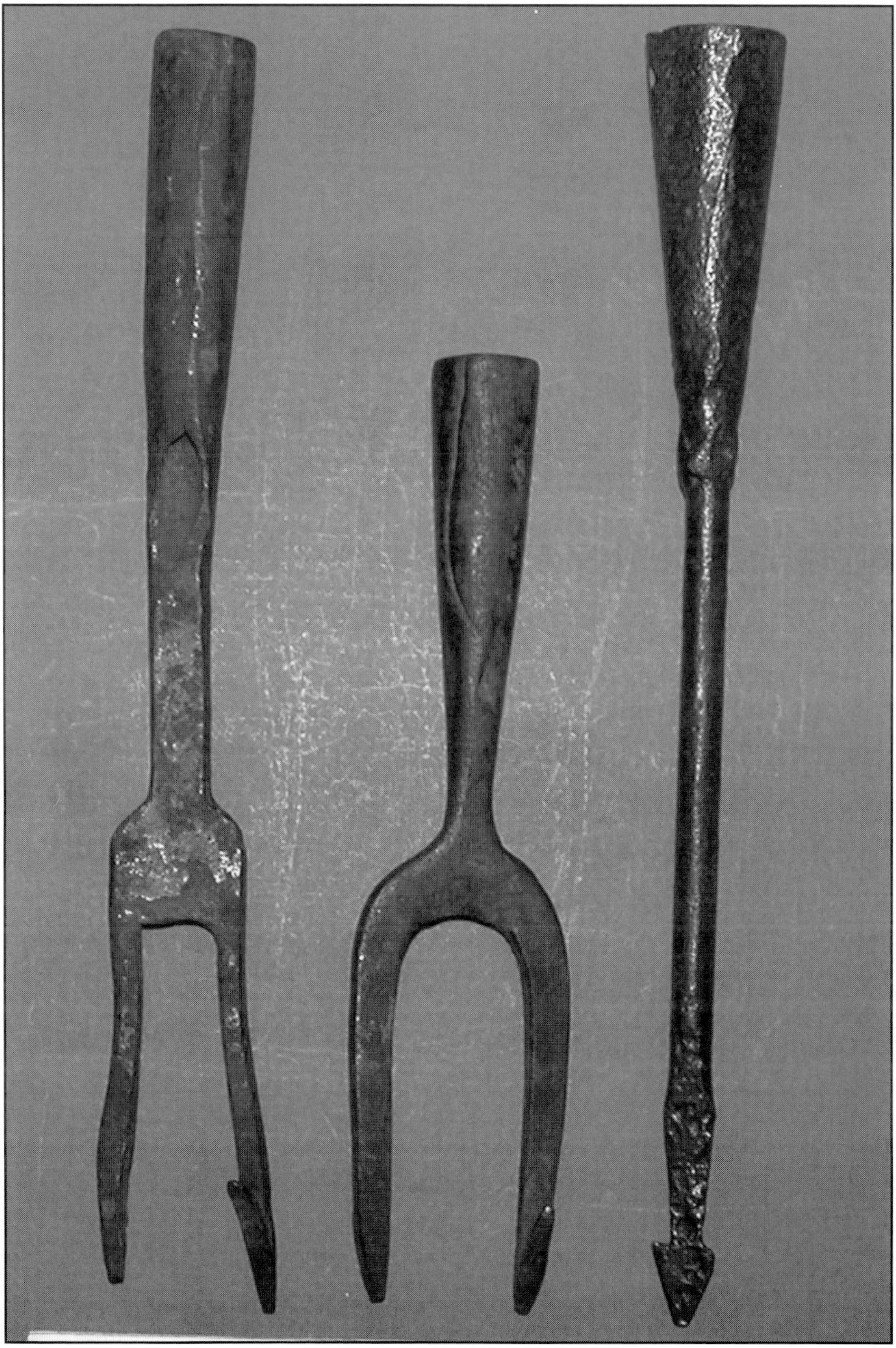

The two-prong on the left is from Des Arc, Iron County, Missouri–probably made by someone without too much blacksmithing skills. The ferule (socket) is well made, but the prongs and the beards are uneven. The center two-prong is also from Des Arc, and it is well made. Mr. Bill Cooper, a blacksmith, made this one in the 1930s, or early 1940s. The single spike on the right also came from Iron County, maker unknown.

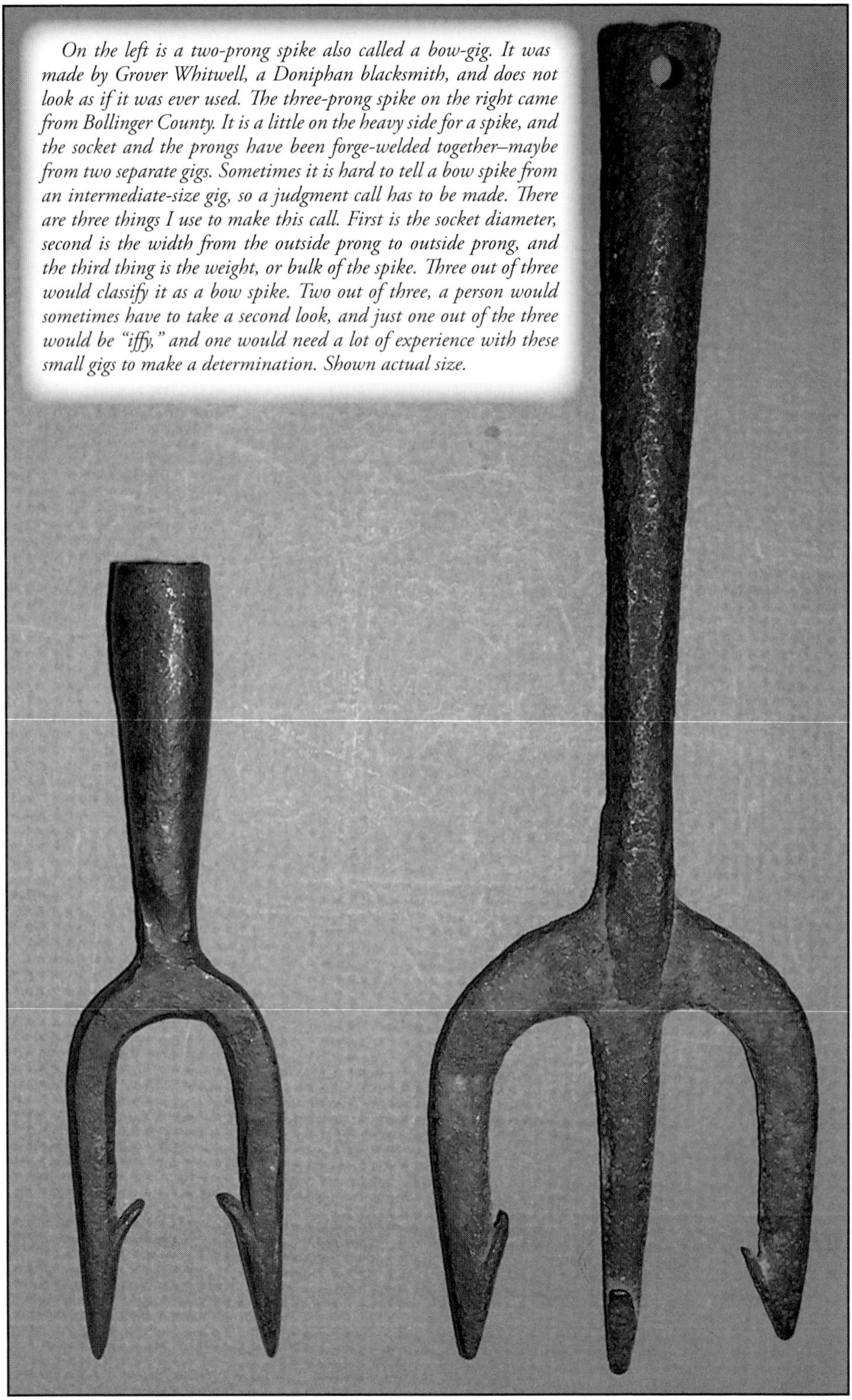

On the left is a two-prong spike also called a bow-gig. It was made by Grover Whitwell, a Doniphan blacksmith, and does not look as if it was ever used. The three-prong spike on the right came from Bollinger County. It is a little on the heavy side for a spike, and the socket and the prongs have been forge-welded together–maybe from two separate gigs. Sometimes it is hard to tell a bow spike from an intermediate-size gig, so a judgment call has to be made. There are three things I use to make this call. First is the socket diameter, second is the width from the outside prong to outside prong, and the third thing is the weight, or bulk of the spike. Three out of three would classify it as a bow spike. Two out of three, a person would sometimes have to take a second look, and just one out of the three would be "iffy," and one would need a lot of experience with these small gigs to make a determination. Shown actual size.

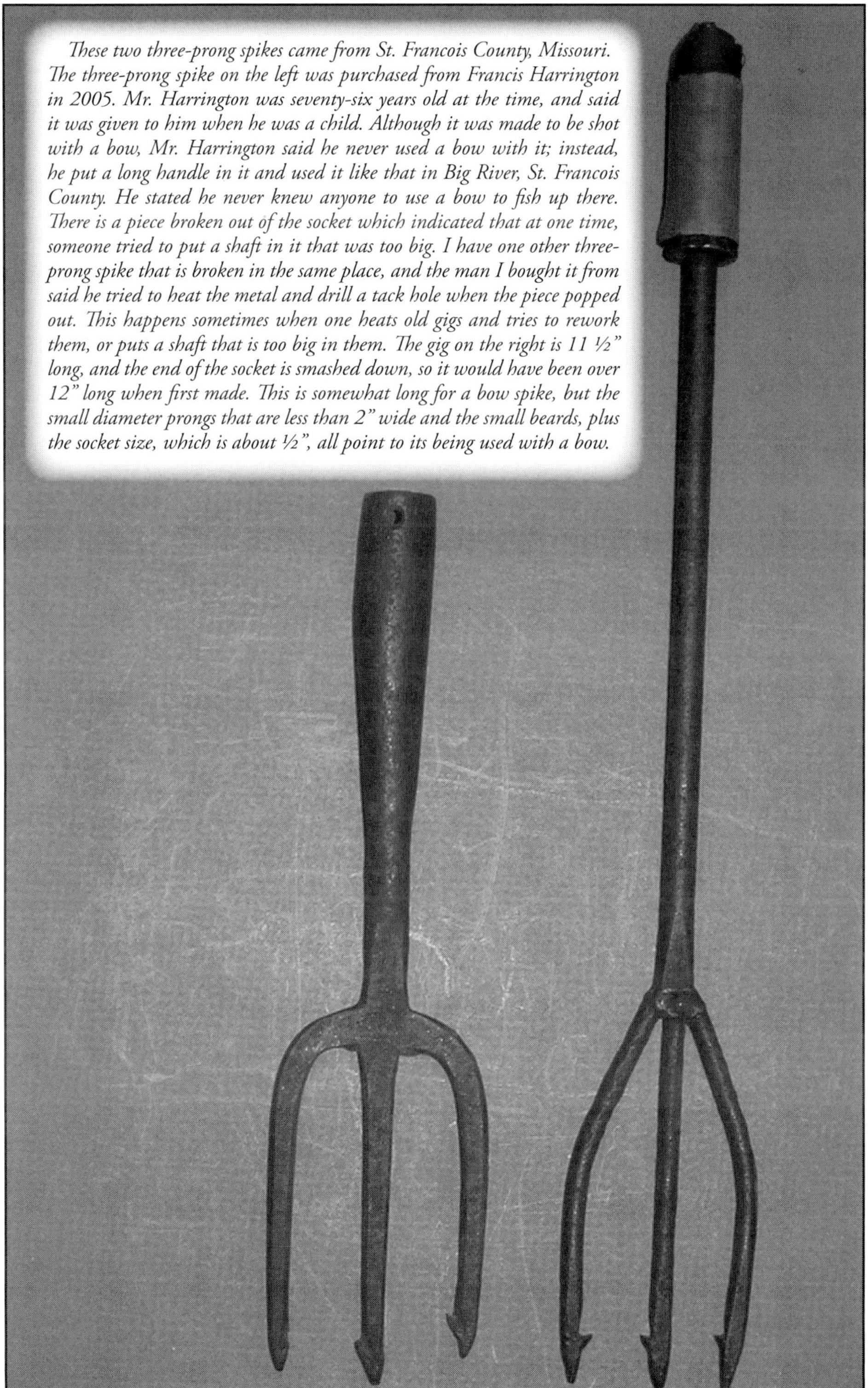

These two three-prong spikes came from St. Francois County, Missouri. The three-prong spike on the left was purchased from Francis Harrington in 2005. Mr. Harrington was seventy-six years old at the time, and said it was given to him when he was a child. Although it was made to be shot with a bow, Mr. Harrington said he never used a bow with it; instead, he put a long handle in it and used it like that in Big River, St. Francois County. He stated he never knew anyone to use a bow to fish up there. There is a piece broken out of the socket which indicated that at one time, someone tried to put a shaft in it that was too big. I have one other three-prong spike that is broken in the same place, and the man I bought it from said he tried to heat the metal and drill a tack hole when the piece popped out. This happens sometimes when one heats old gigs and tries to rework them, or puts a shaft that is too big in them. The gig on the right is 11 ½" long, and the end of the socket is smashed down, so it would have been over 12" long when first made. This is somewhat long for a bow spike, but the small diameter prongs that are less than 2" wide and the small beards, plus the socket size, which is about ½", all point to its being used with a bow.

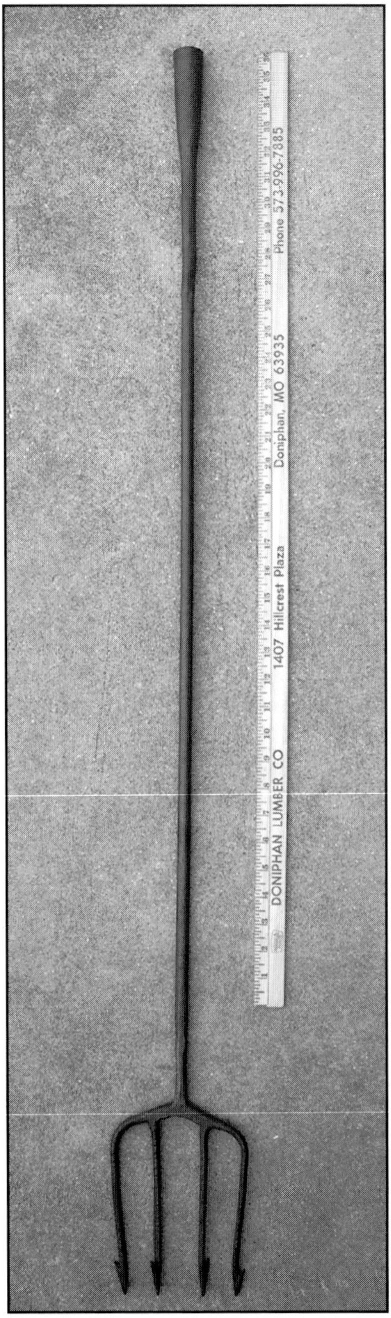

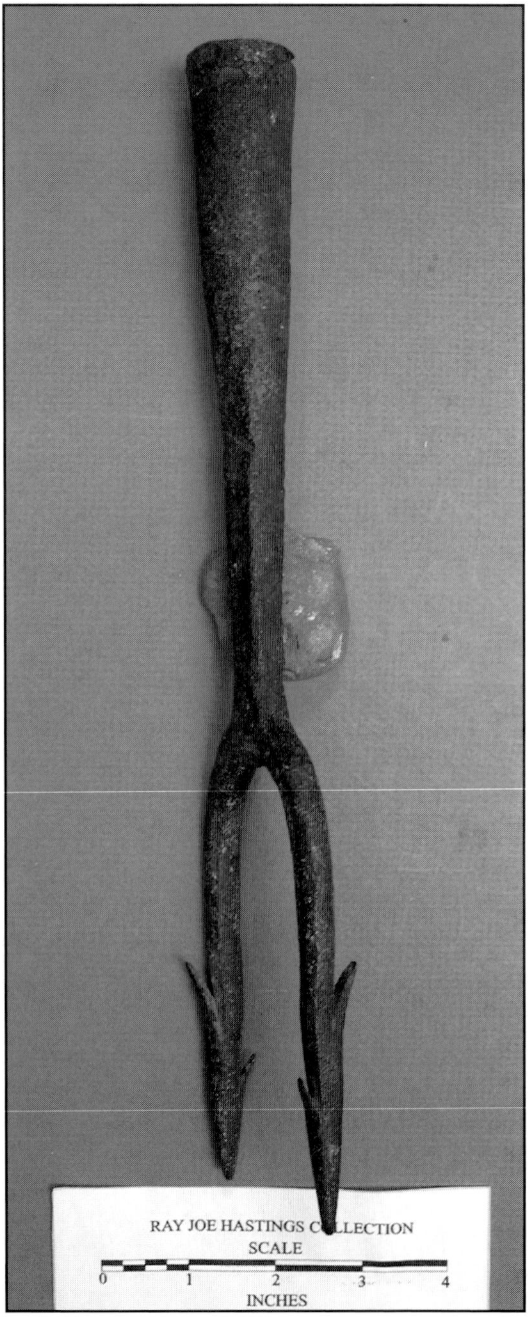

***Left:** A four-prong river gig that is 47" long. This type of gig was probably a deep-water gig and would have been used in real deep water. The major reason for the length of this gig is that in this depth of water, creating more weight and eliminating at least three feet of the gig pole would have prevented the gig pole from having too much buoyancy, and from trying to float up with a lighter gig on it. **Right:** A two-prong river gig I found a few years ago. This one has two beards on each prong. One beard is above the lower beard, and other than holding a fish on the gig better, I can see no other purpose the two beards would serve. This one is nicely made, and it took a good gig-maker to put the two beards on each prong. The beards look as if they were forge-welded, which is explained elsewhere in this book.*

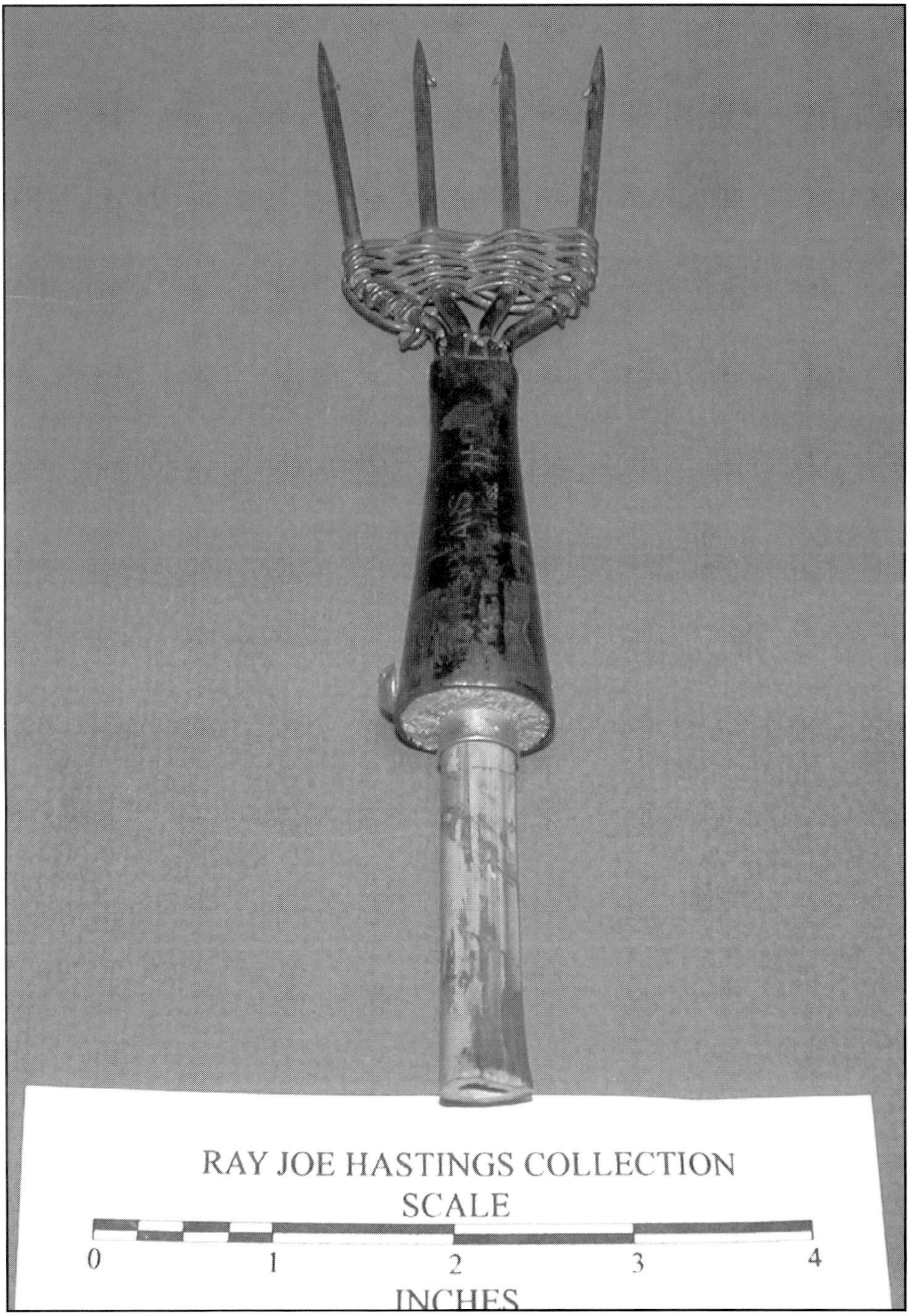

This little four-prong is factory made. The prongs are flimsy, and it would bend easily. Someone went to quite a bit of trouble and work to convert it into a gig to be shot with a bow. Note the cut-off shaft inserted into the piece of wood and fitted into the socket. The short piece made of cane is the right size to be shot with a bow. Also the prongs are reinforced with stiff wire that is woven in and out of the back end of the prongs to reinforce them. Although the points show no use, I believe it was made to be shot from a bow, either for frogs or fish, or perhaps both. Shown actual size.

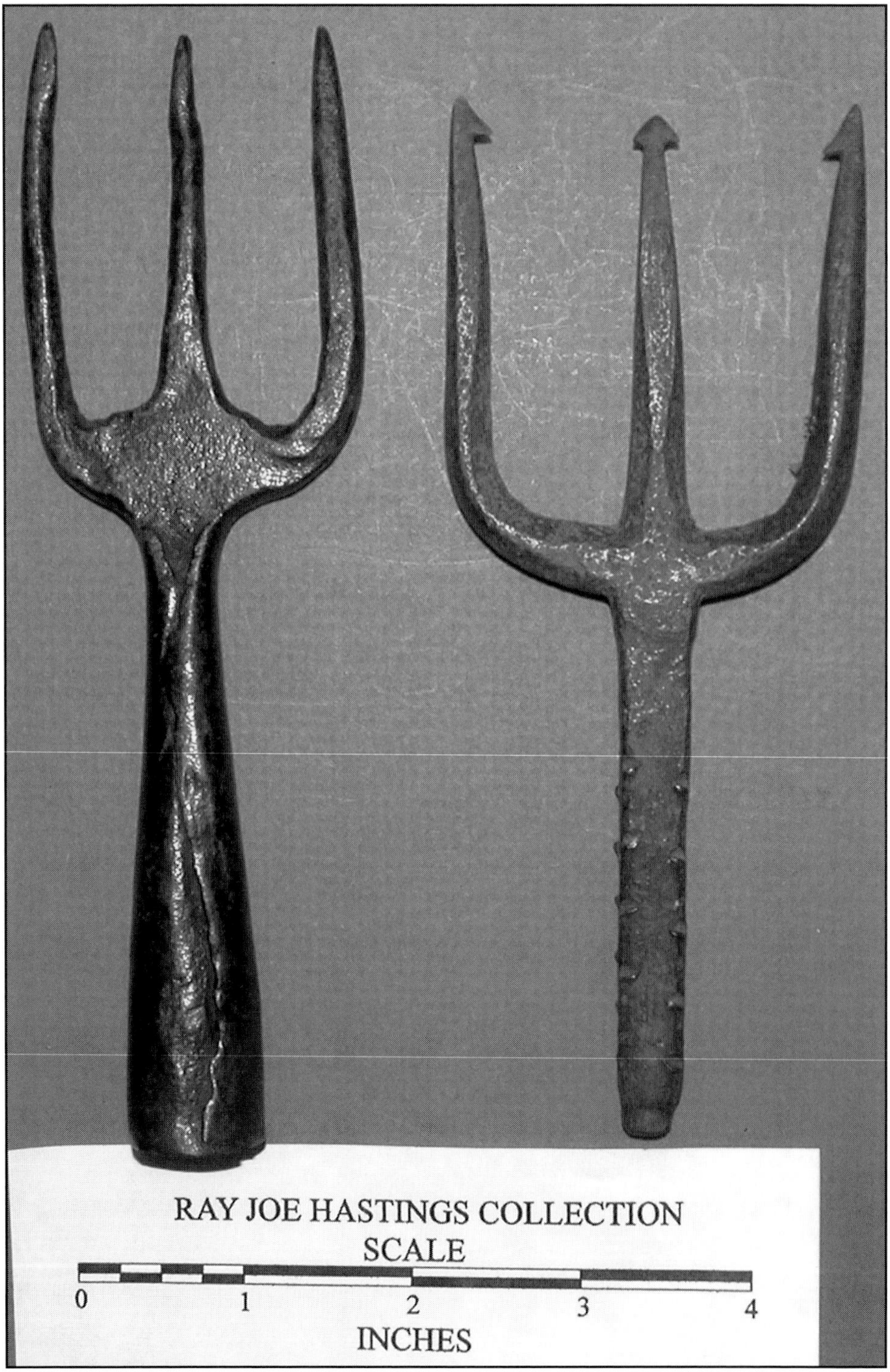

Above and right: *These are what I call intermediate size. Most are too bulky, and the socket sizes are too big for spikes. Most of these four were probably used on a five or six-foot pole to gig with in the creeks. Sometimes one man would carry this size gig to use in deeper water.*

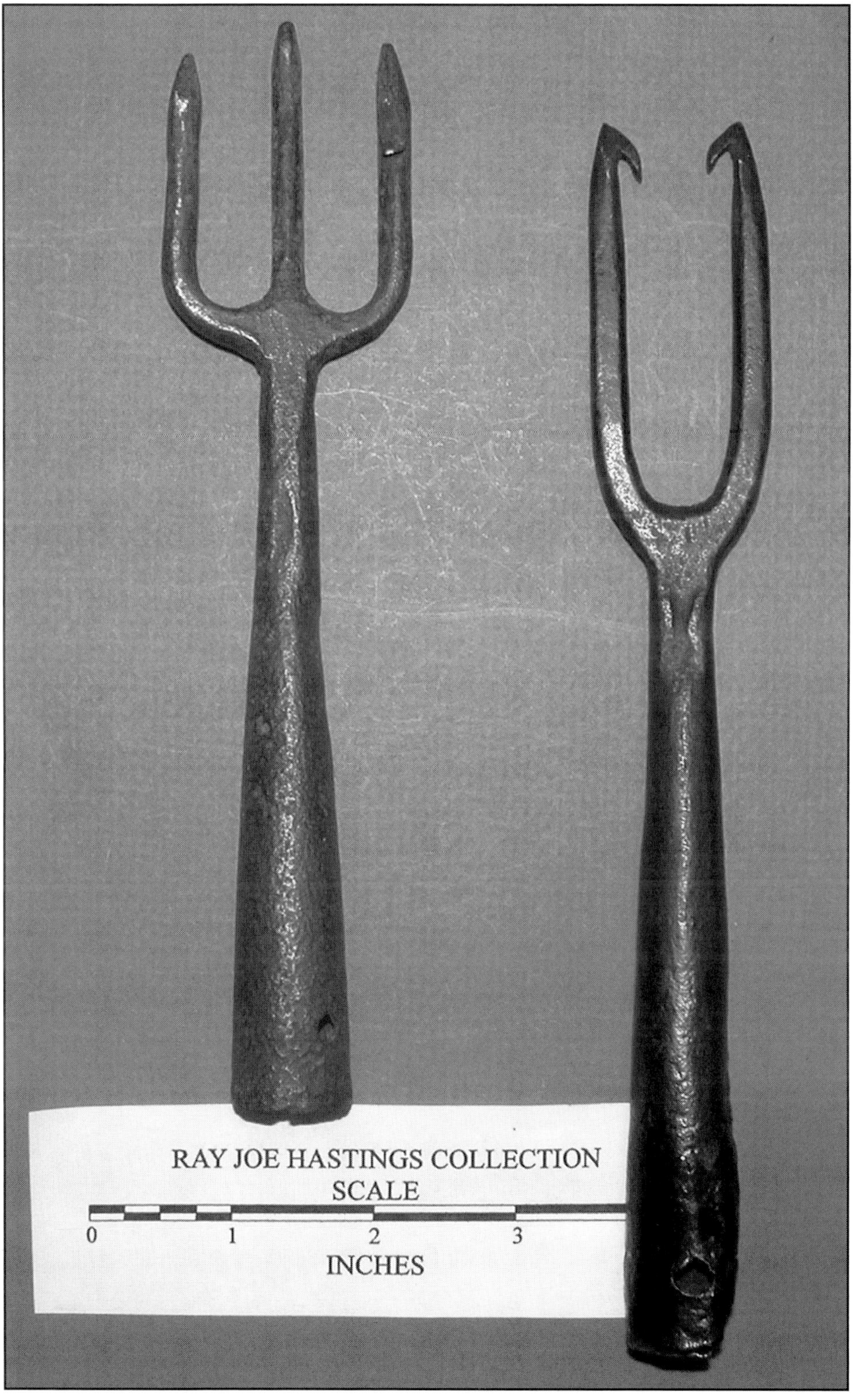
RAY JOE HASTINGS COLLECTION
SCALE
0
1
2
3
INCHES

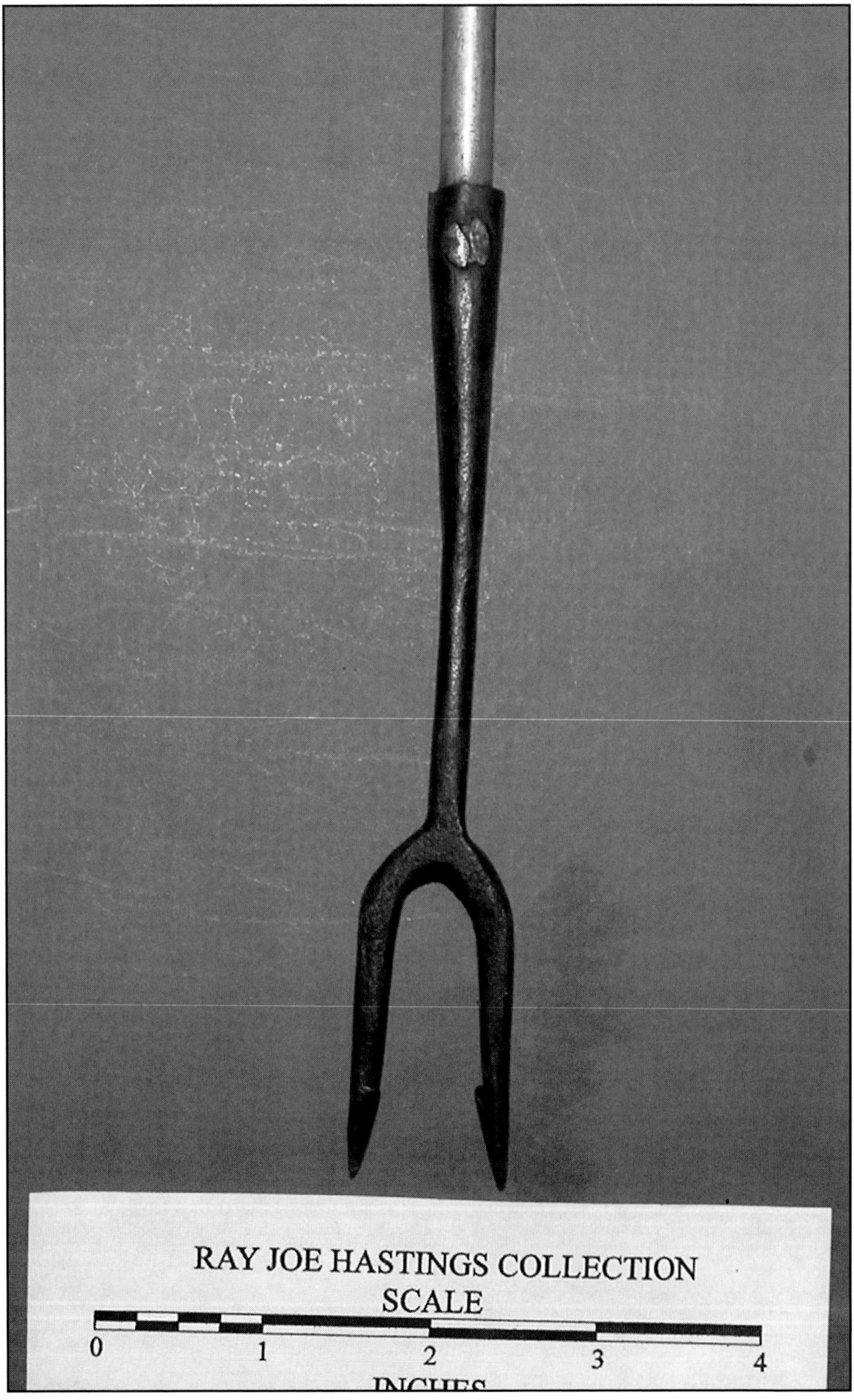
RAY JOE HASTINGS COLLECTION
SCALE
0 1 2 3 4
INCHES

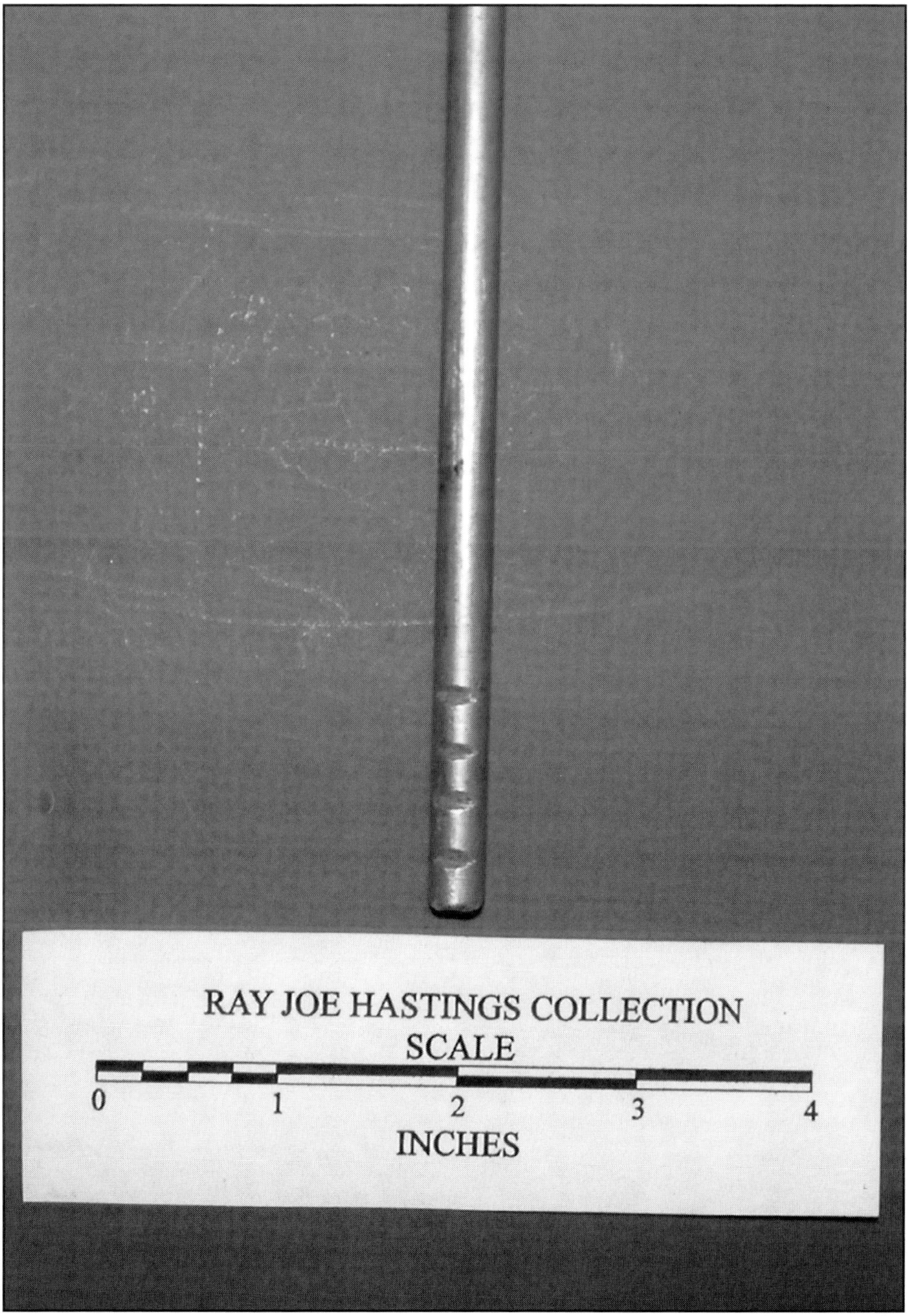

Left and above: *Made about 1950 or '51 by Mr. Thomas Roach, of Lodi, Missouri, Wayne County. The little two-prong spike is 5 ¾" long. The solid aluminum shaft in 37 ¼" long, and has four notches filed on either side of the shaft for thumb and finger gripping when drawing the bow. This solid aluminum shaft was very unusual since almost all shafts were made of wood or cane so when shot, the back end of the shaft would float at the top of the water for easier recovery. Shown actual size.*

The Making of Bow and River Gigs

Making the Spike

Spikes were one, two, three, and four-prongs, and could be from two and one-half inches to over nine inches long. They were forged from scrap metal such as worn-down buggy springs and even from worn-out files. By the early 1900s, some families had a forge to work their spikes into the shape they wanted, sometimes using nothing more than a charcoal fire to heat the metal. As soon as a community was settled, a blacksmith shop would spring-up to make what the people needed, and some of the small towns even had two or three.

I have a three-prong spike that was made by Mr. Frank Nickell with the help of Mr. Harold Nickell, Frank's dad. By using the heating stove and the hot coals to heat the metal, they were finally able to cut the prongs, beards, and the socket out, but had to take the unfinished gig to Grover Whitwell, a well-known Doniphan blacksmith, to heat and hammer out the socket, and then roll the socket over for the shaft to fit into. This was in 1944 when Frank was only ten years old. In later years Frank became a well-known gig-maker, making a few hundred gigs. They were much sought after by giggers in Ripley and surrounding counties. (Read more about Frank in the Legendary Gig Makers.)

The single spike was made by selecting a piece of metal that was just the right size. A hay rake spring, or just a piece of flat metal like a file was often chosen. That piece of metal was heated and cut to the correct size with a hammer and cold chisel. After the desired shape was obtained, the point and beard was made by reheating and cutting the metal as many times as needed to make the spike. The beard and point could be made in two different ways. One way that almost all of the blacksmiths used was to heat and hammer the tip or point to a tapered, flat shape until it could then be bent back on the prong, and forge-welded to it, using either sand or borax as flux, and being careful to leave part of the flattened point sticking out to serve as the beard. The ferule or socket was then cut into a fan shape, heated and hammered flat until it was thin enough to roll over into the size and shape that was needed.

The second method–the one I use–is to cut the beards on the prongs. This takes a little longer because the metal still has to be heated to a cherry red in order to cut it with a cold chisel. The cut beards seem to stand the wear and tear of gigging better in the gravel bottom streams of our Ozarks. Some of the beards on the ones that were forge-welded back on the prongs have dropped off when worn down on the points. A blacksmith had to know his business in order to do a good forge-weld.

A method that Dad and many others used to keep the spike on the shaft was to either drill, or file, a small hole in the gig, and drive a tack or small nail into it. The shaft would swell to a snug fit when placed in the water for a few minutes. Often times when the shaft dried, the spike would fall off as the wood shrank, especially if it did not have a tack in it. Some men chose not to file or drill a hole in their gig, making sure the spike and shaft fit snugly.

All three spikes are from Ripley County. The two-prong on the left and the three-prong on the right were made for Mr. Frank Nickell in 1953 by Mr. Grover Whitwell, a Doniphan blacksmith.

The three-prong in the center was made by Frank and his dad, Mr. Harold Nickell, in 1944 when Frank was only ten years old. The heating stove in the home served to heat the metal to cut out the prongs, beards, and socket. Frank and his dad took the nearly finished gig to Grover Whitwell to roll the socket over. In later years, Frank became a much sought after gig maker, making a few hundred big river gigs for the giggers of Ripley and the surrounding counties.

These two spikes came from Crawford County, Missouri. The four-prong on the left is one of only two that I have found in sixteen years of collecting. The four-prong is the hardest to find of all the small bow spikes. It is 8 1/16" long, and the prongs were brazed onto the socket.

The three-prong was used enough that the beards came off and a chisel was used in an attempt to cut more beards, but the metal was not heated enough to do a good job.

For reasons that I have not figured out, more of the two-prong spikes have been drilled with tack holes. Out of forty-one of my two-prong spikes, nineteen of them have either a hole filed or drilled in them. Three of the forty-one have a piece of the socket missing where a tack hole could have been, so I am unable to determine the exact number. The two-prong spike was often referred to as a bow gig. Out of twenty-five of my three-prong spikes, only six have a tack hole in them, while just three of the twenty-one of my single-prong spikes, which are often called a straight spike, have tack holes. A four-prong spike is very rare. I have only found two in sixteen years of research. One has a tack hole filed in it, and the other one does not. The gullet or gullets between the prongs of the two, three, and four-prong spikes were sometimes filed sharp to let the spikes slice through the water more easily and without splashing as much.

I have also found two broad heads just under five inches long that were probably used in hunting deer (see page 143). One of these appears to have been used and re-sharpened, and it has a tack or nail hole in it with about one-third of the shaft and nail still in the broad head. The other one does not appear to have been used.

Since more two-prong spikes were made, it was probably used more often than the single, three, and four-prong spikes. The two-prong was my choice of spikes, over

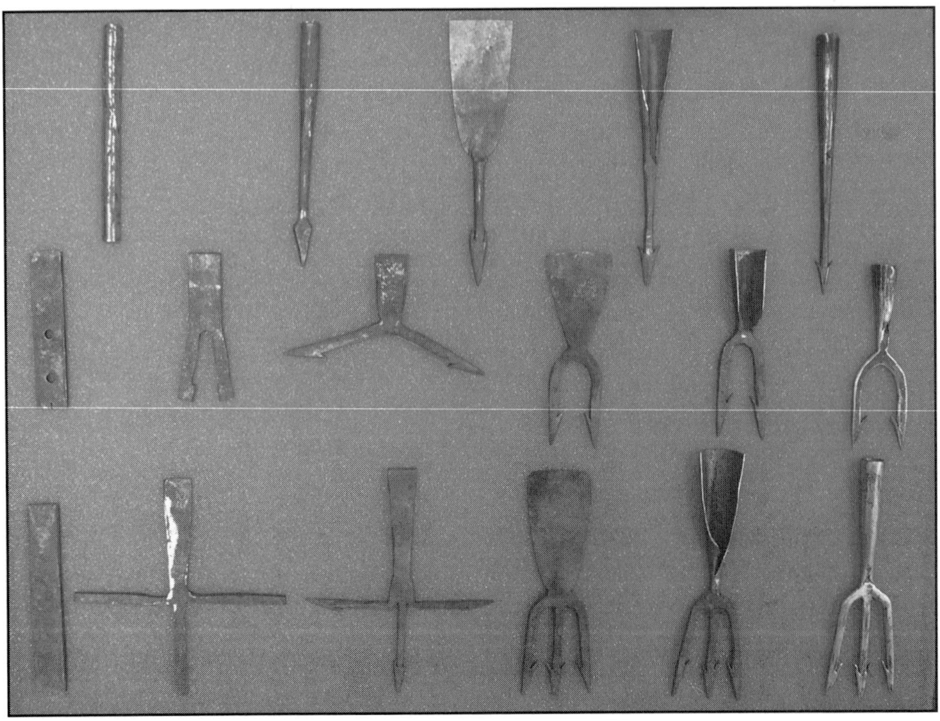

The steps in making a gig are shown here in this picture of the one, two, and three-prong bow spikes. The big-river gig would have been cut out and made using the same procedure. These were made by Mr. Steve Orchard during his apprenticeship training in gig-making, and given to me. Steve has become a very fine gig maker as one can see. Each step in the long process is beautifully done.

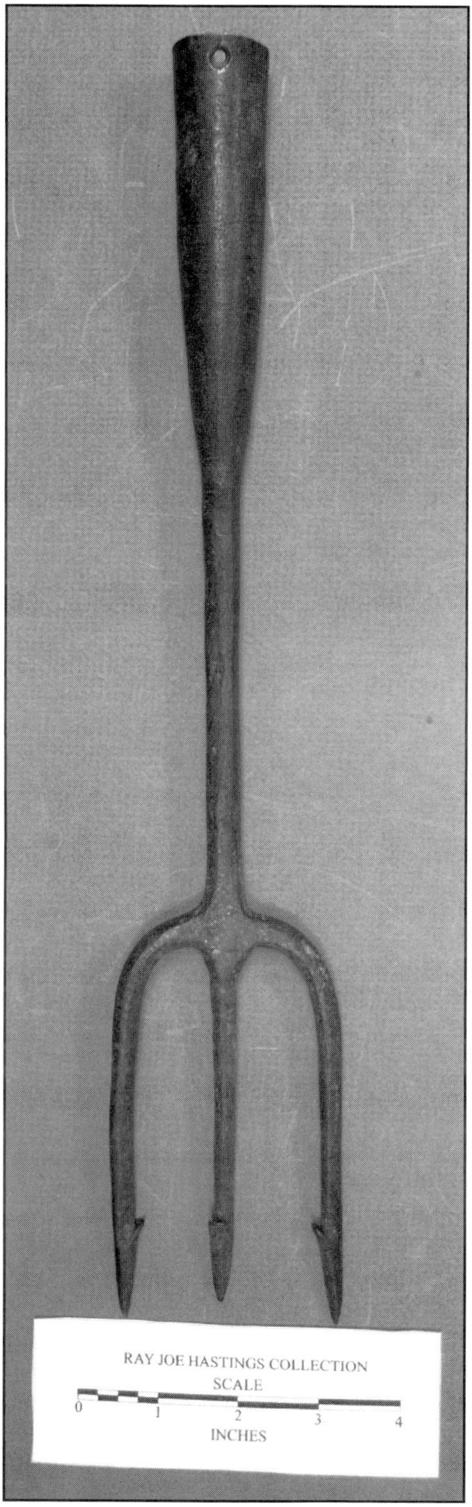

A typical "Hoe-fork gig."

the single, since they were the only two types of spikes we had. Until I started collecting bows and spikes, I had not seen a three or four-prong spike. Some bow and spikers chose the three-prong over the one or two-prong, and, although I personally never used the three-prong when I was growing up, it seems to me to be a bit of overkill on pan-fish. However, it would have had more stopping power on the bigger fish that one sometimes encountered while fishing this way, but on the other hand, the single-spike seems just a bit of underkill.

To make a two-prong spike, all that was needed was a piece of flat spring steel that was one-half inch wide, one-fourth inch thick, and four to six inches long. One cut half way down the center made the prongs. The points, beards, and the socket were then formed the same as described in making the single spike. On the three-prong gig, two cuts were made down the piece of metal, and three cuts were made on the four-prong gig on a slightly wider piece of metal, and then was worked out like the one and the two-prong gigs. The multiple prongs on a gig made it a more time-consuming task. (See the previous page for step by step pictures of how the gigs are made.)

The Blacksmiths and the "Hoe-Fork Gig"

Being a blacksmith meant doing long hours of hard work for the people who brought them worn-down pieces of their working equipment. Whether it was anything from skidding tongs to broken wagon parts, the local blacksmith in each community fixed it all. Wages were low during this time period, so this created a non-stop pounding of hot steel all day long for the blacksmith, and he was always looking for ways to do his work as quickly and as easily as possible.

I have already explained about this type of gig in other pages of this book, but thought it needed further explanation. As I wrote earlier, the blacksmith worked long, hard days during both the winter and the summer for very little pay. Even though he was usually covered up with work, when someone needed a gig, he was obliged to make one. With necessity being the mother of invention, it did not take them long to figure out that the easiest way to make a gig was to find something that was already two-thirds made–enter the garden hoe and pitchfork.

I, having made a few gigs, know the hardest and most time consuming part of the whole process is first cutting out the prongs, then cutting out the socket, and finally heating and hammering the socket out thin enough to roll it over for the gig pole to go into. When using this process of making a gig with a flat piece of spring steel, the very best gig makers could only make two or three a day. There was at least one exceptional gig maker who reportedly could make four in his younger years, and that was Irving Ellerman.

Wages were not only low for the blacksmiths, but for everyone else as well. Little money could be spent on a gig in those days–usually five dollars or less; therefore, the "hoe-fork gig," as I have dubbed it, was the answer. A good smith could make one in as little time as thirty minutes, as opposed to two to three hours when cutting it out of a flat piece of spring steel. This quicker and easier method solved two problems. He could make a gig quicker and cheaper, and doing so, also let him get back to making and repairing things that people depended on to make a living.

In the many years of making this type of gig, from approximately 1920 to 1970, literally hundreds were made in the areas of the many counties that used the gig. These are still fairly common and can be readily found if one knows the right places to look. I have several in my collection that has been accumulated in the last sixteen years.

Making the Arrow Shafts

The arrow shafts that went into the spikes were made of several different kinds of wood, such as pine, white oak, hickory, hazelnut, cedar, and in later years commercial dowel rods. Cane from the river or creek bank was also used, but pine seems to have been the choice because it was easily worked, and available over most of the Ozarks. Each would let the top of the shaft float on the surface of the water while the spike would hang downward.

Like the bows, the shafts also varied in length. The ones that I have range from 24 to 38 ½" long. The diameter runs from ⅜" to ⅝" with only one or two exceptions being slightly over ⅝". No fletching was used on these, since the weight of the spike kept the

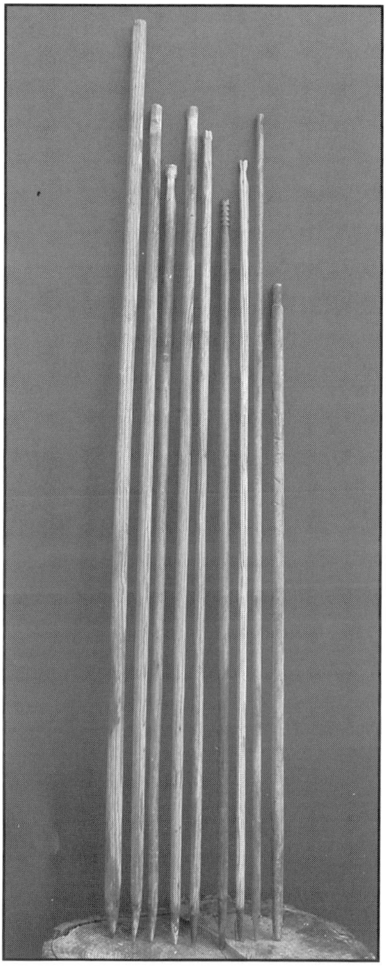

Another item hard to find is the arrow shaft that went into the spikes. The spike shafts in my collection vary in length from 24 to 38 ½", and were made mostly from pine, although other types of wood, and also cane were sometimes used. I have even found one aluminum and one steel shaft. These two would have been attached to the bow by a line to retrieve the arrow after the shot since, unlike the wooden arrow, these would sink.

shaft on a straight course to its target on the close range shots that were usually taken.

On the back end of the shaft, crossed nocks, or sometimes just a single nock, were cut into it for the wire or string to rest in. These are much like the arrow nocks of today only more shallow, and were cut directly into the shaft. Two to four notches were cut into the sides on the back end of the shaft. This was for the thumb and the side of the forefinger to grip when pulling back the wire, string, or band stringing the bow.

To make an arrow, some men chose a second growth sucker from a cutoff hickory stump that was just the right diameter. Still others picked out a hazelnut bush, as these were about the right size and grew thickly in places along stream bottoms. Others took a pine board, and with a handsaw, cut a ⅝" by ⅝" inch square from it, and worked it down by working each

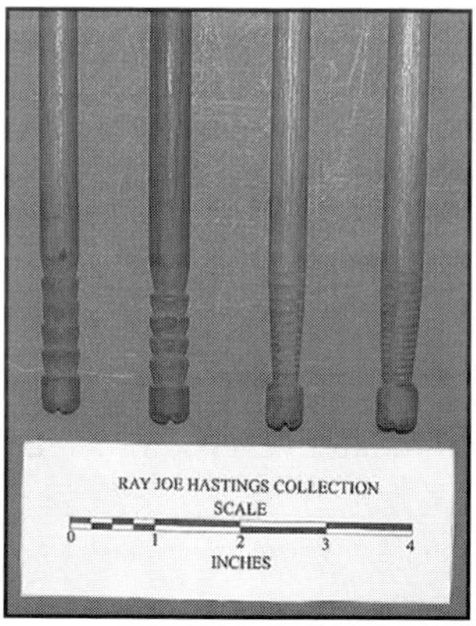

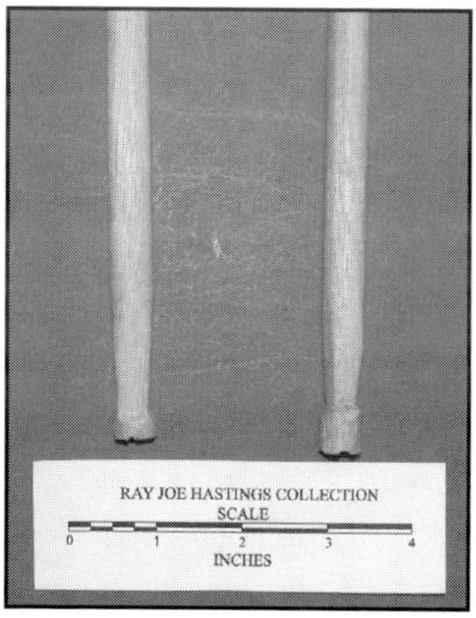

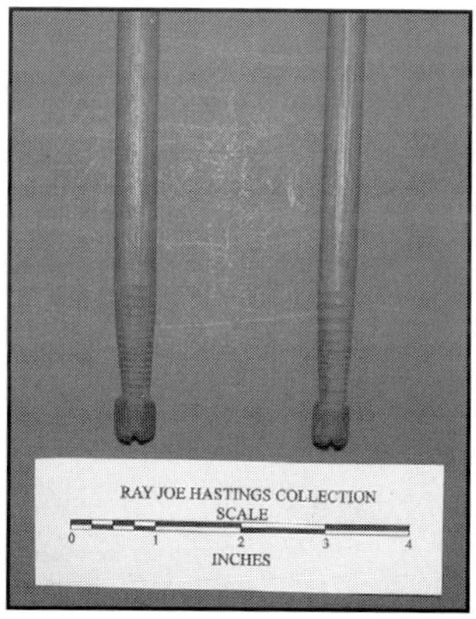

These pictures show the different types of notching on the back end of the arrows to facilitate gripping it when drawing back the bow. The nocks are also clearly visible for the wire or string to lie in. No fletching was used on these. The arrow notches were gripped by the thumb and the side of the forefinger when pulling the bow back. The picture in the center shows the most often used method of cutting the thumb and finger grip in the back of the arrow.

corner until it was the right size of the spike socket. The shafts that I have seen were always round in shape and some so well made as to look like they came directly from a factory. In the last year, this writer has made several spike shafts from the ⅝" squares and is quite happy with the way they have turned out.

Dad often bought dowel rods to put in our spikes, as they came in the right sizes, and were thirty-six inches long. All we had to do then was take a sharp pocket knife and work the taper on the end of the shaft that goes into the socket. Sometimes a file was also used since a person could get a better fit with it. The knife was also used to cut the cross nocks and the notches.

Descriptions of Bow Lengths and Types of Wood

The bows that were used to fish with were made from several different types of wood. Red cedar was the wood most often used because of its availability and long-lasting qualities, and it was also easily worked. Other types of wood used were sassafras, white oak, hickory, bodarc (osage orange), mulberry, persimmon, and ash. I have also even seen one bow that was made out of pine, and other types of wood may have been used.

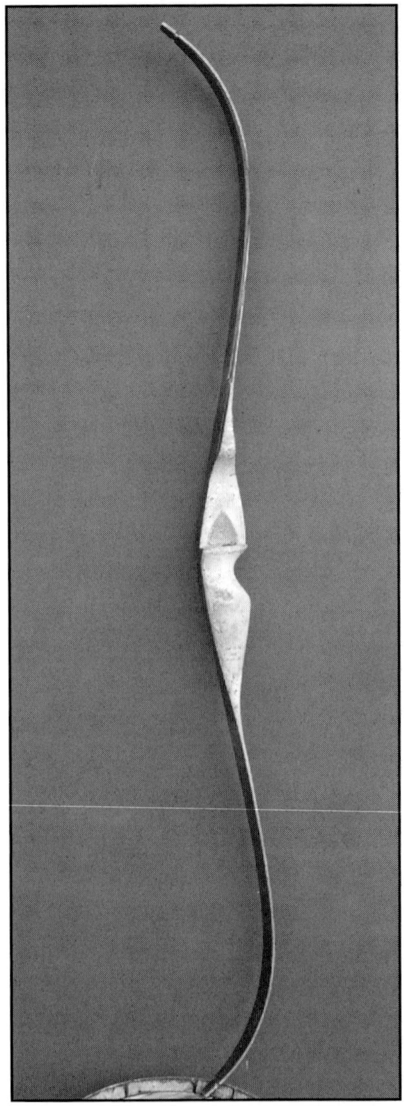

A recurve bow that is forty-eight inches long and was acquired by Ed Holland in 1960, when he was only ten years old. Too young to use the cedar bow his grandpa had made in 1910 for fear of breaking it, this recurve bow worked quite well until 1968, when, after graduating high school, the bow was hung up and retired. For eight years, he and a friend bow and spiked the prongs of Fourche Creek in Ripley County. This bow was procured from Ed a few months ago, and was a welcome addition to my collection, since it is the only factory-made recurve bow I have that was used to bow and spike fish, and was one of the last to be used, as fishing this way was pretty much over by 1968.

In the late 1950s and early 1960s, I know of at least two fiberglass bows that were used, and I know that Mr. Ed Holland used a factory-made recurve bow from 1960 to 1968. This was at the end of fishing with the bow and spike. Also, one other bow that I purchased from Mr. Charles J. Braschler was made by his Uncle Charles V. Braschler, and it was made from three pieces of material. Two pieces were made and glued together, and the third piece was very thin, and glued

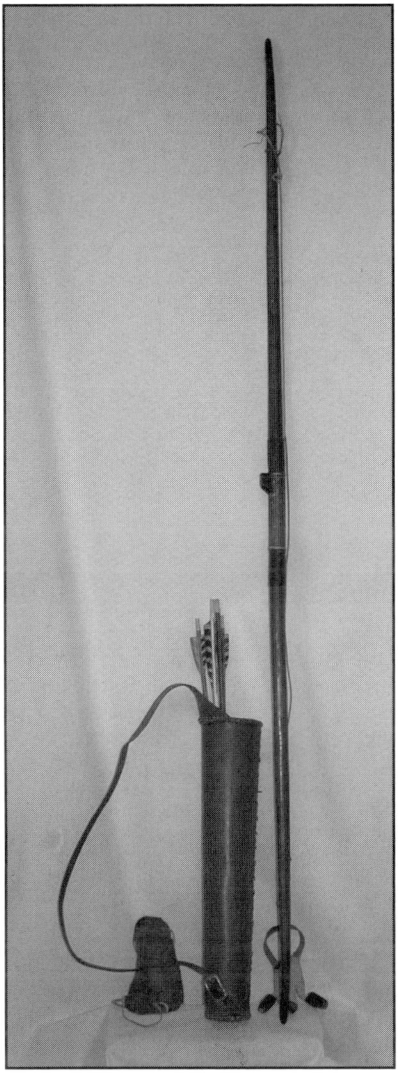

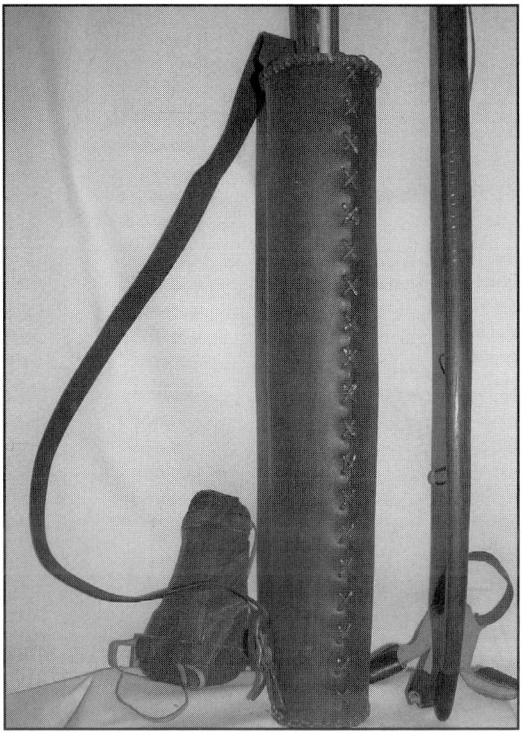

The bow, quiver, and arm guard were made in 1950 to hunt deer. The bow is made out of a piece of Bodarc (Osage Orange). As the story was told, Mr. Murray met a person of Indian descent, and they quickly became friends. His friend had a bow, so Mr. Murray decided to show him that he could make one. Not only did he make a beautiful bow, but the quiver was also a work of art. Old shoe laces were used to tie on the arm guard, although Mr. Murray hunted deer with his bow, none were taken, as there were few deer in Ripley County during that time.

to the back of the bow, perhaps to give it strength. It is a unique bow that was made about 1929, and would rival the finest bows that are made today that are laminated together.

The length of the bow seems to have been chosen by the person making them, or sometimes the length of the bow blank would dictate what length to make them. Of fifteen bows in my collection that I measured, the average length was 61 ½" inches with the longest bow being 76 ½" and the shortest one being 41 ⅞". Some of these bows are beautifully made, while some are just average.

One bow that was owned and used by Mr. Bill Davis in Ripley County, and made by his Uncle O.A. McKinney of Ripley County was made from a knotty cedar sapling. Although the bow was nicely made, one would think it would break with all the knots in it, yet Mr. Davis took a considerable number of fish with the old bow from the time it was made, which was about 1940, until he quit fishing with the bow and spike sometime around 1950.

What kept those fishing bows from breaking? It was probably the fact they only had to be pulled back a few inches, or just enough to shoot through the fish, that prevented them from breaking. Sometimes the bow that a youngster used was made from nothing more than a hickory limb by the boy who was going "bow and spikin'." Most of the time we were not allowed to use the good bows unless we were with Dad.

A good bow was time-consuming to make. First the tree had to be cut down–usually red cedar, hickory, or sassafras–and the log hauled to a barn or shed. The log was usually five to six feet long. Then the material had to dry out for several months before making the bow After it was dry, a section was "rived-out" of the log that would be the bow. It was then shaped with a hatchet to remove most of the material that was not needed. A draw knife, or spoke shaver, took more of the wood off the bow, and a

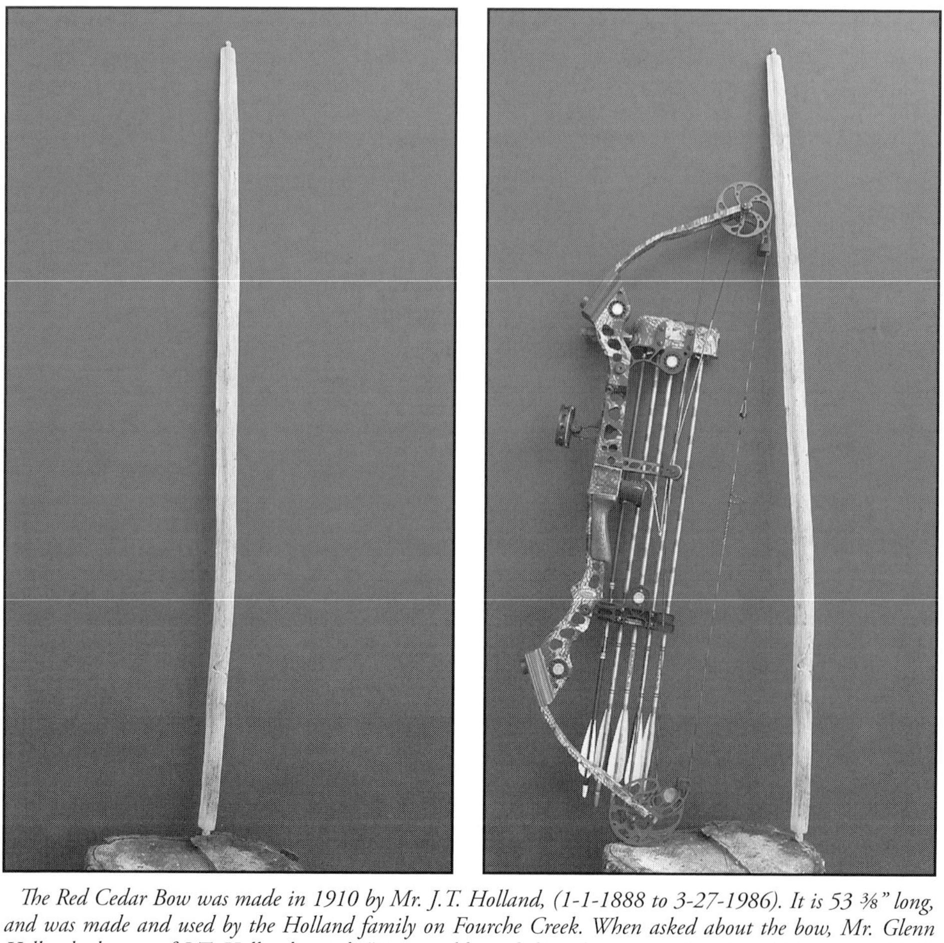

The Red Cedar Bow was made in 1910 by Mr. J.T. Holland, (1-1-1888 to 3-27-1986). It is 53 ⅜" long, and was made and used by the Holland family on Fourche Creek. When asked about the bow, Mr. Glenn Holland, the son of J.T. Holland stated, "You would not believe how many fish that old bow has killed!" The bow on the right was bought by the author in 2004 to deer hunt, and is only displayed to show the vast difference in bow-making in the past ninety-four years.

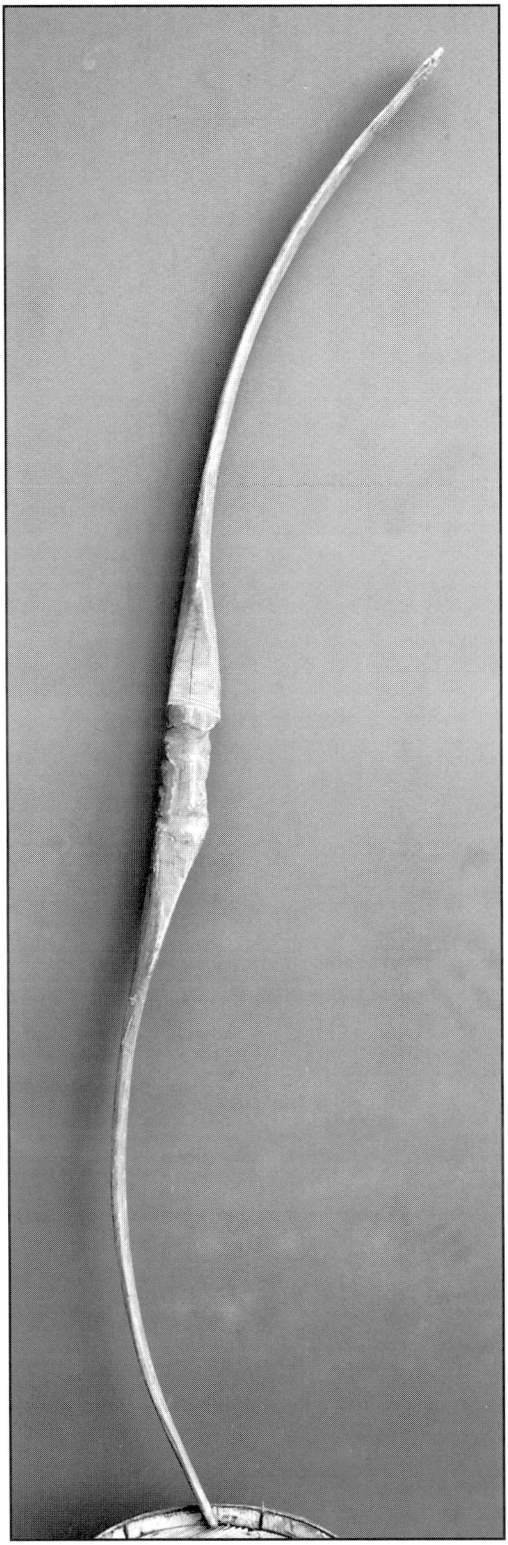

pocket knife, or sometimes a piece of glass, was used in the final finishing. A protrusion on each end of the bow was left to wrap the baling wire, or heavy twine around to string the bow, and sometimes two grooves on each end of the bow were left for the string or baling wire to lie in. My dad, Joe Hastings, always used baling wire for the bow string on his bows.

One other method was used to string the bow. A hickory bow band was made in the spring from the in ner bark of a hickory tree. The inner bark was carefully selected and was twisted, and strung to the bow. One man who had seen them used said when the band was old, it did not look like it would string the bow without breaking, but when soaked in water for awhile, the band came back to life, and worked just as well as when first made. Most bows had to be soaked in water for an hour or so to keep them from breaking when strung.

A bow from Iron County made from a three-inch diameter hickory sapling (some bark shows on each side of bow) left no doubt of its diameter and of the type of wood from which it was made. This is what I call a dual-purpose bow, i.e. it could be used to hunt land animals as small as rabbits and as large as deer, and it could also be used to bow and spike fish. The maker of this old bow put a lot of work into it. It has an arrow shelf built into the bow, so it could have been used for land animals. There are also thumb and finger grips carved into the bow. By turning the bow horizontally (crossways) in front of you, it could also be used to take fish.

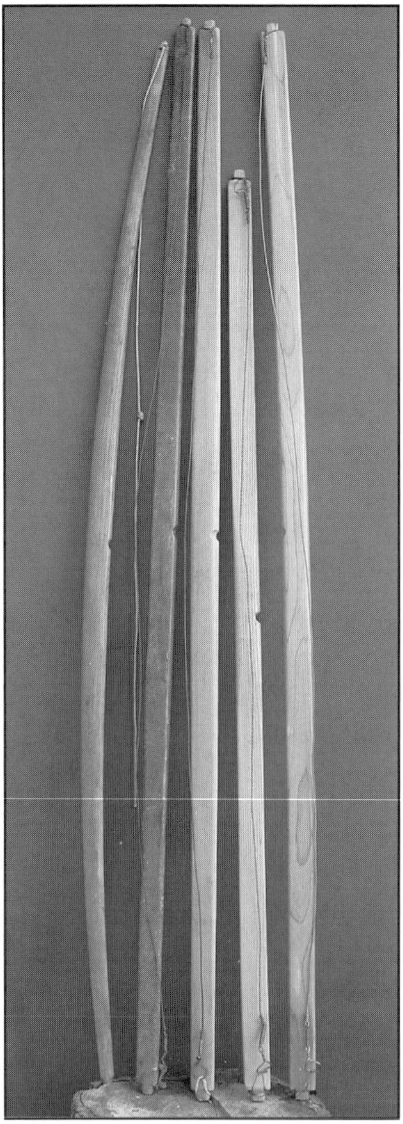

All of these bows were made by Ernest Murray in Ripley County near Doniphan, Missouri. The bow on the left was made out of Sassafras in the late 1920s, and is 60 ⅛" long. The Red Cedar bow second from the left was made about 1933, and is 61 ¼" long. It had a baling wire to string the bow with while the Sassafras had a string.

The next two bows are also made of Sassafras, while the last is made of Red Cedar. The last three were made for the author in 1993 and '94. Mr. Murray always put notches in the center of the bows he made for the arrow shaft to lie in. All of these bows are of top quality workmanship.

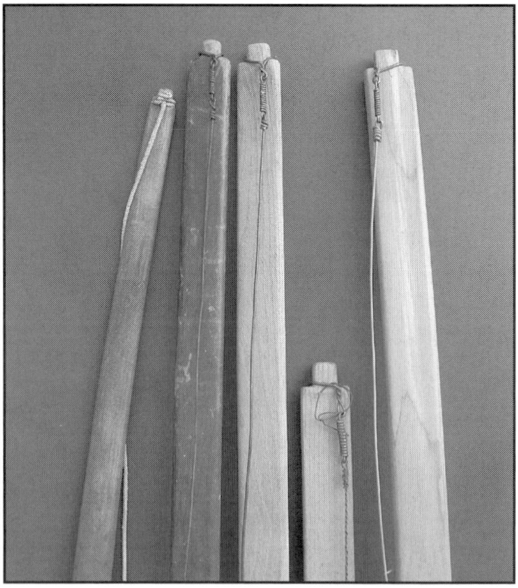

This shows the ends of the same five bows. Notice the protrusion on the end of bows to attach the heavy twine or baling wire. The special tying on the ends of the wire belongs to Ernest Murray. I have not seen another wire attachment like these. This allowed the wire to lie closer to the top of the bow by being off-center like this, but it also put an undue strain on the bow.

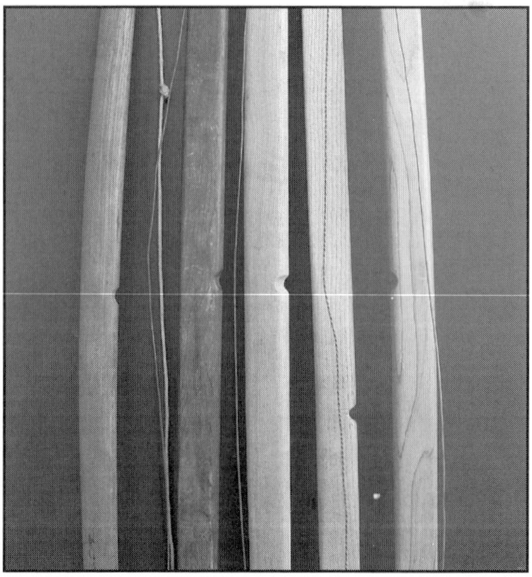

This picture gives a closer view of the notches in the center of the bows.

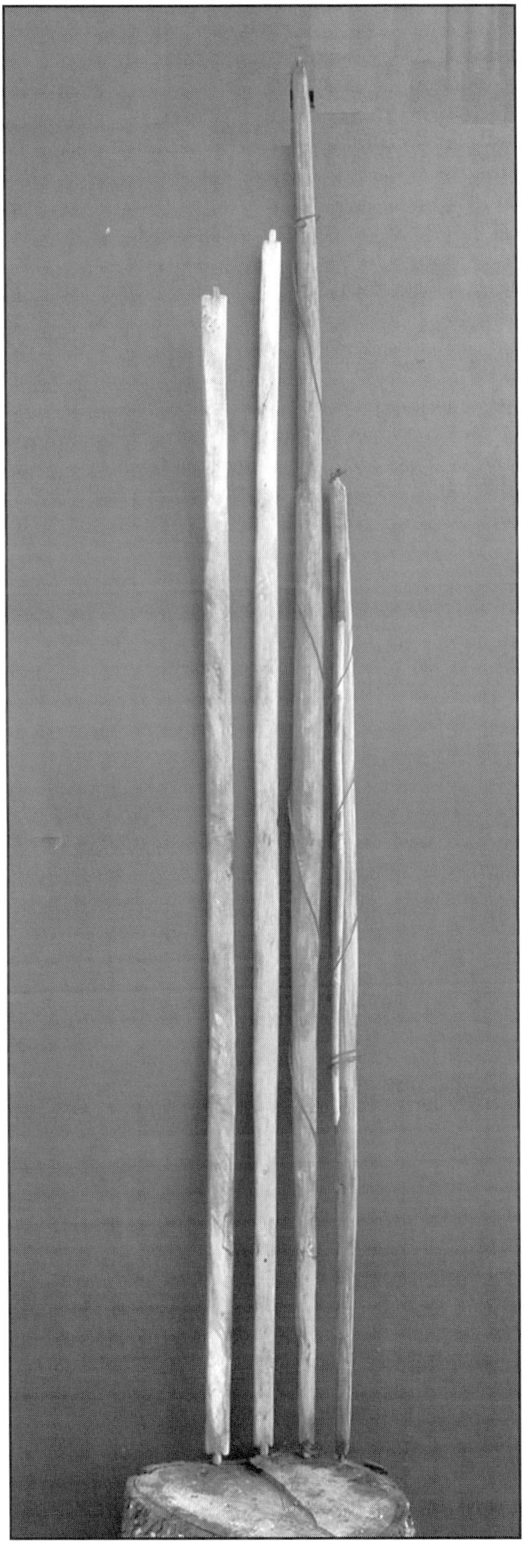

Left: *All four bows are from Ripley County and made out of Red Cedar. The two bows on the left were used by the Dave Marek family. Jim Marek was the fisherman in the family. These two bows were probably made in the early 1930s. All four bows were used in the clear streams in Ripley County.*

The third bow from the left is 76 ½" long, and has the baling wire to string the bow attached. The fourth bow from the left is 52" long, and has a cane shaft with a single spike on it. The cane shaft is held to the bow with the baling wire wrapped around the shaft and bow. The baling wire was also used to string the bow. Both bows were used by the Earl Emmons family from the early1930s -1950s.

Above: *Close up view.*

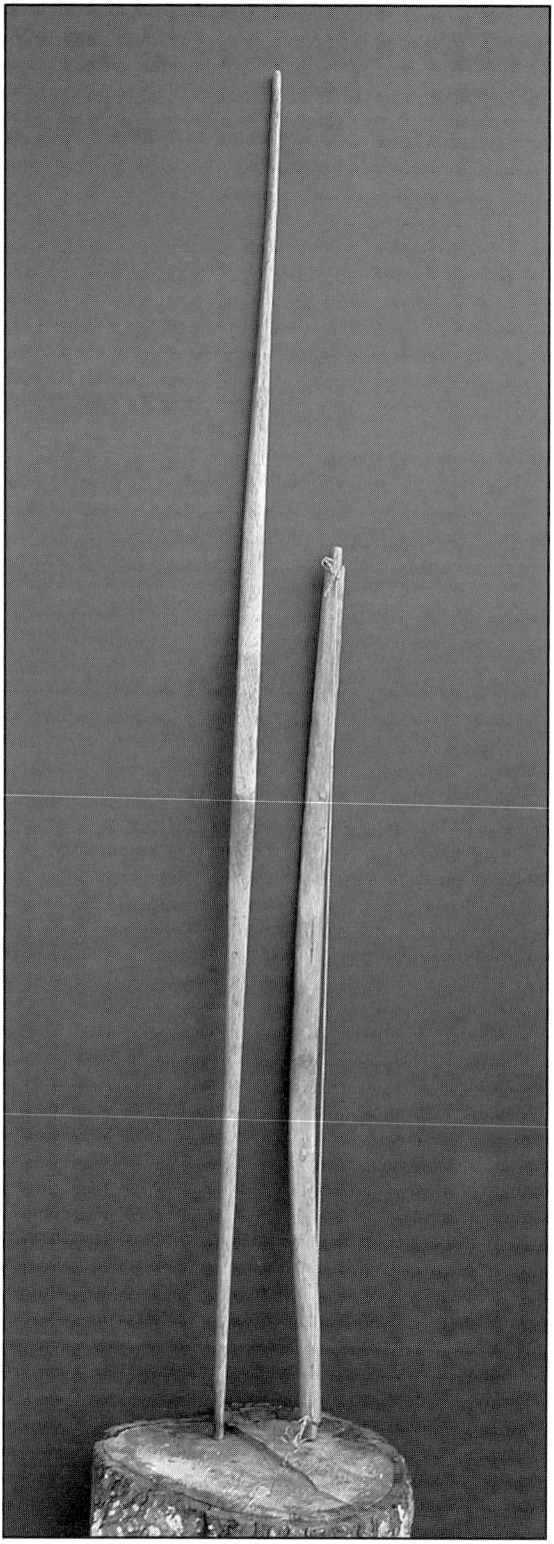

Left: *The bow on the left appears to be made from White Oak, and is 65 ⅞" long. This old bow is well made, but has no tips to attach a string or wire. Maybe the owner had a different method of stringing it, or maybe it was never finished. The bow on the right is 41 ⅞" long, and appears to be made out of Red Cedar or Hickory, but it is hard to determine. There was a shaft with this old bow but the spike was missing.*

Above: *Shows end of short bow.*

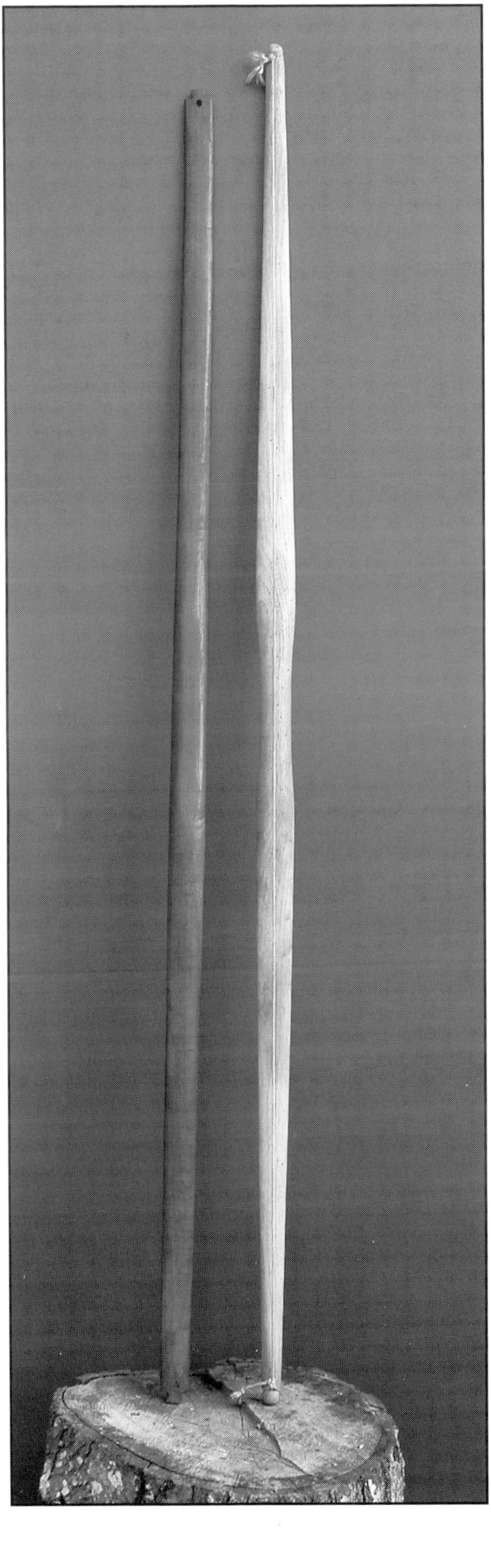

Left: *The bow on the left is 56" long, and it looks like it was made from Sassafras. It came from Ellsinore, Missouri, Carter County, and it was made about 1935. There is a small hole drilled in each end to run the string through, then over the protrusion to string the bow. This is the only bow that I have ever seen made like this. The bow on the right is 58 ¼" long. It appears to be made out of Ash, and it also came from Carter County, Missouri. It is a very well made bow. The Sassafras bow on the left was given to me in 1995 by the previous owner, Mr. Ed Stucker of Ellsinore, Missouri, Carter County. The bow on the right was previously owned by Mr. Glen (Buck) Warfel.*

Above: *Shows the end of bows.*

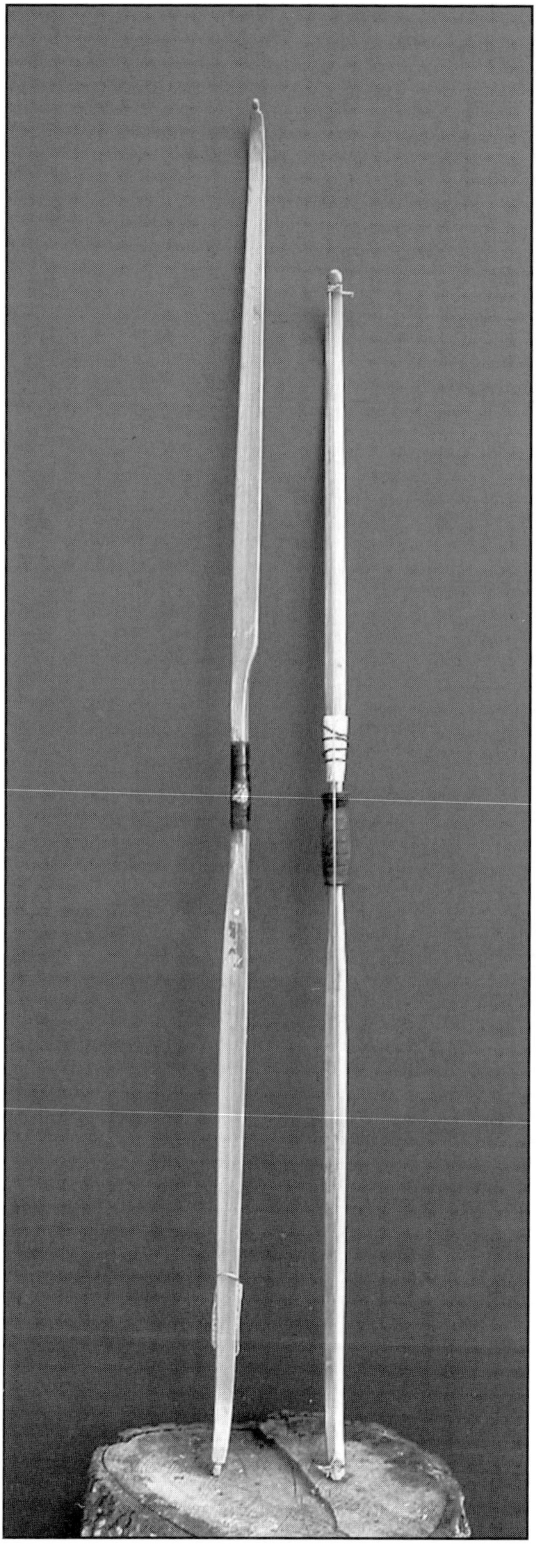

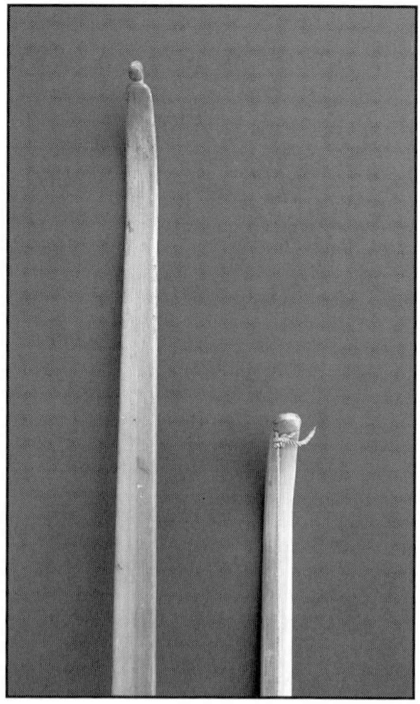

Left: *The fiberglass bows were some of the last bows used to bow and spike. These two were used in the early 1960s as bow and spikin' was winding down. The one on the left was used in Ripley County, and is 54 ¾" long. The one on the right was used in Carter County, and is 48 ⅝" long.*
Above: *Ends of bows.*

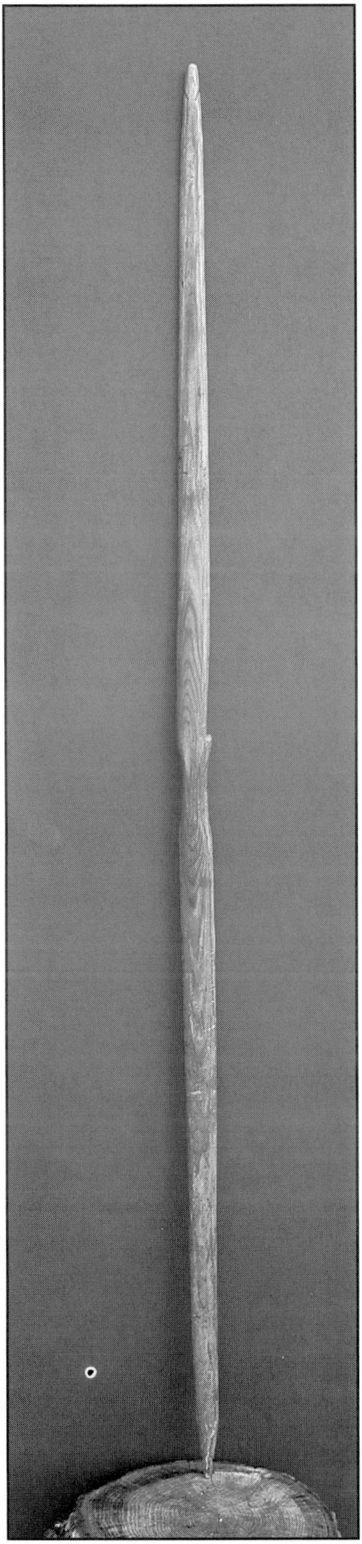

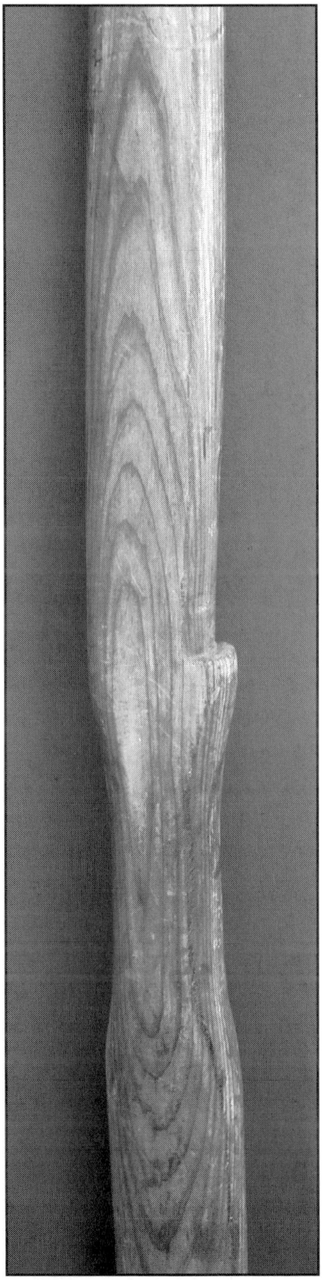

Left: *Red Cedar Bow with shelf for arrow rest. It is 64 ⅞" long, and was made for a left-handed person. The arrow shelf made into the bow was to be held perpendicularly to hunt rabbits and deer. Fishing bows were held horizontally. Further study of these old bows with the arrow rest in the center reveals that they could also be used to bow and spike fish. This would give the person using it a two-way bow to use on land and water.*

Above: *Close up view of the arrow shelf.*

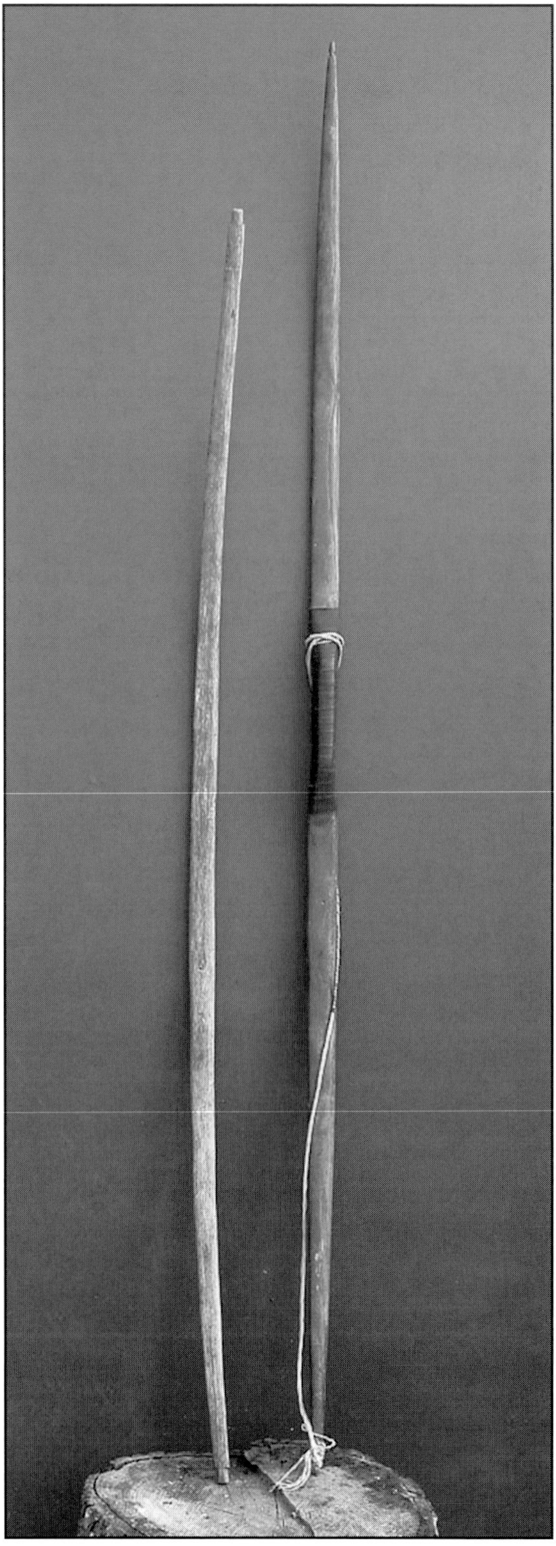

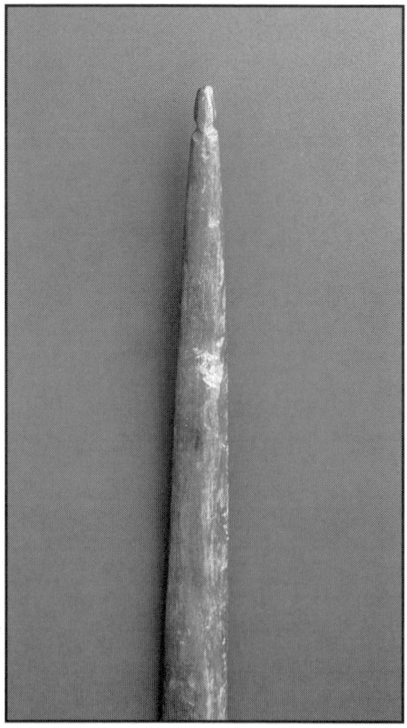

Left: *The bow on the left is 53 ¼" long, and was made from Hickory in 1949 by Elva Tillman, and used in Briar and Harris Creeks and Little Black River in Ripley County. The bow on the right is three pieces laminated together, and is 60 ¾" long. This bow took both rabbits and fish. It was made about 1929 by Charles V. Braschler for his nephew Charles J. Braschler.*

Above: *Close up view of end.*

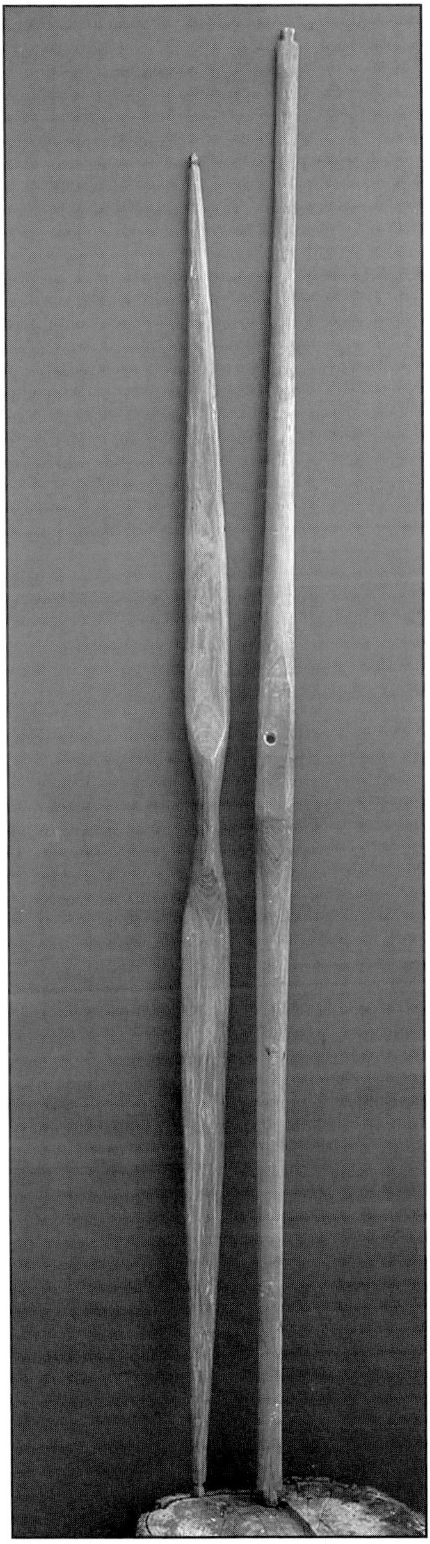

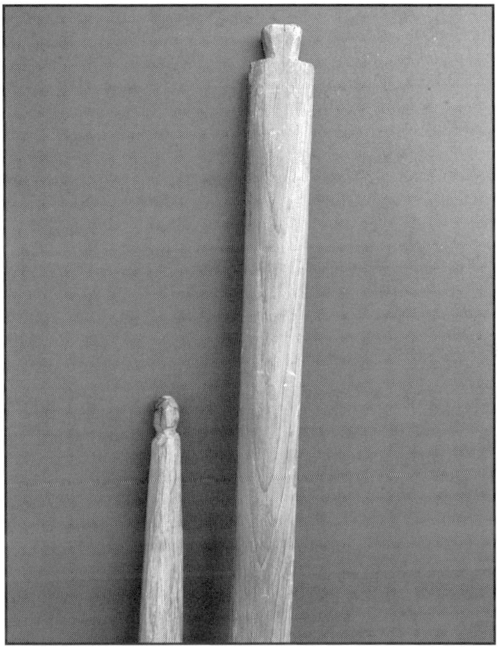

Left: *The bow on the left looks like Osage Orange, and is 65 3⁄16" long. It was probably used both for hunting and fishing. The bow on the right is made of Red Cedar, and is 72" long. The hole in the center looks like it was match-drilled from both sides with a pocketknife. The hole may have been drilled by some young boy to shoot horseweeds through, etc., or maybe the spike shaft.*
Above: *Close up view of ends.*

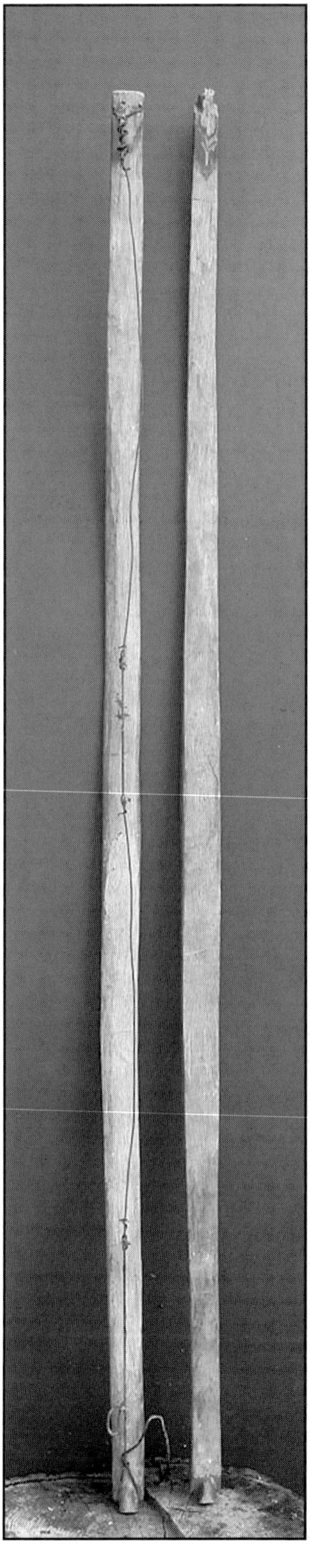

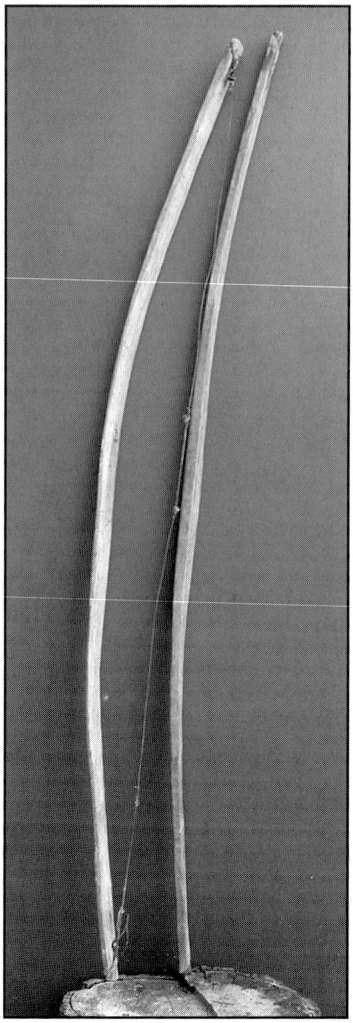

Far left: *Both of these bows were procured from Mr. Clayton Stevenson of Poplar Bluff, Missouri, Butler County in 1994. These two bows were used in Lick Log Creek in Bollinger County, and Bear Creek in Wayne County. The bow on the left in 54 5⁄8" long, and the bow on the right is 55" long. Mr. Stevenson said he and his brothers began bowin' and spikin' about 1925, and continued until around 1937 or '38. He also stated both of the bows were made about 1930 by his older brothers, but that he helped make them. A single spike made from a horseshoe nail was used to impale the fish, and a carbide light was also used at night to see the fish.*

Left top: *This picture shows the ends of the two bows made of white oak and how the string or wire is looped around the end to string the bow. The bow on the left has a string and baling wire combination.*

Left bottom: *Shows side views.*

This bow looks like it is made out of Hickory and is 45" long. It has a small hole in each end to attach what looks like a catgut string to the bow. (No known provenance)

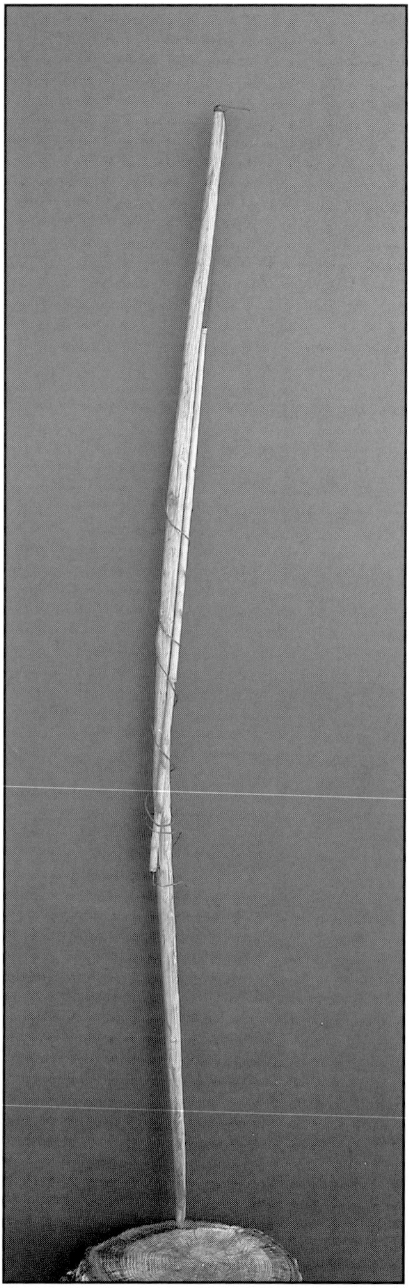

Red Cedar Bow 64 ½" long, was made around 1940 by O.A. McKinney for Bill Davis. A cane shaft 30 ½" long is attached to the bow by baling wire. The spike is missing. Used mostly in Little Black River, Ripley County, Missouri.

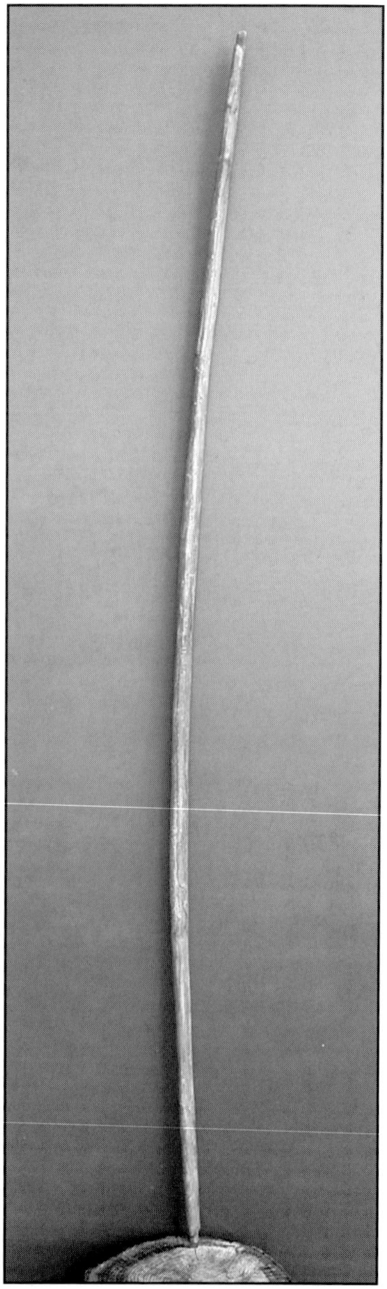

Red Cedar Bow 69" long from Iron County, Missouri. One must have to wonder how many fish this old bow helped take, which creeks it was used on, and what person made it.

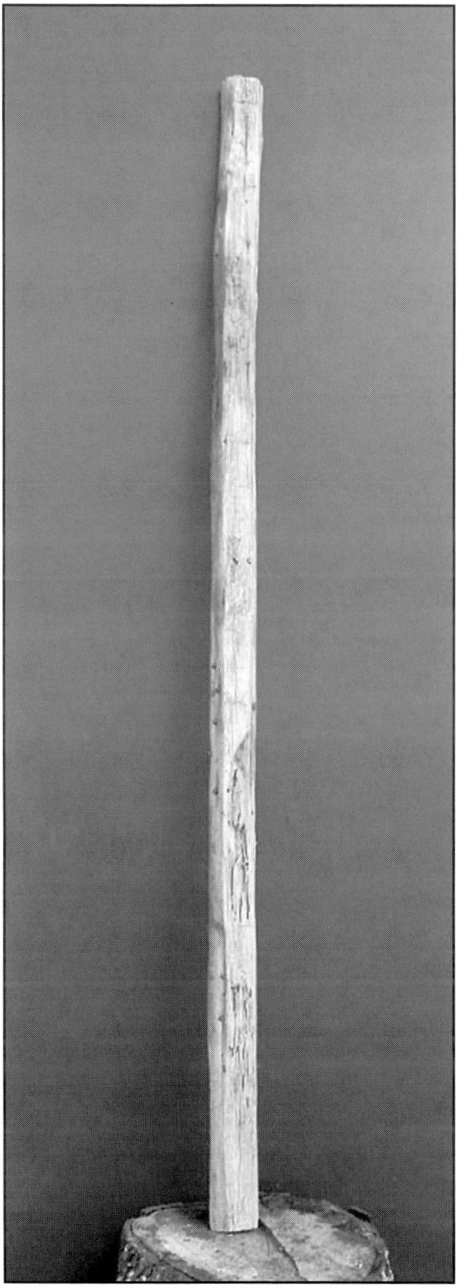

Red Cedar bow blank from the Little Black River area of Ripley County, this blank also had a single spike with it, and the shaft still in it. This is the only bow blank that I have found in my sixteen years of collecting. As well as being hard to find, it also is a good example of what the bow maker started with.

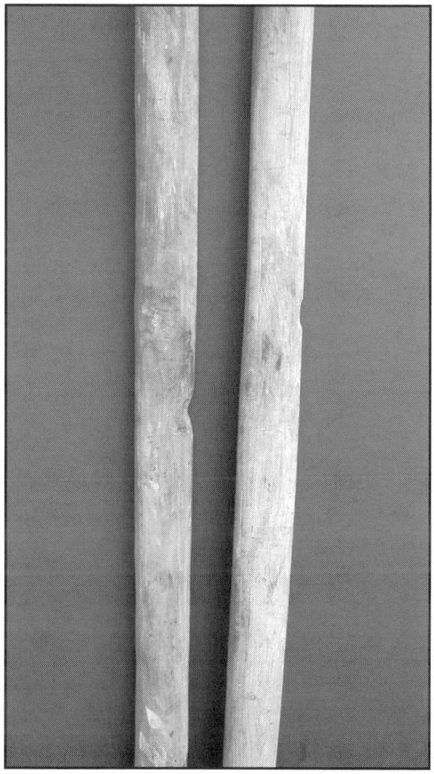

A picture of two Red Cedar bows made and used by the Dave Marek family, Ripley County. Looking closely in the center of the bows, the notches carved in the bows for the gig shaft to lay in can be seen. Most bow and spikers did not cut these in their bows, but let the shaft rest against their hand that held the bow.

All three spikes are from Ripley County. The two-prong on the left was made in 1954 by Mr. Melvin Lassen, a blacksmith in the northern part of Ripley County. The two-prong in the center was used by Joe Rush. Mr. Rush was elected Collector of Ripley County, and held that position for many years. Mr. Rush said he did not use it much, but when he did, it was used in Fourche Creek where he owned a farm. The two-prong on the right was made by Willard Borth in the late 1930s, and was used in the Little Black River around Highway 21 North. Mr. Borth was not a blacksmith, but made a nice enough little gig to do the job.

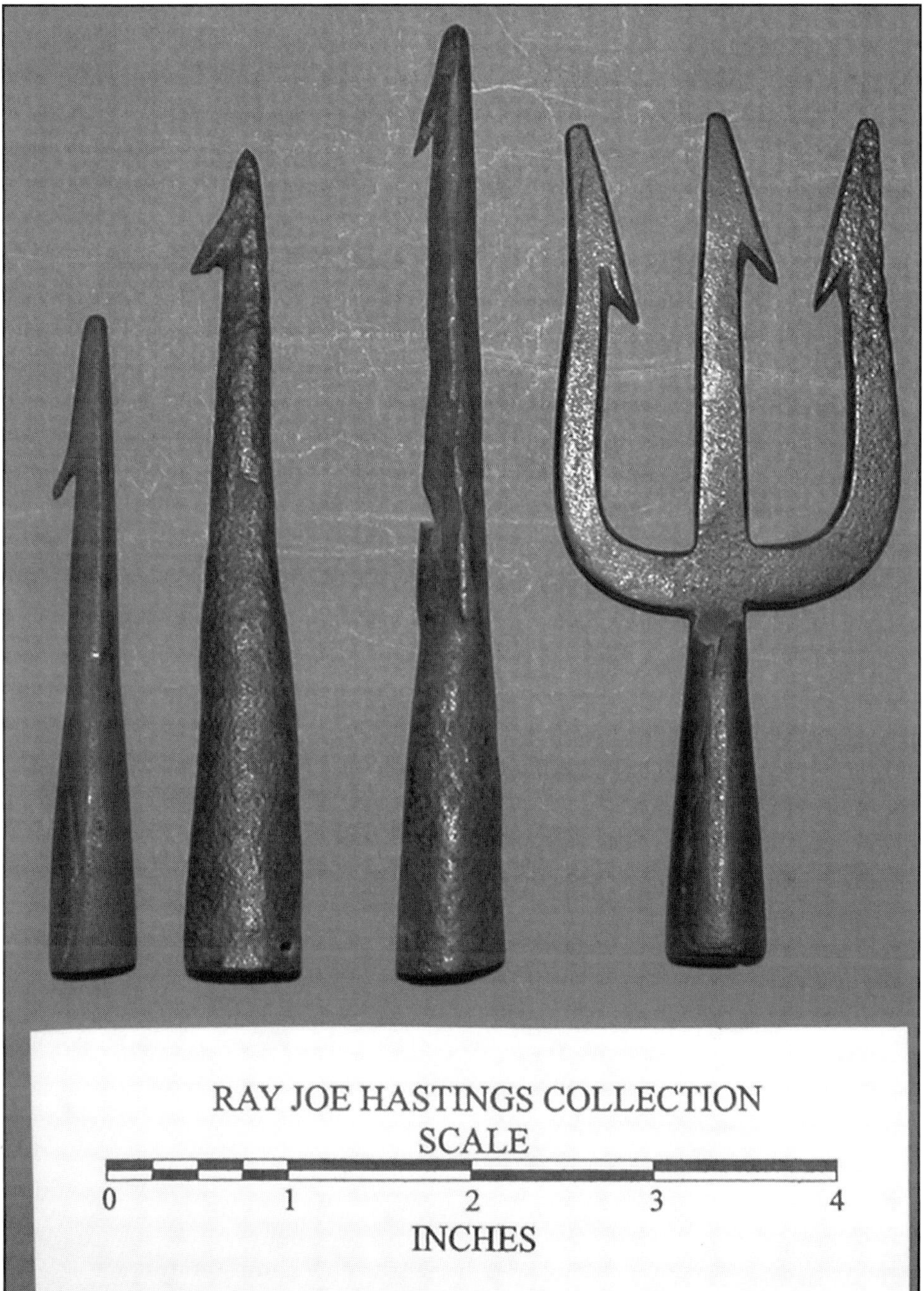

All four spikes are from Ripley County, Missouri. Mr. Bill Yates bought a shed that was full of different things from Mr. Eugene Marek, and these four spikes and two red cedar bows were in the shed. Mr. James Marek was a brother to Eugene, and people who knew him told me that he was the fisherman in the family. Even so, four spikes and two bows suggest that there was more than one fisherman that used them, so maybe in his younger days Eugene also fished with bows and spikes. Also, it was not unusual for a friend or two to go along who had no bow or spikes, and these extras could be used by them. The two cedar bows and four spikes were a very good find. Shown actual size.

The two-prong on the left was made in the late 1940s by Grover Whitwell for my dad, Joe Hastings. Mr. Whitwell was a blacksmith in Doniphan for several years, and made a large number of small bow spikes and large river gigs in his day. The blunt points on the two-prong were done by me and my younger brother Truman, while bow-spikin' for crawdads and fish in Briar Creek after their dad, Joe Hastings had quit using it in the early 1950s. The three-prong on the right was made by Mr. Ed Murray of Ripley County, and was used by the family many years in Simpson Creek. The Murrays, though not true blacksmiths, could and did make some of the nicest bows and spikes around. They were truly works of art. One has only to look at the points worn down to the beards to know "a heck of a lot of fish" were taken with this little three-prong spike. Shown actual size.

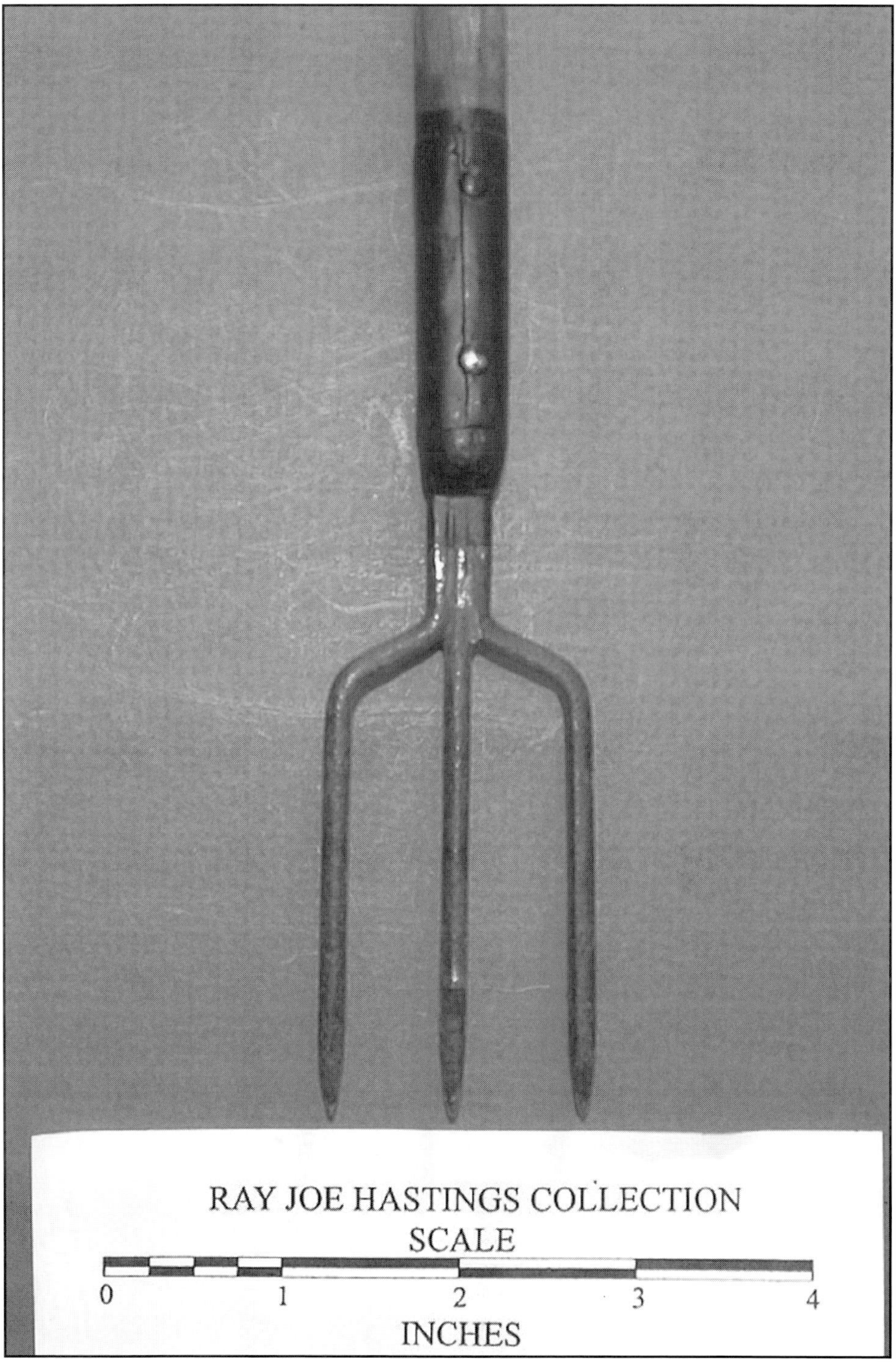

Mr. Ernest Murray hand made a shaft to go in this factory made gig. After attaching the shaft, he wrapped a piece of metal around the shaft, and put two brads through them to hold them together. I have used this little three-prong several times to bow and spike. Although one beard was knocked off, it is still as solid as the day he put it together for me several years ago. Shown actual size.

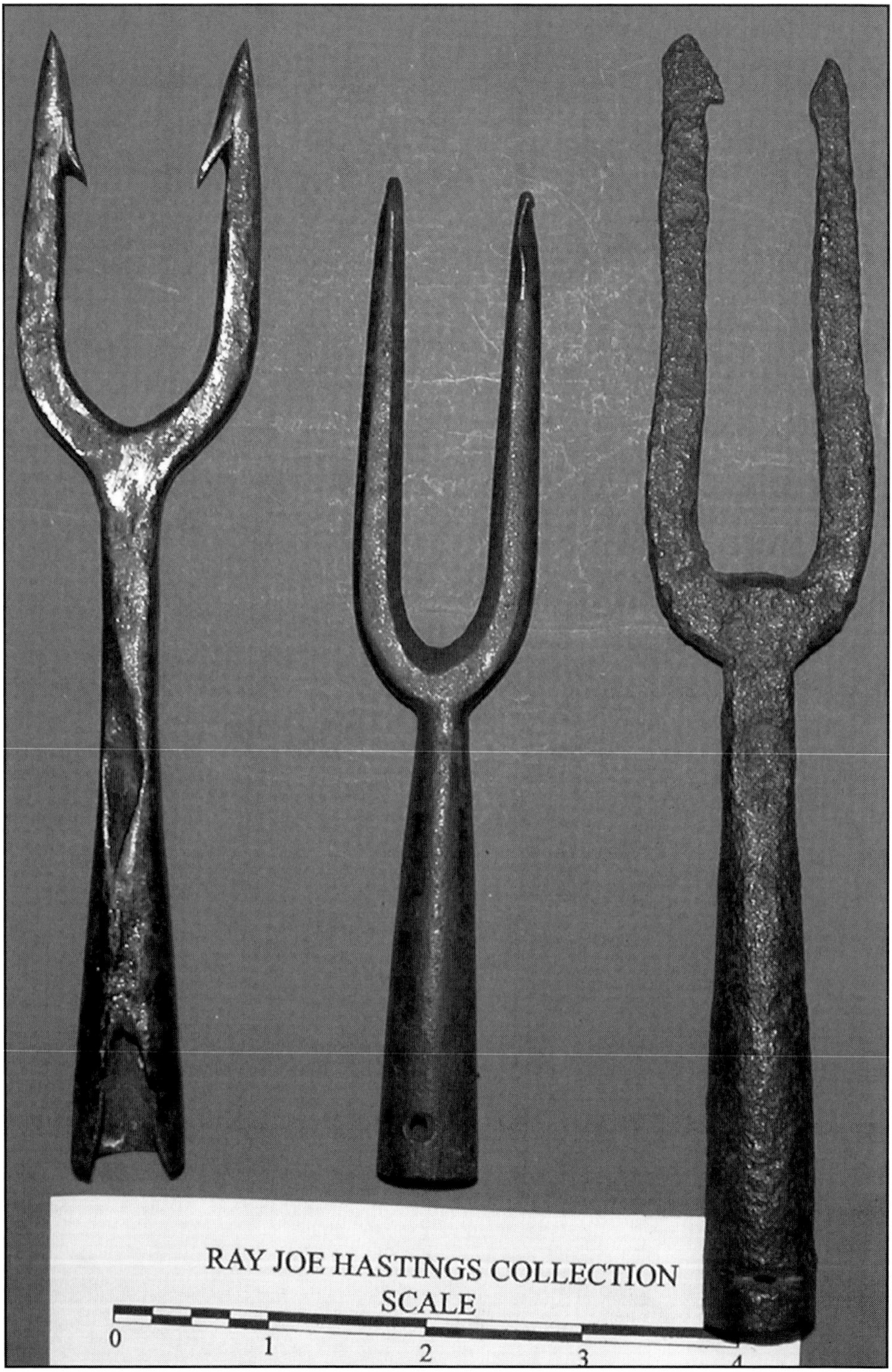

No provenance on the two-prong on the left. The two-prong in the center is from a flea market in Washington County. The two-prong on the right is from Dent County. This one is badly damaged and rusted from lying on the ground for many years. It is 8" long.

No provenance on these, just an interesting variety of bow spikes. The two-prong on the left was filed and re-sharpened. The three-prong in the center was used to the point that the center prong beard came off, and the two outer prongs had almost lost their beards. The two-prong on the right is a well-made gig with the beards on the face of the prongs, instead of the inside of the prongs like most were made.

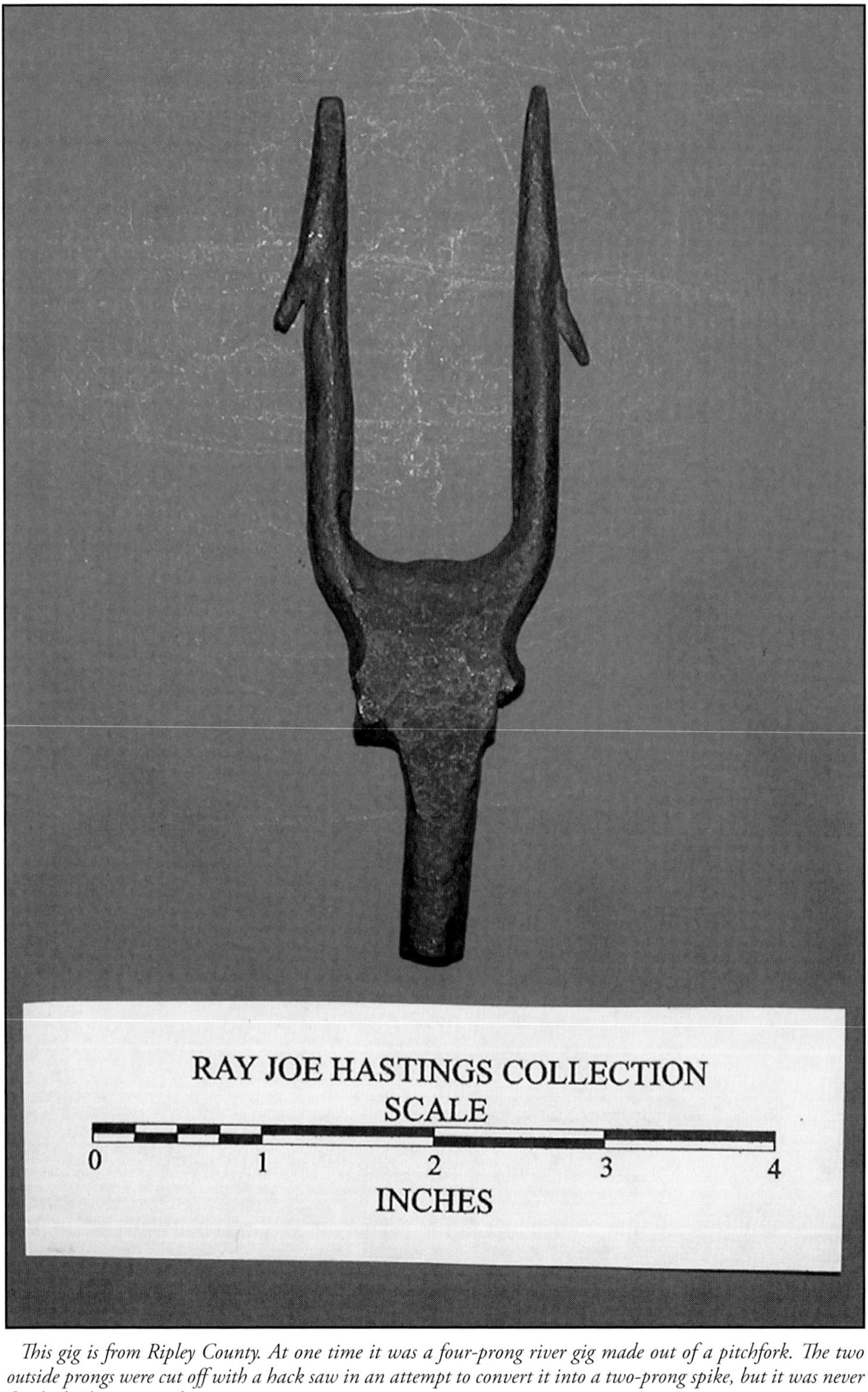

This gig is from Ripley County. At one time it was a four-prong river gig made out of a pitchfork. The two outside prongs were cut off with a hack saw in an attempt to convert it into a two-prong spike, but it was never finished. Shown actual size.

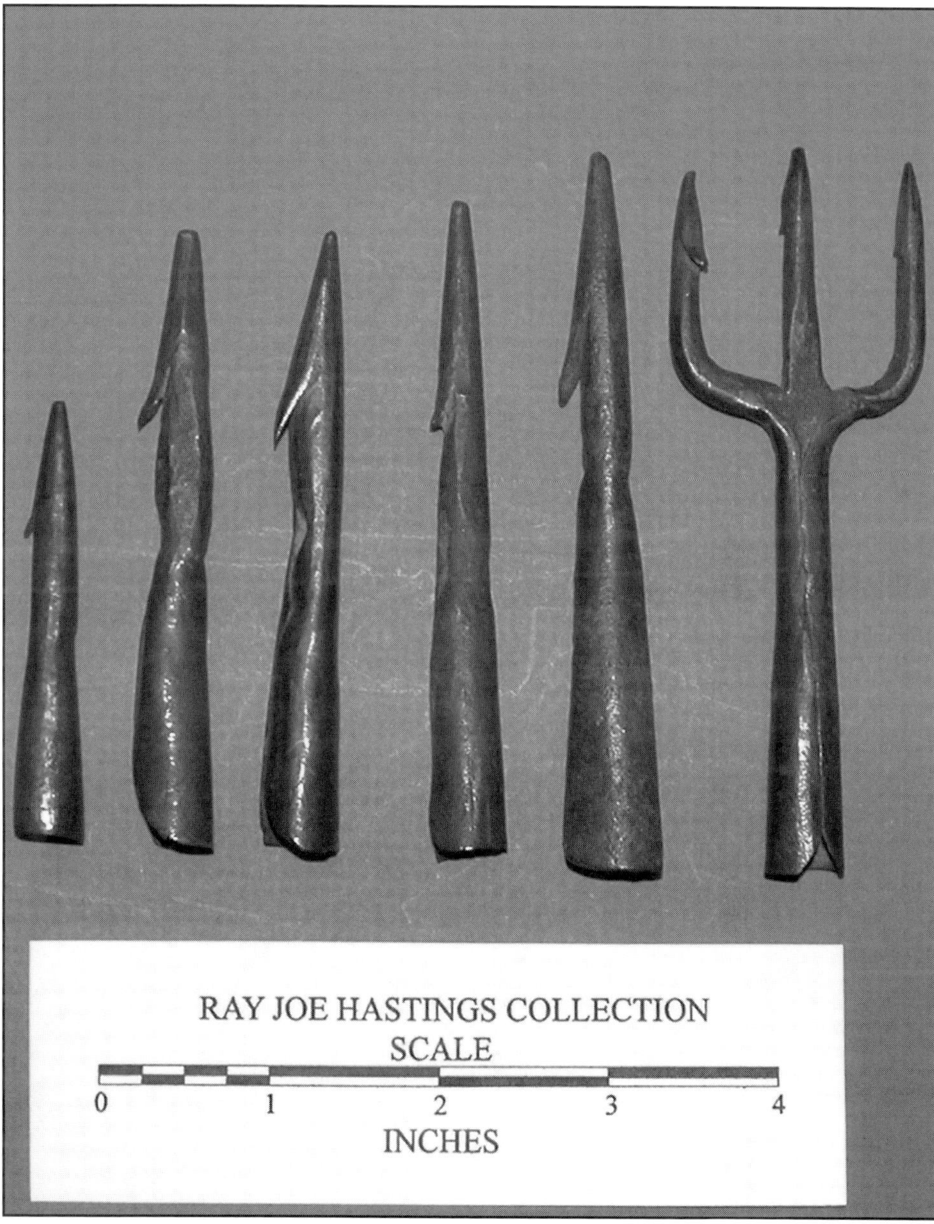

All six spikes are from Ripley County. They were procured from Mr. Melvin Rogers, whose dad was Mr. Ireneaus Rogers. A worker by the name of Bill Hur stayed with the Rogers and other families some, and worked for his room and board and for some extra money. Melvin told me that his dad, Ireneaus Rogers, made some of the spikes, and Mr. Hur made some; but he could not remember which were made by his dad, or which were made by Bill Hur. They were made about 1923, and they did a remarkable job on them. There was another two-prong that went with these, but years ago it was loaned out to a neighbor, and shot into a big fish on Little Black River and never recovered. To find six spikes in one bunch like this is almost too good to be true. The little spike on the left is only 2 9⁄16" long and to date is the shortest spike the author has found.

From Ripley County–another Winfield Bell two-prong spike. This one was owned and used by my Uncle Bob Belcher of Briar, Missouri in Buffalo and Fourche Creeks. Note the tack hole. Instead of being drilled, a six or an eight-inch file turned on its edge was used to cut the hole. Many people including my dad, Joe Hastings, used this method, because most of the families had no drills in those days. Shown actual size.

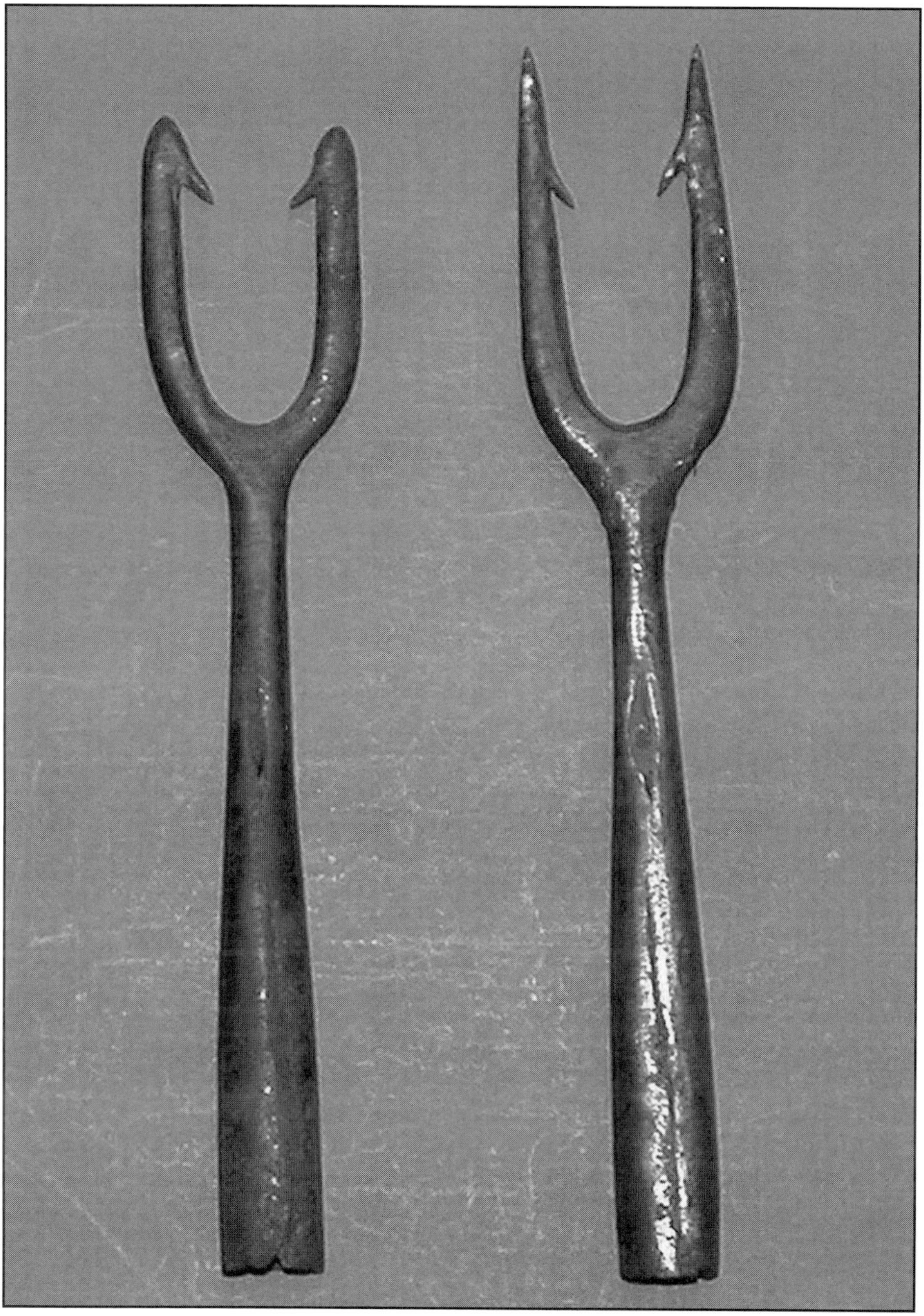

Both spikes are from Ripley County, Missouri. Young Ernest Christian worked with his dad in his blacksmith shop in Poynor, Missouri. learning the trade. He was born in 1906, and by the time he was fourteen years old, he was making his own gigs. These two were made in 1920 and are a fine pieces of work. The two-prong on the left was worn down almost to the beards, and not re-sharpened. The two-prong on the right was also worn down. Many years later, in the mid 1990s Ernest's son, Mickey, heated the points with a torch, and with a hammer drew the points out (like father, like son). He did an admirable job. These two bow gigs were used in Fourche, Briar, and Logan Creeks in Ripley County. Shown actual size.

From Ripley County, Missouri. This two-prong bow gig–as the two-prong was often called–belonged to Mr. Glenn Holland and was made by Mr. Winfield Bell–a blacksmith in Doniphan, Missouri–from the late 1890s, to the late 1940s. Glenn, together with his son and his dad, used this on Fourche Creek for many years. Shown actual size.

From Sharp County, Arkansas, this little three-prong is 4 ¼" long, and shows extensive use. The points on this three-prong are worn down to the beard that is left. The other two came off as the points wore down past the beards. A few counties in Arkansas along the Missouri border used the bow and spike to fish. As I talked to one elderly gentleman in the area, he informed me that he had done quite a bit of bow and spikin' in years past on Martin's Creek in Sharp County, Arkansas. Shown actual size.

The three-prong on the left was bought at a yard sale in, or near Poplar Bluff, Missouri, Butler County. The man who found it graciously sold it to me. The two-prong on the right also came from Butler County. The man I purchased it from lived in Poplar Bluff, Missouri, and he bought it at a farm sale in either Butler or Ripley County. Shown actual size.

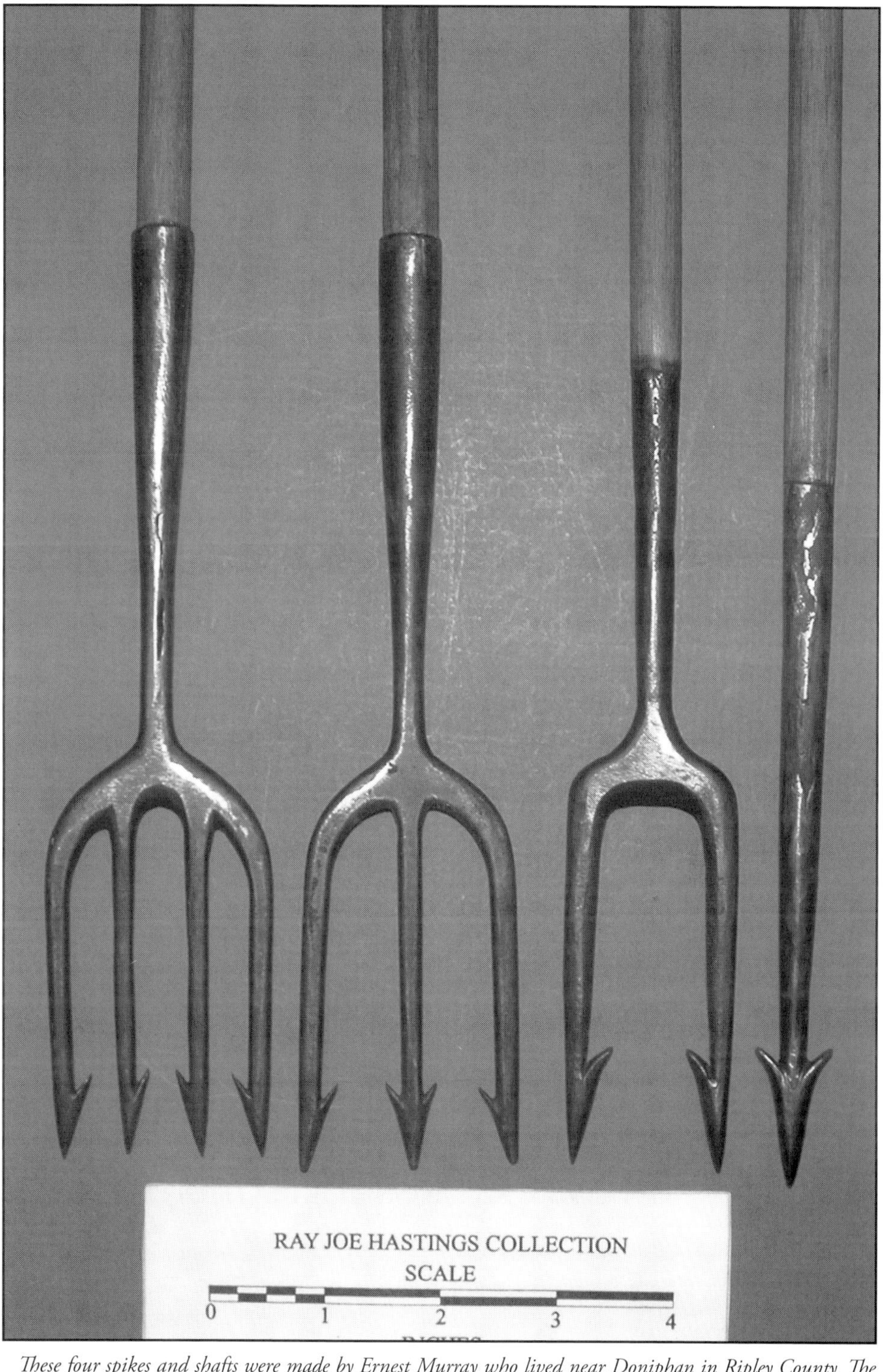

These four spikes and shafts were made by Ernest Murray who lived near Doniphan in Ripley County. The four and three prongs were made in 1933. The two prong and the single spike were made for me in 1992. These show the superb workmanship that Mr. Murray put into all four spikes.

Legendary Gig Makers from Ripley County, Missouri

Doniphan, Missouri is just another small town in the southeastern part of the Missouri Ozarks, with one exception. It sits on the banks of the Current River with the main part of the town being on the east bank, but just across the river on the west bank is an area known as West Doniphan. It is no wonder, with its location, there would arise some of the best gig makers in the country. Some of these gig makers made many gigs over a long period of time, and the gigs were not only durable, but were also so beautifully made that one would have to classify the makers of the gigs as "Legends."

I will go a step further and include the ones who not only made a small number of fine gigs, but could also make johnboats, paddles, pike poles, wildcat calls, bows and arrows; in fact, just about anything that was needed. The worst thing about being a legend is one has usually passed away before anyone has noticed that that person was the best at what he or she did. Unfortunately this is true with most of the gig makers who are included in this chapter, but many of their gigs are still around, and are still being used when gigging season comes around. It is my pleasure to tell about some of the many gig makers whose gigs I have had the opportunity to collect and to see their handiwork. I have listed them in alphabetical order according to their last names with the exception of Melvin Lassen and Oatman Tanner, who were gig-making friends, and their pictures are shown together.

Winfield Bell

Born 1871, Died April 16, 1949.

His obituary printed in the *Prospect News* on April 21, 1949 states:

> Robert Winfield Bell, aged 78, died in a Poplar Bluff hospital last Saturday following a few weeks illness. Mr. Bell is a native of this city and had lived here most of his life. He was a blacksmith by trade, and had run a shop here for half a century or more.

Although Doniphan had a great many blacksmiths before 1900, this one is the earliest I have knowledge of. Winfield Bell was his name, and by the late 1890s he was already in the "smithing business." Everyone says he was a good one, and I know his gigs were of the finest-quality workmanship. Like the other blacksmiths of this era, his gigs were made mostly from a pitchfork and a garden hoe. The pitchfork tines were cut off to the chosen length and the points heated and forge-welded back on themselves, leaving enough of the point unwelded to serve as the beard. The garden hoe was also cut to the necessary length and the two pieces were then forge-welded together. The gig pole was inserted into the hoe socket. Using this method, a good blacksmith could make a good gig in just a short time.

I have only one Winfield Bell gig; it is a three-prong, and can be seen in the Current River Heritage Museum at Doniphan, Missouri. I have several of his one and two-prong spikes that are very well made. Mr. Bell died April 16, 1949, and there is no way of knowing how many gigs he made. It is almost impossible to find one of his gigs today; however, there is no doubt in my mind that Mr. Bell is one of the earliest "Legends" of the gig makers in Ripley County!

ANDREW CHRISTIAN, ERNEST CHRISTIAN (Father and Son)

Andrew J. "Andy" Christian, Born June 17, 1882, Died May 6, 1952.
Ernest Christian, Born October 5, 1906, Died November 9, 1980.

Ernest Christian

Ernest Christian worked with his dad who owned a small blacksmith shop at Poynor, Missouri in Ripley County, a few miles southwest of Doniphan. By 1920, when Ernest was only fourteen years old, he was already making some of the finest gigs I have ever seen.

I do not know how many gigs he made, but the couple of two-prong bow gigs that I have that he made in 1920 are very well-made. Would this make him a legend? Probably not, but it does show how gifted some men were at the forge, and undoubtedly if he had continued working at his trade, he would have continued improving his skills. Ernest soon quit the blacksmith trade and moved on to other jobs. There is little doubt he learned most of his skills from his dad, and if he would have continued he would have had a name long remembered by the people of Ripley County as one of the "legendary gig makers!"

Mr. Christian's dad, Andrew, moved his blacksmith shop from Poynor, Missouri to Doniphan for a few years, and then down to Currentview, Missouri, which is on the Arkansas/Missouri border, where he continued the blacksmith trade for many more years. Although I do not have any of Mr. Andrew Christian's gigs, judging by his son's work, I am quite certain that his work would be of the same quality, and that he could also be referred to as a "Legend!"

JOHN DUSZA (Oxly, Missouri)

Born September 17, 1897, Died November 9, 1980.

John Dusza ran a blacksmith shop at Oxly about eight miles southeast of Doniphan. He may have done some "smithing" before going to work in Rockford, Illinois, but by 1930, he was back in Oxly working at his blacksmith shop, which he continued at for many years before finally quitting about 1970. In his forty-plus years at this trade, he made a vast quantity of gigs for people in the surrounding area.

I have one of his river gigs that was made like most blacksmiths made them. (A garden hoe was used for the socket, and a pitch fork for the tines.) It is little wonder a pitch fork was chosen, since the tines are just the right size and the quality of steel was as good as one could find. Also, the fact that the tines did not have to be cut out, or the socked did not have to be rolled over, saved a considerable amount of time in making a gig. The one that I have that was made by Mr. Dusza is a very well-made gig and is very highly prized. Although Mr. Dusza reportedly made hundreds of gigs, they are just about impossible to find today. Add one more "Legendary Gig Maker" to the list.

Tom Kennon (Doniphan, Missouri)

Born July 2, 1884, Died 1988.

Tom operated a blacksmith shop in Ripley County for approximately sixty years, 1920-1980. Although I have never seen any of the gigs that he made, I am sure that, like all of the rest of the blacksmiths that I have mentioned in these articles, he made his share of them. I am still looking for one of his gigs and would like to obtain one. If anyone has a gig that he made, or knows where it could be acquired, I would appreciate any additional information on this item.

Melvin Lassen

Born 1888, Died 1967.

He had his blacksmith shop on "O" highway in northern Ripley County when I knew of him. Mr. Lassen also made a large quantity of both the large gigs and the small spikes. I have one of each, a little two-prong bow gig, and a four-prong river gig made in 1956. The four-prong river gig is just beautifully made, and was never used. I feel very fortunate to have it in my collection. I feel that Mr. Lassen could certainly qualify as a "Legend" when it comes to describing gig makers or blacksmiths!

Melvin Lassen, left, and Oatman Tanner, right.

Mr. Lassen had a close friend who was also a "Legendary Gig Maker," by the name of Oatman Tanner. The two spent a good amount of time together hunting, fishing, and gigging, and were very competitive in their gig making, each one trying to make a better gig than the other. Looking at their gigs, I would say it was a toss-up on who made the better one, as both men's gigs were durable and very pretty to look at. Both great gig makers are gone now, but their memories live on for those who are the collectors of their work, and to the giggers who live in this place they call "Current River Country."

Oatman Tanner

Born March 17, 1890, Died January 31, 1976.

Taken from the *Prospect News*, February 4, 1976.

> Mr. Tanner worked in the blacksmith trade and auto mechanics from age 14 to the late 1930s. He was an equipment and mechanic foreman of the CCC (Civilian Conservation Corp) Camp at Bardley, Missouri for five years. In 1944, he opened the garage on Washington St., and became the franchised Chrysler-Plymouth dealer of Tanner and Sons Motor Sales and operated it until his retirement in 1956. He had a good reputation as an expert craftsman in metal and woodwork. He was an avid hunter and fisherman, and was well-known for his hand-made gigs. One of Tanner's gigs is on display in the Missouri State Capitol Museum, and gigs made by the self-taught craftsman are now prized as collector's items, as well as useful instruments.

According to Mr. Gene Ryan, who was a friend of mine, Mr. Tanner made his first gig while employed at the CCC Camp in the late 1930s. Although making gigs was a side-line for Mr. Tanner, during the twenty-five or thirty-year time period, he made many of them. I have a couple of his river gigs, and they are works of art. One man stated that he had lavished a lot of work on gigs that he had made to just sell them for $10 a piece. So it was with Mr. Oatman Tanner, who took a great deal of pride in his work and whose gigs sell for many times that amount today–if you can find them! Mr. Oatman Tanner is another one of the great and "Legendary Gig Makers" of Ripley County!

Ernest Murray

Born June 24, 1912, Died January 18, 2001.

Here was a man I knew quite well, and was one of the few men who could, and did, make just about anything: paddles, johnboats, and gigs, just to name a few. The four bow spikes I have that he made, a three and a four-prong in 1933, and a one and a two-prong made in 1992 were made to perfection. He also made the shafts that went into these, as well as the bows to shoot them. All were works of art.

I have a number of things that Mr. Murray made for me such as a miniature johnboat that is twenty-six inches long. This johnboat can be seen at the Current River Heritage Museum in Doniphan, Missouri. Even in the modern times, Mr.

Murray somehow got by with never having electricity, and he carried his water from a rock-lined dug well. He was never married, and to many he may have appeared to have lived a very simple lifestyle. However, he did not seem to miss the "luxuries of life." Mr. Murray was one of those rare individuals who just "made do" with what he had, and he did quite well in my opinion. If anyone could be called a "Legend," then I think Ernest Murray earned the title!

Ernest Murray

Frank Eugene Nickell

Born January 23, 1934, Died May 22, 2004.

Frank Nickell grew up in Ripley County on Well's Creek, just a few miles northwest of Doniphan, Missouri. At an early age his enthusiasm for fishing was already evident. At only ten years of age Frank knew of the bow and spike as a method for taking fish, and so with the help of his dad, Harold, they partially made a three-prong spike using only the coals in a wood burning heating stove. They later took the spike to Grover Whitwell for him to hammer out and roll the socket over for a shaft to fit into.

A young Frank Nickell

Frank had a sister named Corrine who later married my older brother Prientus. This gave me the opportunity to visit with Frank down through the years, and he told me this story: There was a long, deep hole of water on Well's Creek near his house, and as he spotted this large fish, he slipped up close enough to shoot a single-prong spike into it. The spike did not have enough stopping power to anchor the fish, and it started to swim toward the other end of the hole of water with Frank close behind. He finally got the fish after a long chase, and remarked to me that he was fishing for something to eat for supper, not just having fun. But so it was with many of the Ozark hill people who used the bow and spike to put food on the table; a way of procuring food was also a way of having fun.

In the 1950s Frank moved to St. Louis where he worked at a Chevrolet plant for the next twenty years. In the mid 1970s he moved back to Doniphan and opened

Old Harold Nickell home on Well's Creek, Ripley County, where Frank Nickell grew up.

a repair shop and started making river gigs. Over a period of a few years, he reportedly made around two hundred gigs, but then he moved to Kentucky where he ran a sawmill for a number of years. When he later moved back to Doniphan, he once again started making gigs. Frank did not make his gigs with a forge; he preferred to cut them out with a torch. In the 1970s, and then in the late 1990s, he found a company that would machine cut the lower half of the gig and prongs, and Frank would then cut the beards on the prongs and use a lug wrench for the neck of the gig. To this he would add a socket he had made and would weld them together. He would grind this down, and it was almost impossible to see the weld.

Frank probably made in excess of three hundred gigs during the 1990s-2004. This would be a total of five hundred plus fishing gigs made during his lifetime. His gigs were very well made and had the eye appeal that drew giggers to them. Frank is gone now, but the giggers of Ripley and surrounding counties will keep the memory of this "Legendary Gig Maker" alive for may years to come when they use his gigs on a regular basis during gigging season!

George Pierce (Pratt, Missouri)

Born January 5, 1888, Died October 6, 1967.

Although I have not seen his work, my friend, Gene Braschler, stated that Mr. George Pierce was a very good gig maker and made quite a few gigs. He was a blacksmith beginning sometime around 1920 to about 1950. Gene also said Mr. Pierce showed him several tips on the art of gig making. He made gigs in his blacksmith shop that was located in Pratt, Missouri. Like most of the other blacksmiths, gig making was a part of the work he performed for the people in the community. I would like to see one of his gigs. My guess is that it would be nice to look at and worthy of throwing into a fish!

George Pierce

Alvin Price

Born June 7, 1913, Died January 4, 1990.

Taken from the Prospect News of January 10, 1990.

A lifetime resident of Ripley County, and a retired employee of the Missouri State Highway Department.

I knew Mr. Price for a number of years, but did not know he made gigs until a friend gave me one of his gigs. I do not believe Mr. Price made many gigs, but the one I have is well made and looks almost identical to the ones made by Grover Whitwell. I would classify his work as very good, and based on that information, thought he was worthy of being included in this book as one of the better, if not a master gig maker in Ripley County.

James William Rawlings

Born June 14, 1888, Died November 7, 1969.

A grandson of Mr. James Rawlings, Lloyd Towell of Poyner, Missouri gave me this information about his grandfather, Mr. Rawlings. He stated that his grandfather was born in Stoddard County, Missouri. He knew that his grandfather was nineteen years old when he worked for the Gibson Family in Poyner, Missouri. Mr. Towell could not pinpoint when Mr. Rawlings started blacksmithing, but states it was quite some time before 1945. He retired about 1964 as the times were changing, and we were moving into a "throw away" society. The *Prospect News* obituary of November 13, 1969, stated that he moved to Ripley County in 1906, and he was married to Margaret Riley.

James William Rawlings

I have seen at least one gig that Mr. Rawlings made, and believe that it was a three-prong river gig, and of the finest workmanship that can be found anywhere. Because I have taken gig-making lessons myself, and know how long it takes for the average individual to learn how to make a decent gig, it is my opinion that Mr. Rawlings must have made quite a number of gigs in his many years of blacksmithing to produce the type of quality gig that I have seen. He would be labeled a Master Gig Maker by anyone seeing his work!

The Ryan Brothers, Thomas Ryan and Ed Ryan

Thomas Ryan, Born September 7, 1891, Died March 23, 1959.

PVT. ARMY TNG CORPS WORLD WAR I

Ed Ryan, Born unknown, Died unknown.

I do not know how much blacksmith work Mr. Thomas Ryan did, if any, before serving in World War I (1914-1918), but by the 1930s, he had a shop on Highway 142 West between Ponder and Gatewood in Ripley County. Tom, as he was called, had a younger brother Ed Ryan, who may have worked at the blacksmith shop with his brother Tom, since his gig making was honed to a sharp edge, as I can attest to.

I saw some big-river gigs and a couple of three-pronged spikes that Ed made. Gene Braschler, who also wrote a short story in this book Bows and Spikes of Pratt, knew Tom and Ed quite well, and Ed gave Gene a lesson or two on gig making. According to Gene, Ed must have been experienced in making gigs, as he was very smooth and good at it. I have also seen a few that Tom Ryan made, and they are of the same quality workmanship as his brother Ed's gigs. It would be impossible to know just how many gigs these gig makers made during their time at this work. However, judging from the workmanship on each one, I would say that between the two it would have been a large number, and they could both be classified as Master Gig Makers!

Grover Cleveland Whitwell

This information was obtained from the obituary column of the *Prospect News* of September 26, 1963.

> Grover Cleveland Whitwell, June 24, 1885-September 25, 1963. Mr. Whitwell, 78 years old, was a retired blacksmith, having operated a shop for 35 years in Doniphan, Missouri.

Having a shop for thirty-five years would have put his blacksmith business starting about 1925, since his shop was still open around 1960, unless he was learning the trade a few years earlier. I remember watching Mr. Whitwell in the late 1940s make a two-prong bow gig for my dad, and I still

Fred Boyles, Grover C. Whitwell, and Gary Boyles about 6 years old. Picture was taken about 1960. The little mule was named Rabbit.

have this one in my collection. Mr. Whitwell, in his many years of blacksmithing, made a large number of gigs, both the large river gigs and the small bow spikes. Mr. Whitwell passed away almost forty-five years ago, but a person can still occasionally find one of his gigs, and only a few weeks ago, I acquired a little two-prong bow gig that appears to have been unused, that he made.

Although most of Mr. Whitwell's river gigs were made from a garden hoe and a pitch fork, his small gigs (spikes) were made out of a small piece of spring steel like a buggy or pickup spring. These were heated and split out with a hammer and chisel (explained elsewhere in this book) if making several gigs while staying busy doing other blacksmith work. I would definitely add the word "Legend" to the name of Mr. Grover Cleveland Whitwell!

Legendary Gig Makers from Surrounding Counties

Not only was Ripley County gifted for having "Legendary Gig Makers," surrounding counties had many whom I am sure were just as gifted as the ones in Ripley County. As stated earlier, I have been collecting gigs for several years, and my quest has led me to many sales in other counties where I have met many people who have told me stories about some of these people. Unfortunately space will not allow me to include everyone, but I feel there are some who must be included in my story. These men were true "Legends," and I feel that my book would not be complete if I did not mention them in it.

JOE CORBY (Van Buren, Missouri, Carter County)
RAYMOND SMITH (Eminence, Missouri, Shannon County)
RAY HICKS (Winona, Missouri, Carter County)

I do not have much information on these three gig makers except that I have heard they were exceptional at their craft, and very skilled gig makers. However, if I failed to include them in the list of "Legendary Gig Makers" I do not think my list, or my story, would be complete. So I have added their names to the list just so they will be remembered as the "Legends" that they obviously were. I am sure there were many other great gig makers that needed to be added to this list, but I did not have their names or the information on them, and I am sorry that I was not able to include their names.

THE ELLERMANS

In a July 25, 1995 interview with Mr. Lloyd Ellerman, a nephew to Irv, related this information to me. There were five Ellerman brothers who made gigs; some made more than others. Their dad, William Henry Ellerman (2-26-1855 to 12-1-1942) came to Shannon County in 1897, and was a master blacksmith and a gig maker.

Matthew Columbus Ellerman, the oldest son (2-8-1877 to 1945) made quite a few gigs. Irving Dewitte Ellerman, the second oldest son (6-10-1891 to 1-16-1973) made a large number of gigs. The third oldest son, Thomas Henry Ellerman, (9-23-1894 to 8-9-1965) also made a lot of gigs. Another brother, the fourth oldest son, Leslie True Ellerman (1-19-1897 to 11-28-1969) made a few gigs, and the youngest son, Webster Leland Ellerman (1-2-1904 to 7-4-1976) made an estimated twenty-five to fifty gigs. I have gigs made by Irv and Thomas Henry Ellerman, and I am sure that all of these brothers made gigs in the same tradition and most, if not all, were "Legendary Gig Makers!"

Even though Mr. Lloyd Ellerman, who was a son of Webster Leland Ellerman, passed away a while back, I want to personally thank his family, and let them know how much I appreciate the information that was given to me for this book. It is my hope that all of the remaining Ellerman families will find this information useful.

Irving Dewitte Ellerman

Born June 10, 1891, Died January 16, 1973.

Irving Dewitte and Osie Martha Ellerman

It was June 24, 1995 when a sale bill with an Ellerman gig on it caught my eye. I had already been collecting gigs for nearly four years, and was always ready to add to my growing collection of not only big gigs, but also the small bow spikes, which I was most interested in. The sale was in Eminence, a small town in Shannon County, Missouri, almost eighty miles north of Doniphan, Missouri where I live. After some back and forth bidding, I was able to get the gig. And what a gig it was! Very beautifully made and without a doubt as sturdy as it was pretty! The man who made it was a "Legendary Gig Maker" from Shannon and Reynolds County, Missouri, who in his younger days reportedly could make as many as four gigs a day, which was quite a feat. This was told to me by my gig-making teacher, Mr. Paul Martin of Bunker, Missouri, who had watched Mr. Irving (Irv) Ellerman make several gigs.

Included in this story is a picture of Irving Dewitte Ellerman and his wife Osie Martha Ellerman. At an age when hands like steel used to hold a hammer and tongs like a vise could no longer do so, Irv's wife Osie stepped in to help hold the steel while Irv was making a gig. One of the three-prong river gigs I have was made by Irv and probably his wife Osie, as it was one of the last gigs he made. This makes this gig historically more important since not too many women were known to have helped make gigs.

PAUL MARTIN (Bunker, Missouri)

Born 1929, Died, around 2004.

Paul Martin

When it comes to gig making, or maybe who made more gigs than anyone else in the country, Paul Martin, who lived in Bunker, Missouri at the time I knew him, would be at, or near the top of the list. Starting in 1960, and up to the year 2000, he estimated that he made around three thousand gigs. He stated that in his younger days he could make two gigs a day, and three if he hurried. At that time he sold his gigs for twenty dollars each; in his own words, forty dollars was real good money back then.

As I wrote earlier in the book, I took gig-making lessons from Mr. Martin in the fall of 1995 through the spring of 1996, and often marveled at how fast he could make a gig, and how nice it looked when he finished. He never had to file out any rough spots, since everything was completely done with just a hammer and chisel.

While I was taking lessons, I asked Mr. Martin to make me a few bow spikes. This he gladly did, and the quality of workmanship that he applied to his big-river gigs, was equally bestowed on the smaller ones. According to Mr. Martin, these are the only spikes he had ever made. By the time he started making gigs in 1960, few people were using the bow and spike, as its heyday was pretty well over by then. I feel very fortunate to have the only ones he ever made, but more fortunate to have known Paul Martin as my friend and my instructor. I say to this "Legendary Gig Maker"–MAY HE REST IN PEACE....

"May They All Rest In Peace"

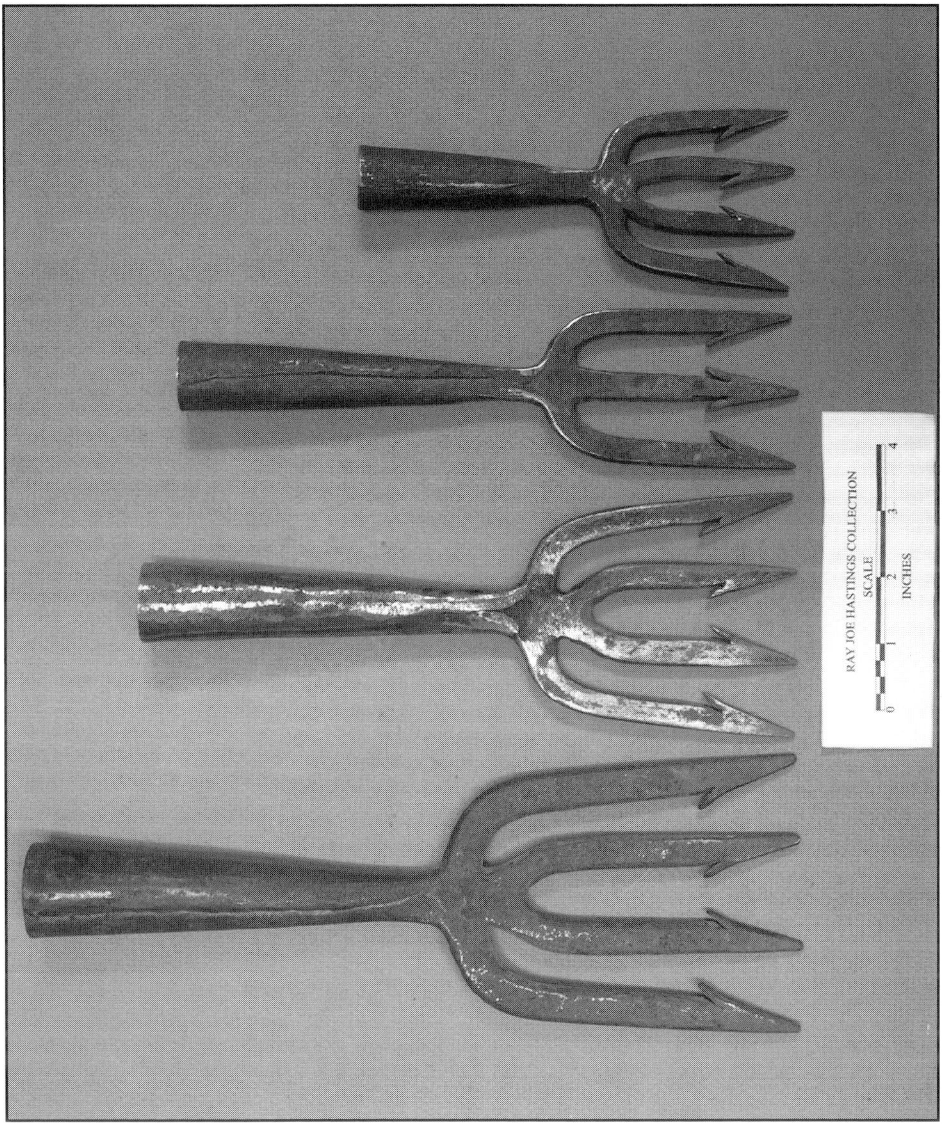

Here are four river gigs made by Paul Martin of Bunker, Missouri in the fall of 1995 and the spring of 1996, when Mr. Martin taught me gig-making through the Missouri Traditional Arts Apprenticeship Program. Mr. Martin made some 3,000 gigs in the 40 years he spent at his craft from 1960 to 2000, and was one of the finest gig-makers around. Mr. Martin's beards on his gigs were always cut out with a chisel instead of the old blacksmith way where the point was drawn out and forge-welded back on the prong.

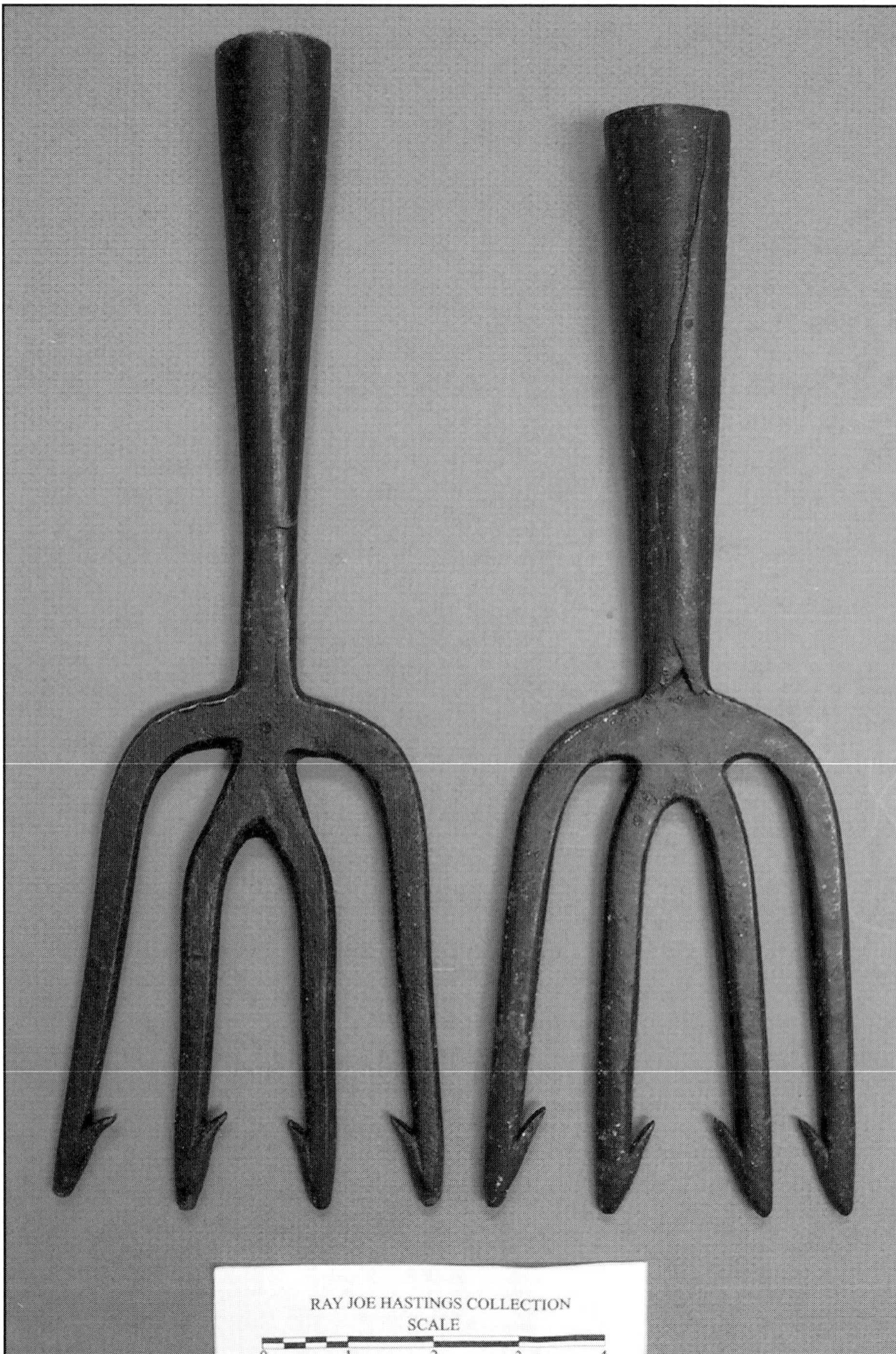

These two river gigs were made by Thomas Henry Ellerman, a brother to Irv Ellerman. The similarity to Irv's gigs is plain to see. These are well-made gigs with a great deal of eye appeal. No doubt there were many fish taken with these, as the points are worn down from striking rocks and gravel in our clear, swift-flowing streams here in the Missouri Ozarks. A dot was put on one side of the throat to tell his gigs from his brother Irv's gigs.

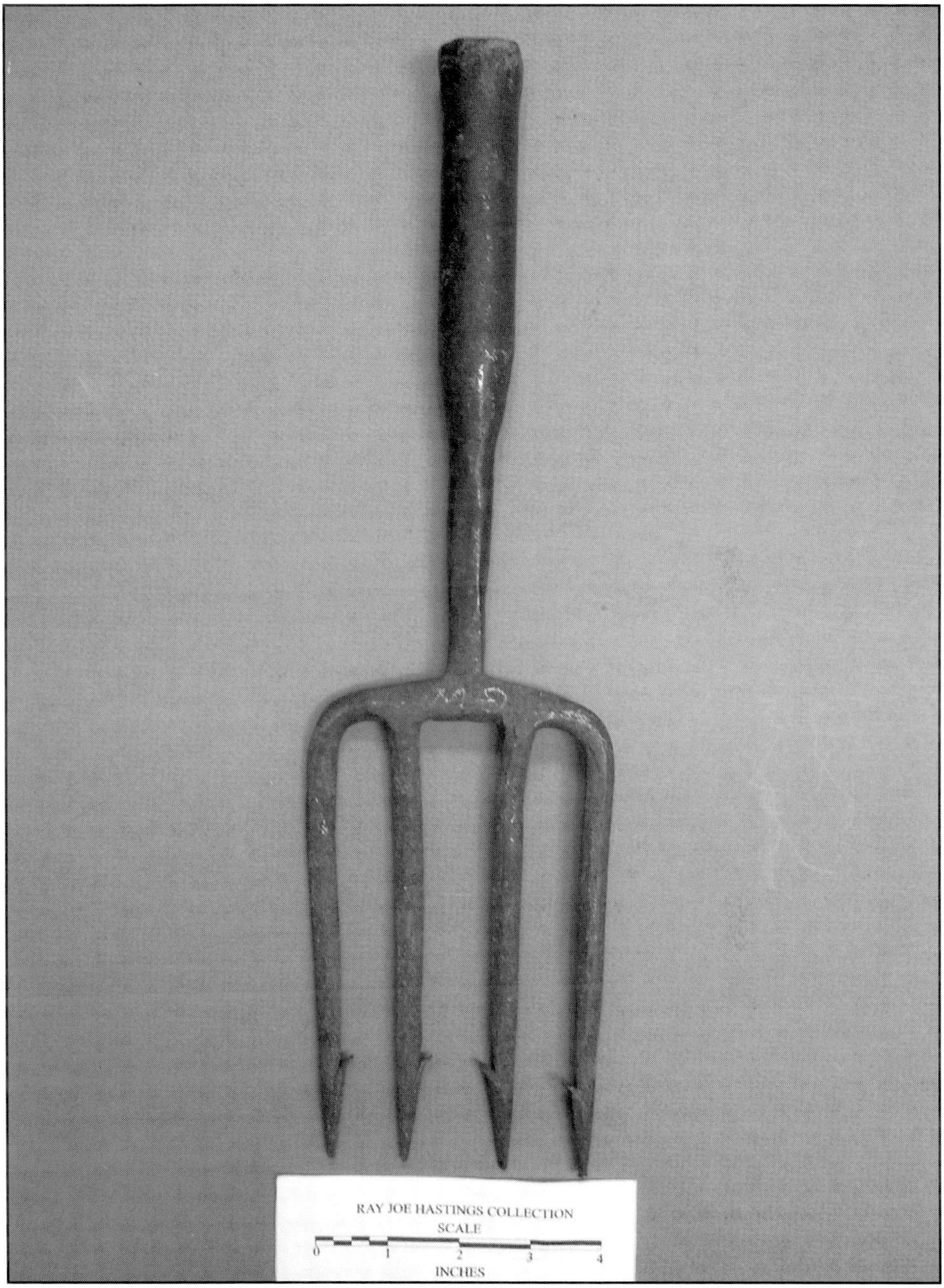

Made by Grover Whitwell probably in the 1940s or 1950s. His blacksmith shop closed about 1960. By then most of the other blacksmith shops in and around Ripley County also had closed down due to a lack of work, as people were using mail-order catalogues to get what they needed, or would just go into town to pick it up at the local hardware store. The long history of the blacksmith making what people needed finally had come to an end.

The socket on this gig was from a worn-out garden hoe. The gig was made from a pitchfork. The points were heated and drawn out by striking with a hammer. The points were then re-heated and bent back and forge-welded to the prongs, leaving enough material un-welded to serve as the beards. The two pieces were then heated to a high temperature, and using either sand or borax as a flux, were forge-welded together to finish the gig. Using this method, Mr. Whitwell could make a gig in as little time as thirty minutes.

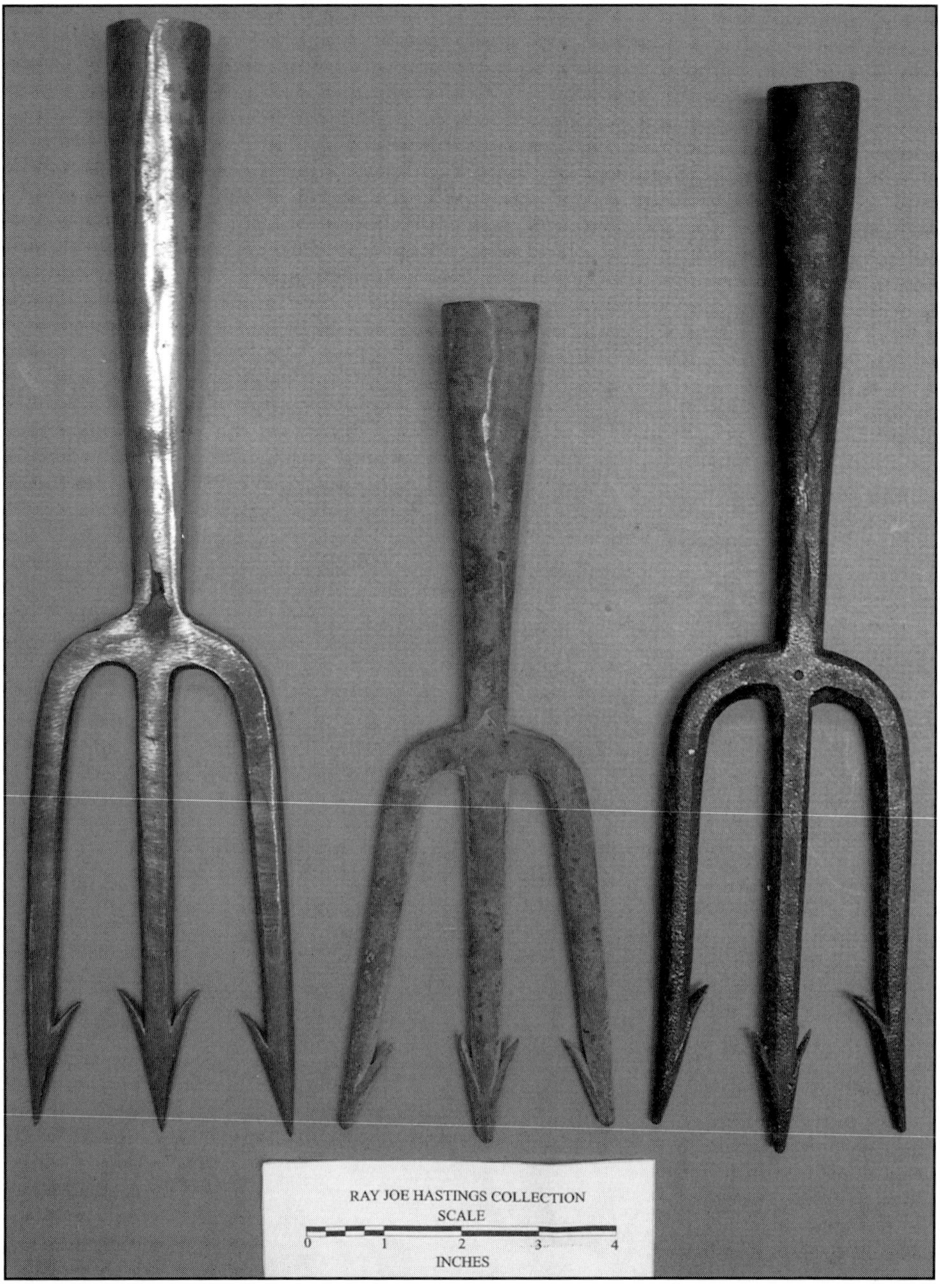

These fine gigs were made by Irving (Irv) Ellerman. Irv, as he was called by his friends was a master gig-maker from Shannon County. The one on the left and the one on the right were never used. After seeing a sale bill from Eminence, Missouri in 1995, with the gig on the left listed, I drove up to the sale. After some competitive bidding, I finally bought the gig. It was one of the last gigs that Mr. Ellerman had made–this was in the late 1960s. In earlier years, Irv had brothers, Matthew, Thomas, Leslie, and Webster who made gigs. One brother, Thomas, made a lot of gigs that looked like Irv's work, so their solution to this problem was solved when Irv put a dot on each side of the throat area of his gigs, and his brother just put one. The gig on the left, and in the middle does not have the dots on them, which indicates his brother was no longer making gigs at this later date. The gig on the right has the dots. Mr. Irv Ellerman's gigs are hard to find, and harder to buy when found.

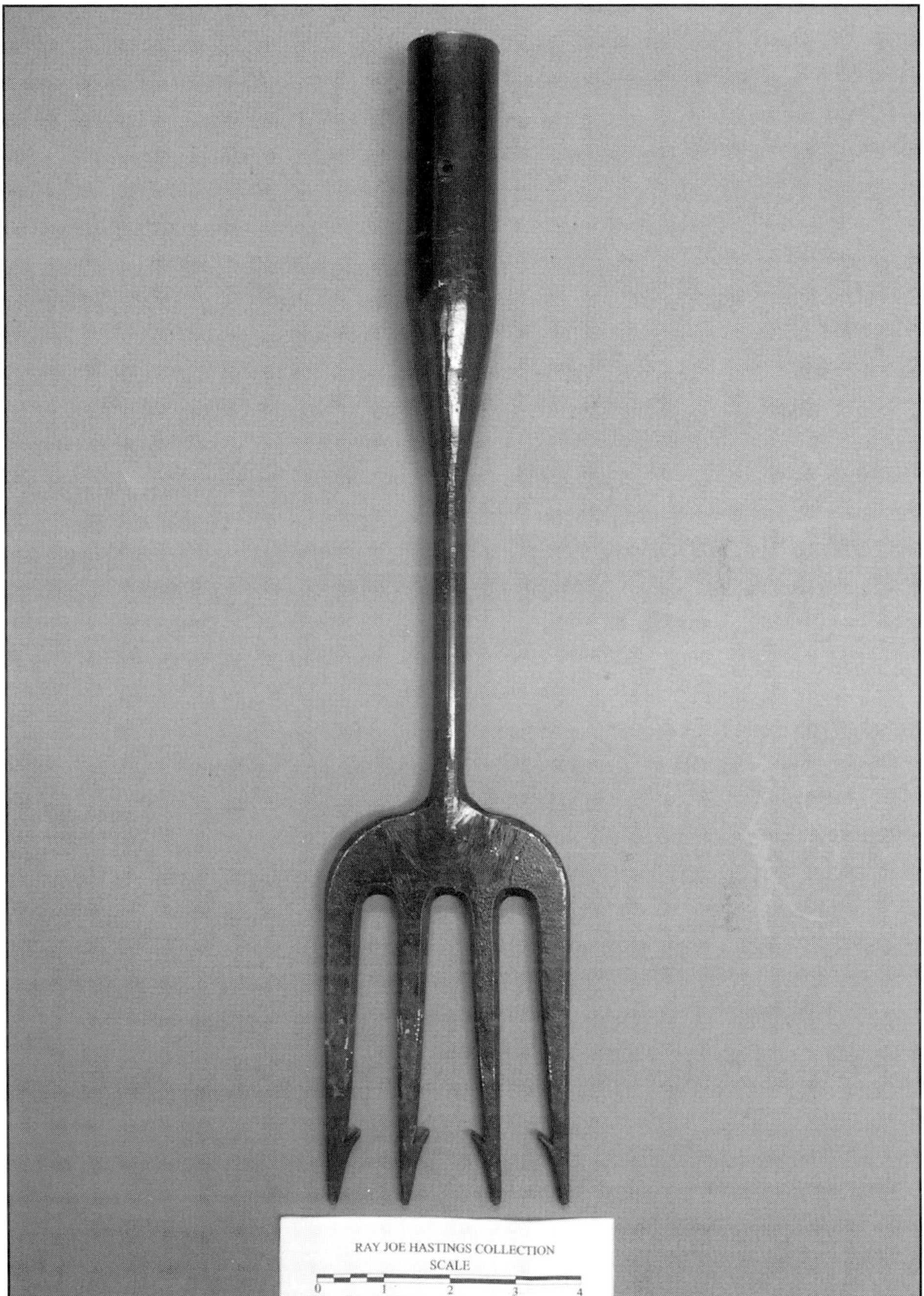

A four-prong Frank Nickell river-gig that has his last name stamped on the socket. Frank grew up in Ripley County, and made his first gig which was a three prong spike in 1944 at the age of ten. Frank was part of the family–his sister Corrine married my brother Prientus. This gave me an "in" when I started collecting bows and spikes. Frank sold me the little three-prong he made as a youngster, and another three-prong that Grover Whitwell, a Doniphan blacksmith had made for Frank in 1953. During the years 1970-2004 Frank made a few hundred river gigs. All of these were beautifully made and very durable. It is sad to note that with Frank's passing away in May 2004, Ripley County lost another great gig-maker.

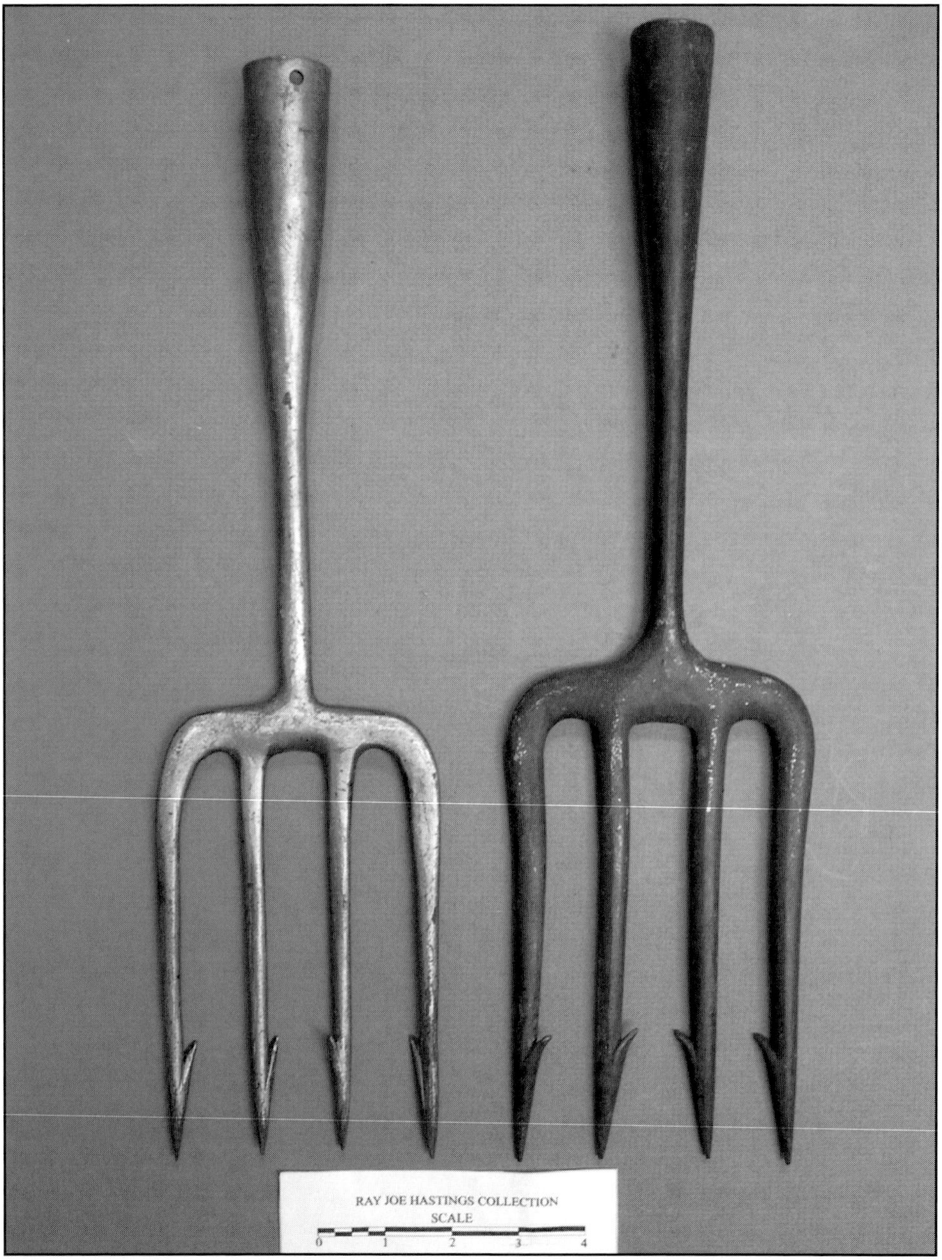

Two beautiful, well-made gigs, made by two different Ripley County gig makers. The gig on the left was made in 1956 for Roy Borth, Jr., by Melvin Lassen, and was never used. The gig on the right was made by Oatman Tanner, probably close to the time period the other gig was made. It has also never been used. The Tanner gig was bought near Bonne Terre, Missouri by another person and sold to me, and I identified it the moment I saw it. Both gigs are that distinctive, and are made so much alike that some people would have trouble telling them apart. This could be because both men were good friends who hunted and fished together. They also did quite a bit of gigging, and made their gigs in a friendly, competitive way to see who could make the nicest gig. I felt lucky indeed to find two unused gigs made by two close friends, but to have this story about their competitiveness related to me by a good friend of mine, and Melvin Lassen's grandson, Dr. Ray A. Lassen, O.D., of Doniphan really added to the story.

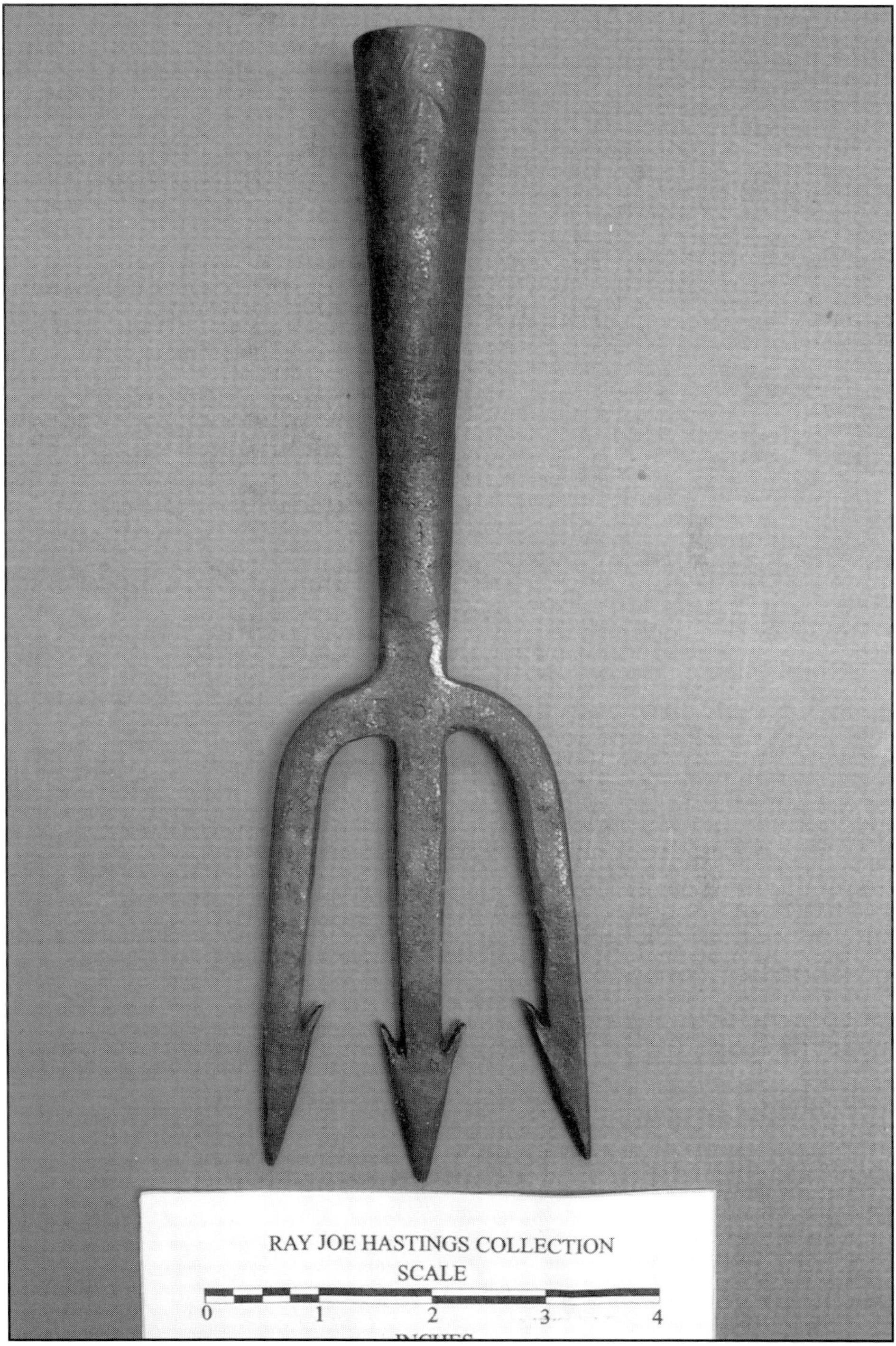

A beautiful, well-made three-prong river gig made by Steve Orchard of Van Buren during his gig-making training with me through the Missouri Traditional Arts Apprenticeship Program. One has only to look at this gig to see the fine workmanship Steve possesses that went into this gig. Steve has already fooled one man who looked at it, and remarked that it was an Ellerman gig, because the two styles look that much alike.

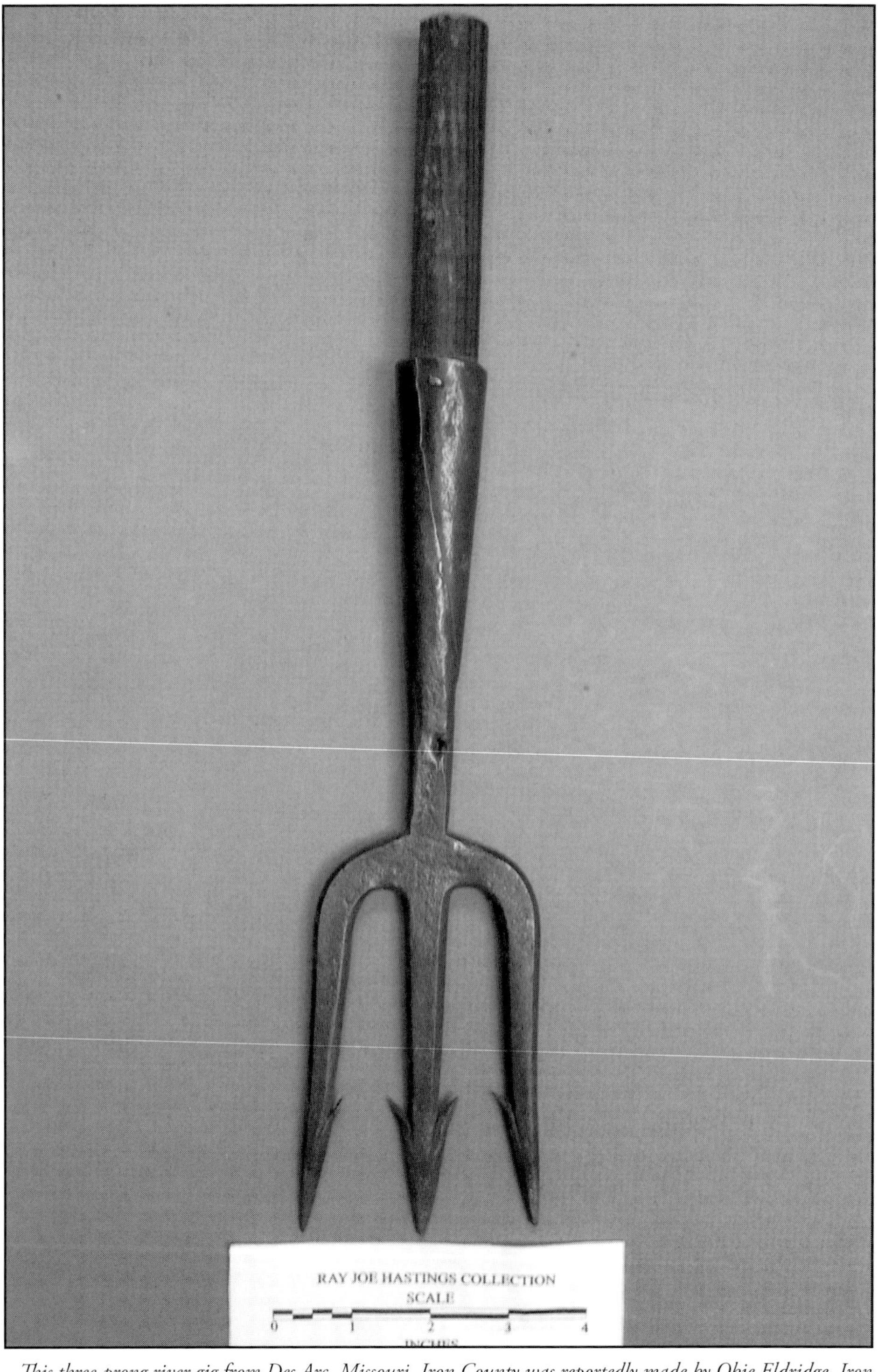

This three-prong river gig from Des Arc, Missouri, Iron County was reportedly made by Obie Eldridge. Iron County had its share of men who used the bow and spike and the bigger river gigs. I have a few of both kinds from this area and all are very well-made.

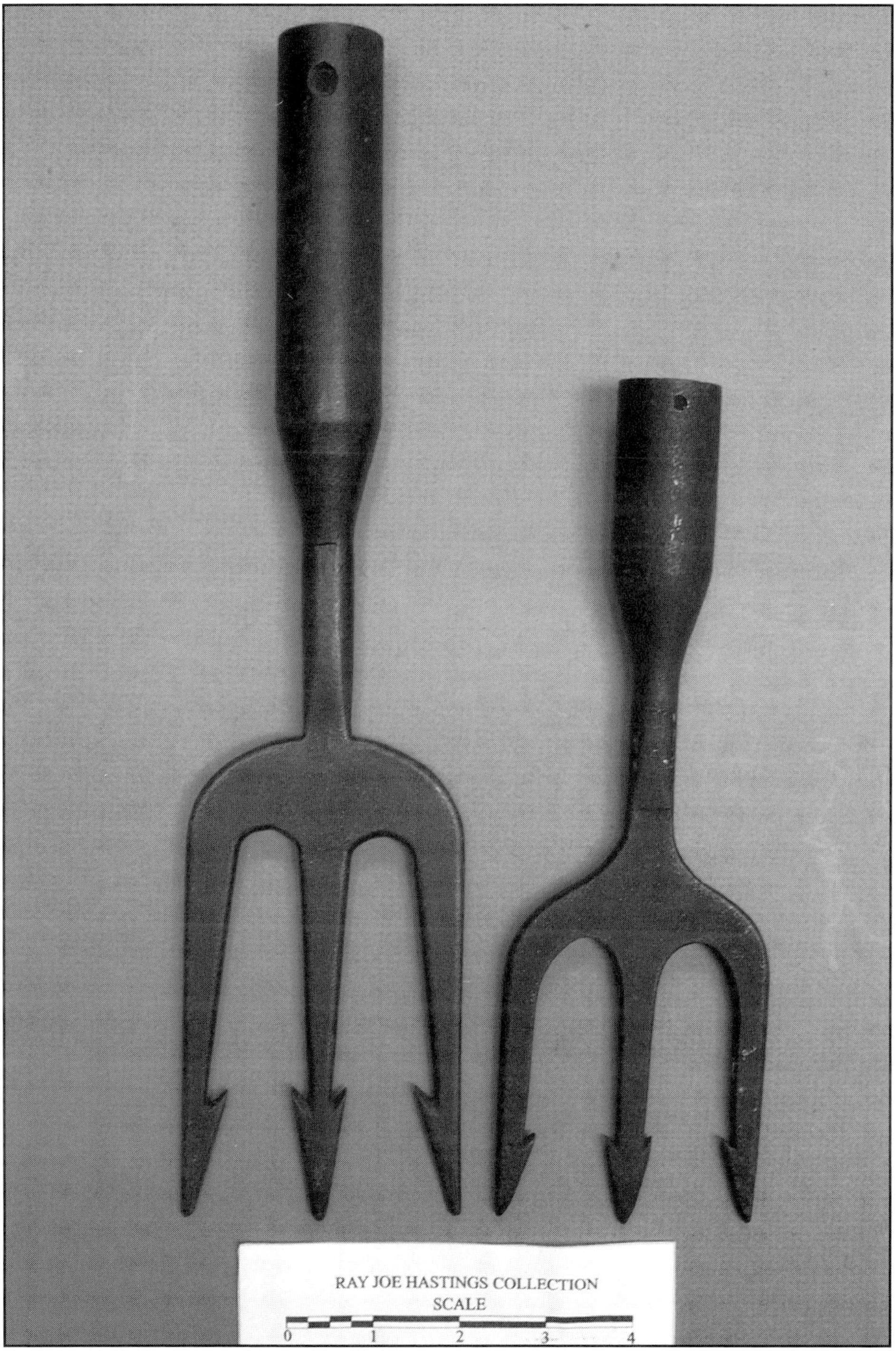

A pair of river gigs made by Boyd Kester of Van Buren, Missouri. The gig on the right is signed by Mr. Kester. In a conversation, with Mr. Kester, he identified the gig on the left as one he also made. He also stated he only made a total of five or six river gigs, and I feel fortunate to have these two. As one can see, they are of excellent workmanship, and pleasant to look at.

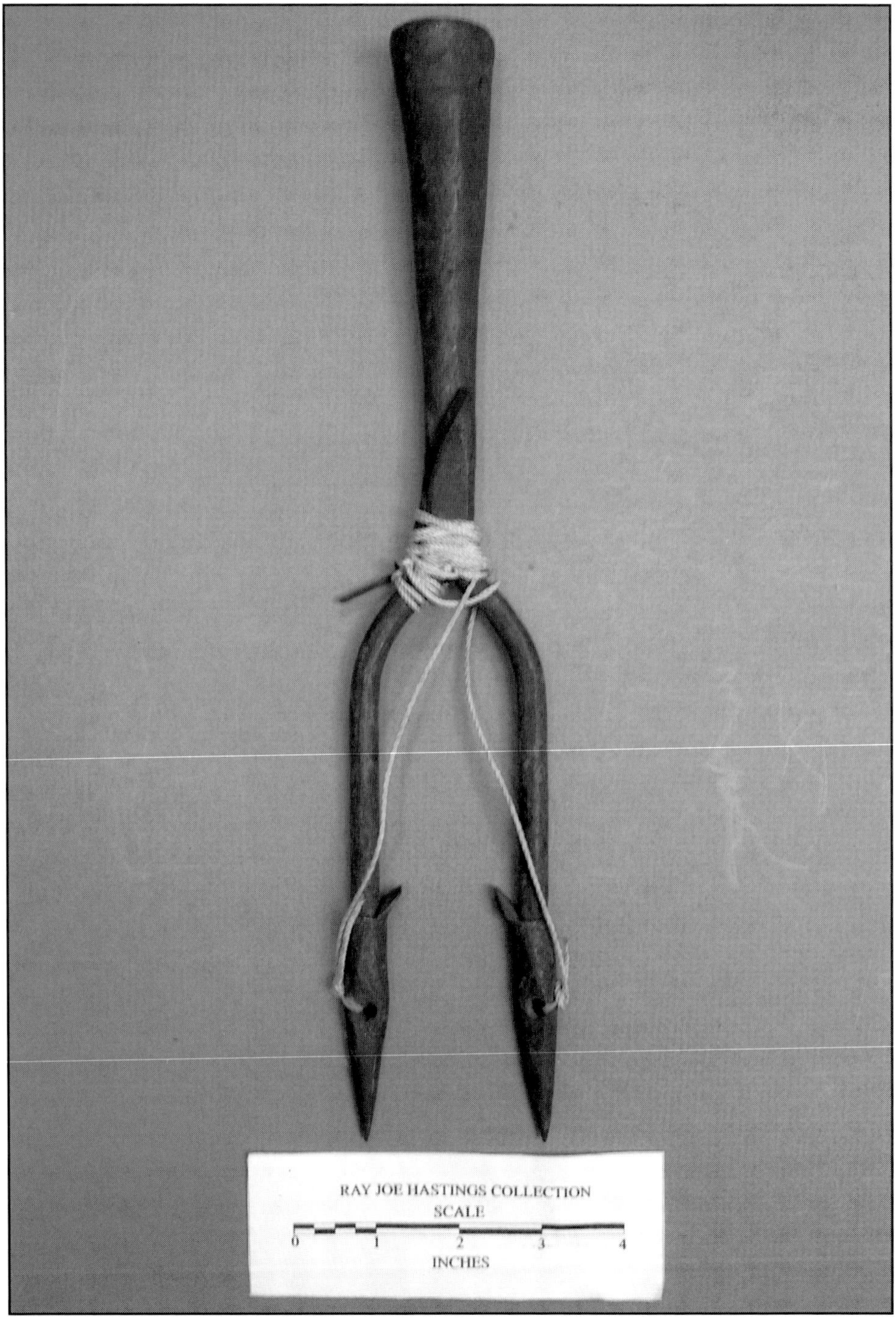

A two-prong river gig with removable points and beards from Iron County, also shown on the following page. It was made about 1956, and thought to have been made by Tom Brawley. This gig is a work of art, and was made to gig a big catfish that bedded in a log in a river near Des Arc, Missouri. Reportedly, too big a fish to handle by hand, the catfish was to be gigged, and when the points were pulled off the gig, the attached lines were there to play the fish until it tired.

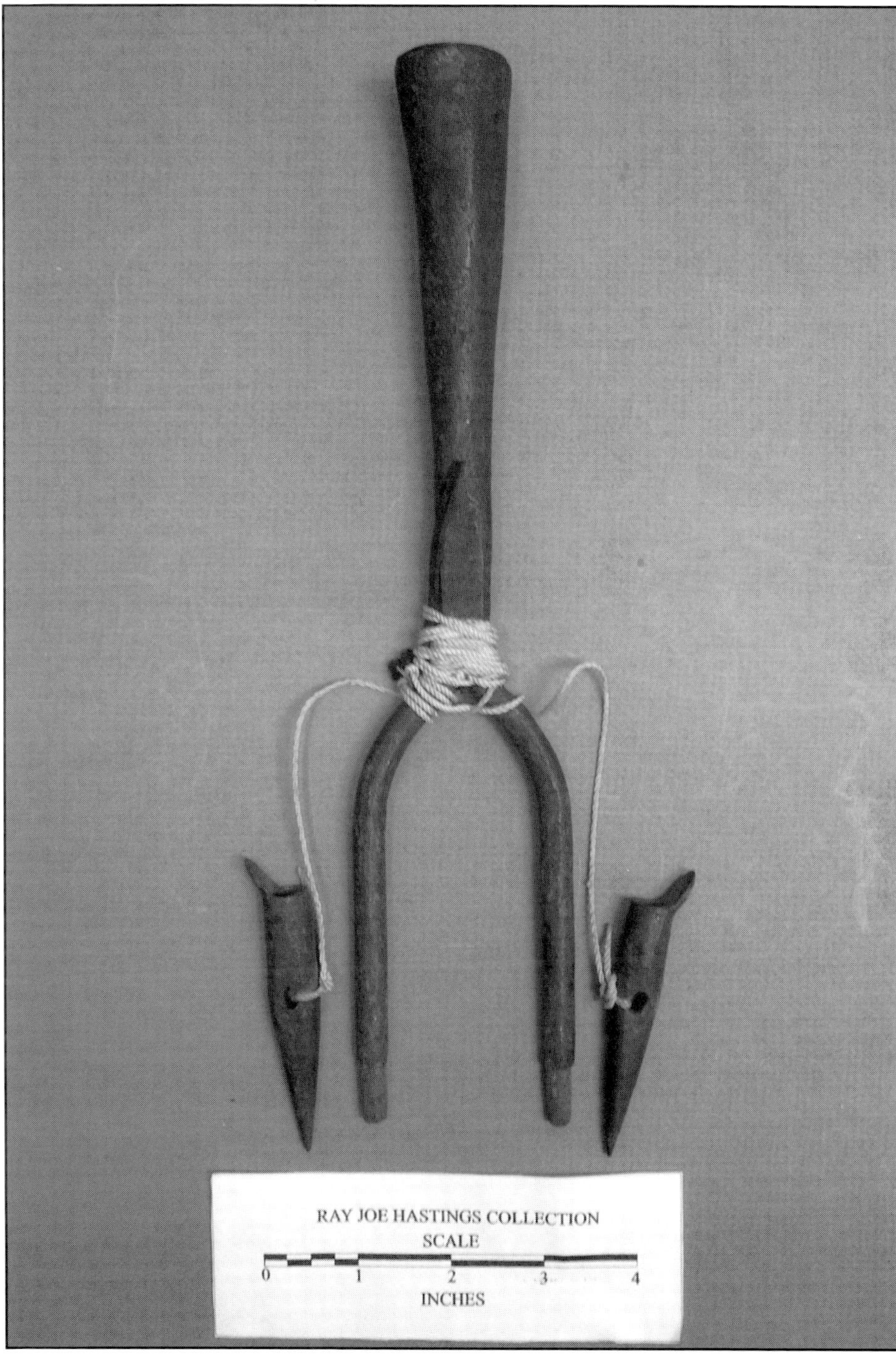

There is a small strip of inner tube to hold the points on the gig until the fish was gigged, and then the strip of rubber would stretch to let the points come off. Before the gig could be tried out, a big flood changed things around, and the river moved over enough that the catfish never used the log to bed (spawn) in again. This may be "one of a kind" gig and I was lucky to acquire it.

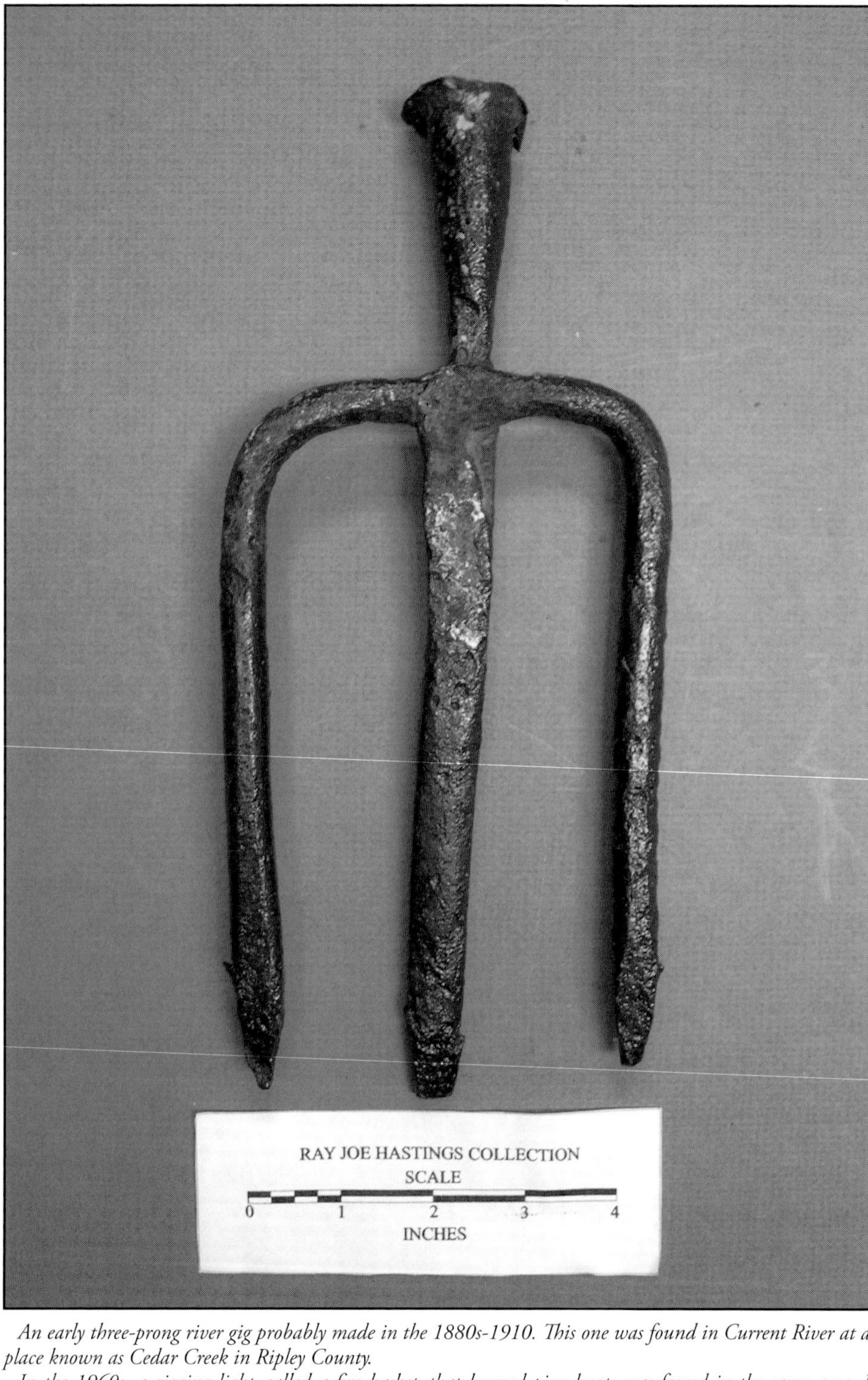

An early three-prong river gig probably made in the 1880s-1910. This one was found in Current River at a place known as Cedar Creek in Ripley County.

In the 1960s, a gigging light–called a fire basket–that burned pine knots was found in the same area. I acquired this old relic years later. A commissary store stood on the east bank of Current River at this place years ago, but as early as 1950, there was no visible sign left of the old store.

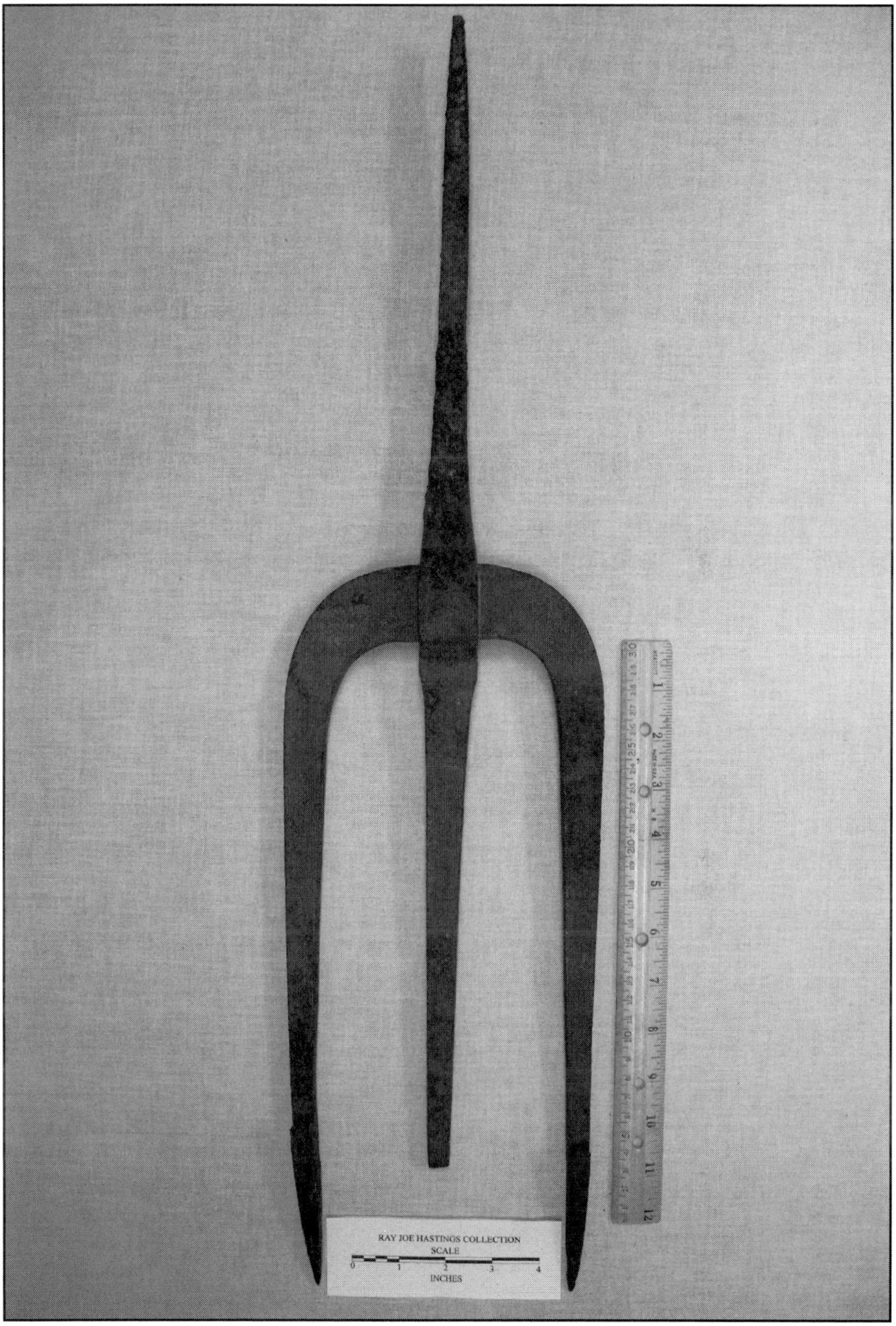

I call this my "Gator Gig." This 26-inch, 6-pound gig still has me puzzled as to the purpose of why and what a gig this size was made for. It was found in an old house that was being torn down. The middle prong was broken off at the beard. I believe the missing beard and point may have been intentionally cut off, since it is hard to visualize a fish big enough to break a piece of steel nearly one-half inch thick. This gig will probably always remain a mystery and the question of who, how, and why may never be answered.

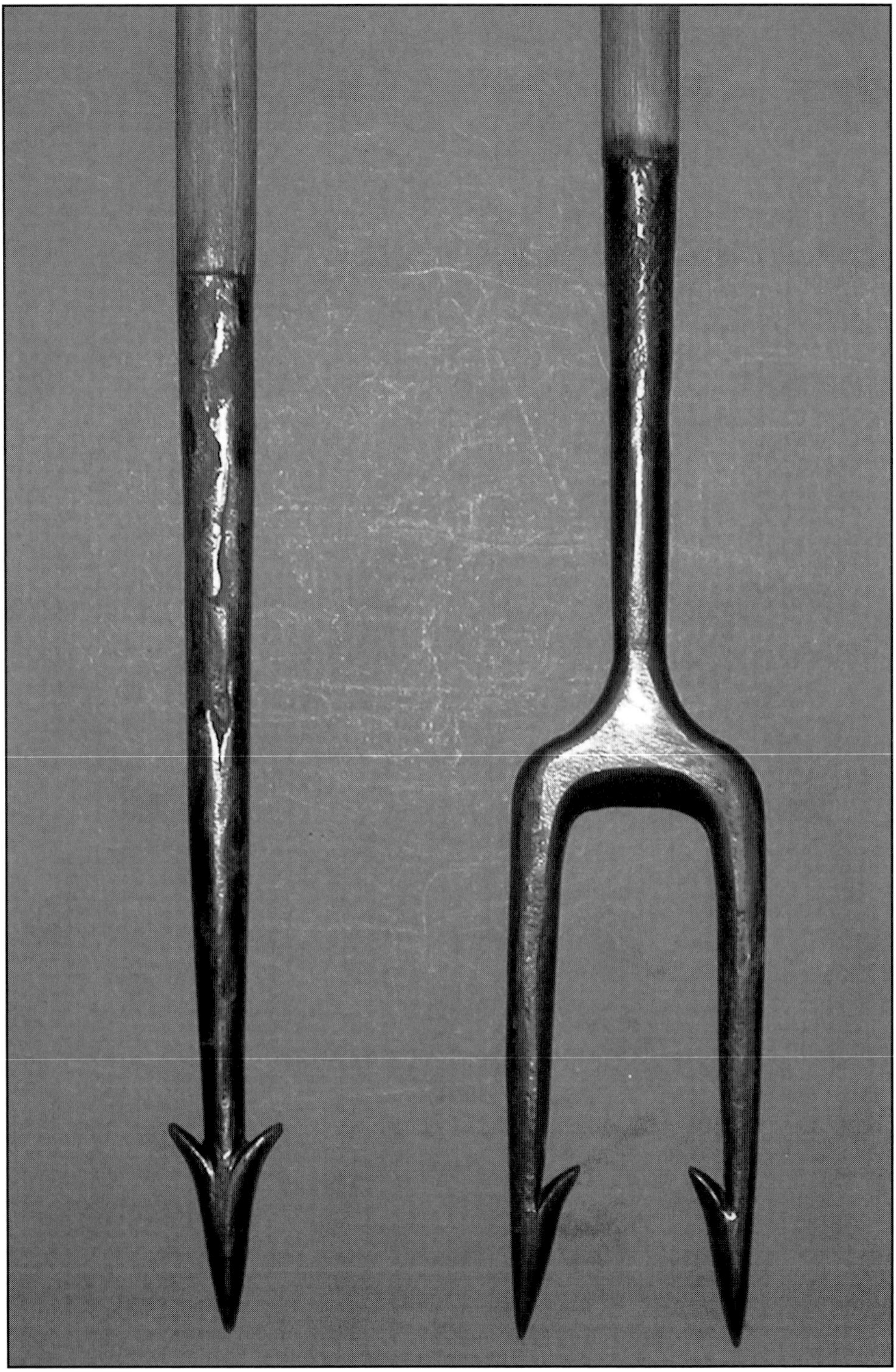

These two spikes were made by Mr. Ernest (Punk) Murray for me in 1992. Nearly sixty years had passed since Mr. Murray had made the three and four-prong spikes. It is easy to see that he had not lost his skills. Note the filed gullet on the two-prong. This would let it slice through the water with minimal resistance. Shown actual size.

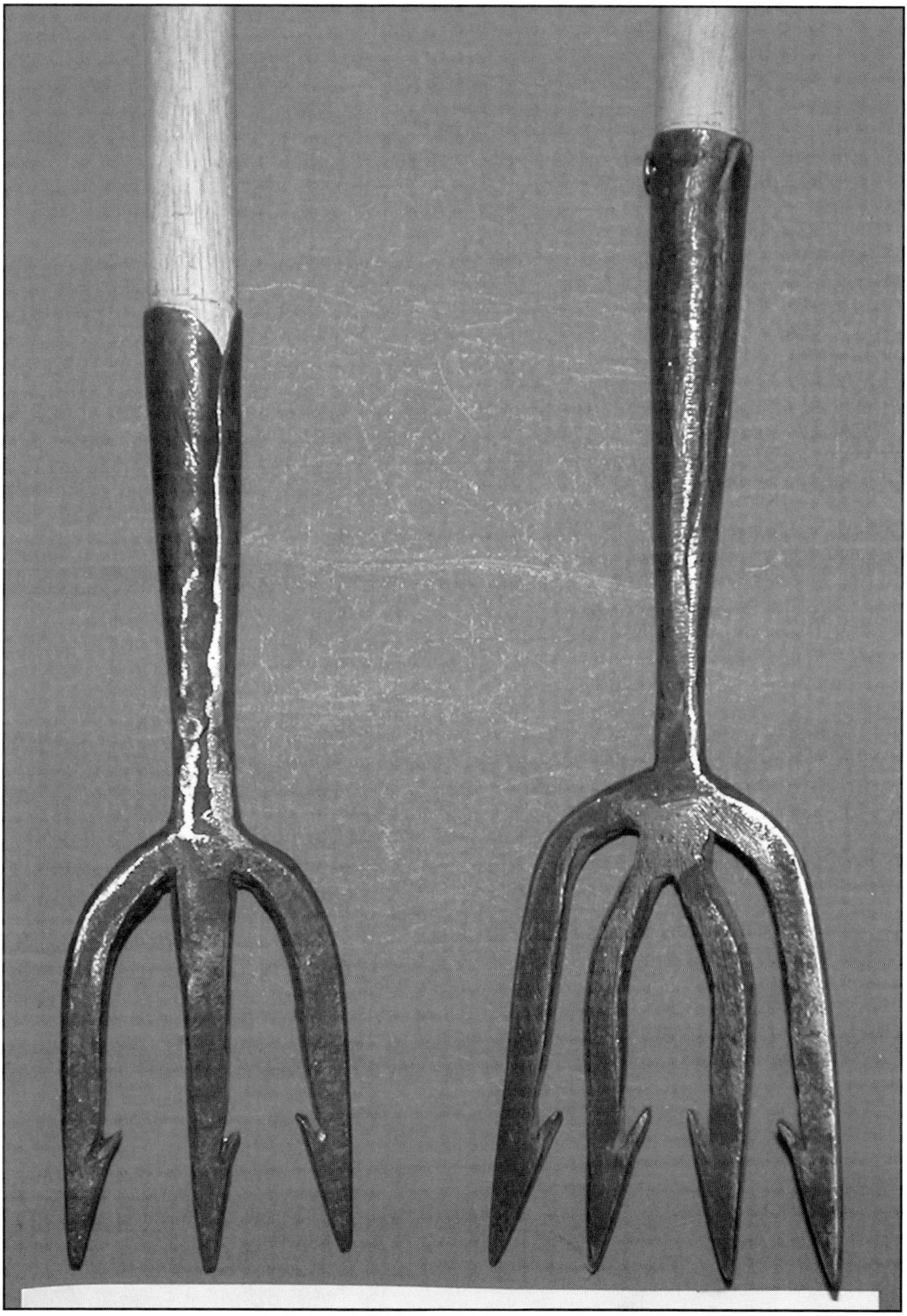

Made by Mr. Paul Martin in 1995 for me. I took gig-making lessons from Mr. Martin for six months in 1995 and 1996. Mr. Martin made gigs from about 1960 to 2000, and he told me that he had probably made 3,000 gigs during that time. In my opinion, Paul Martin was one of the best gig-makers around these parts who made gigs with a forge, chisel, and hammer. He made them from one piece of spring steel, and he was also one of the last to make a gig the old-fashioned way. The few bow spikes he made for me were the only ones he said he ever made. By the time he started making river gigs, bow and spikin' had run its course. Shown actual size.

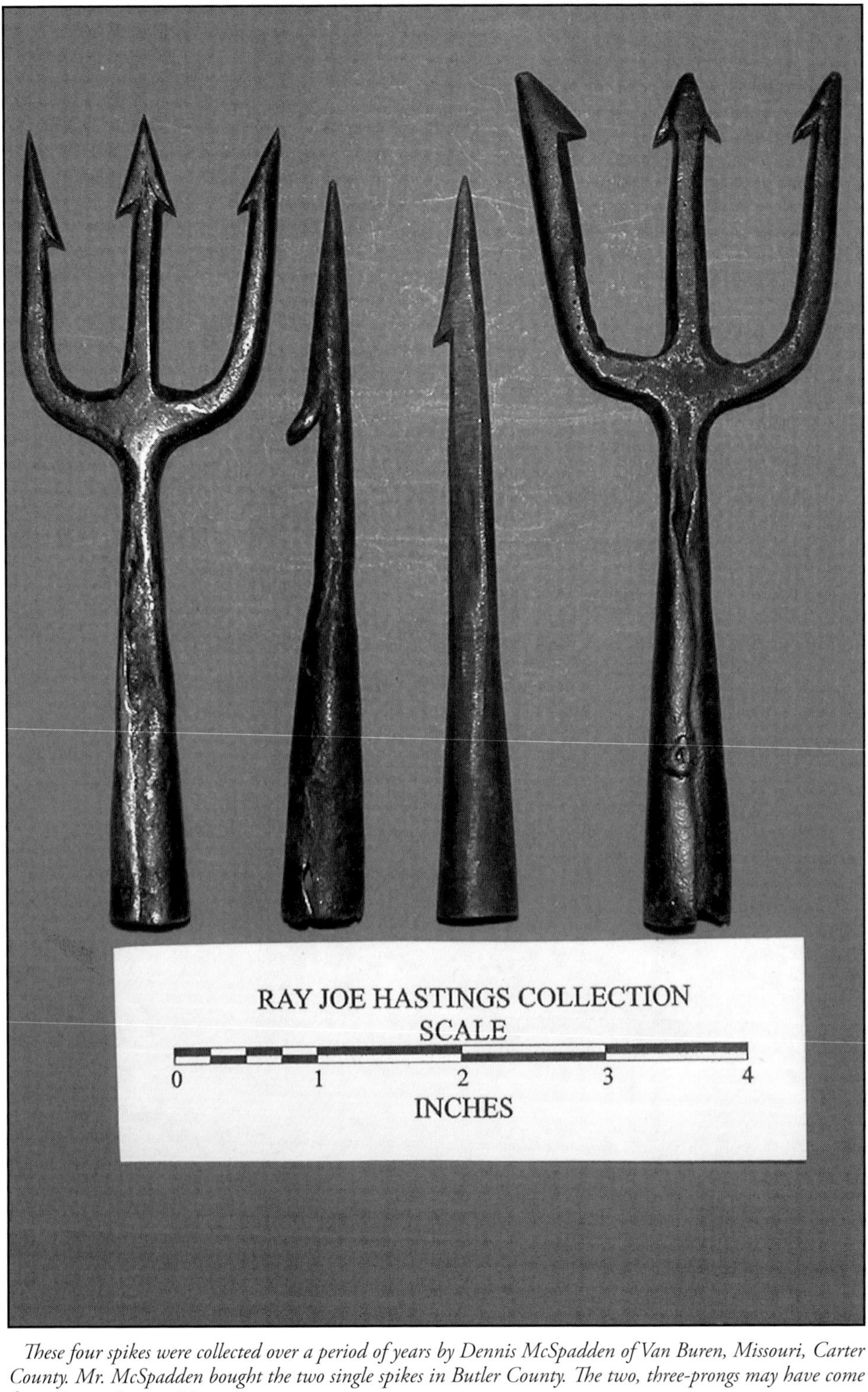

These four spikes were collected over a period of years by Dennis McSpadden of Van Buren, Missouri, Carter County. Mr. McSpadden bought the two single spikes in Butler County. The two, three-prongs may have come from Carter County, Missouri.

All three spikes came from Carter County, Missouri. The two-prong on the left came from a farm auction halfway between Grandin and Hunter, Missouri. The three-prong on the right came from Ellsinore, Missouri. The two-prong in the center started out as a three-prong, but the center prong was burned off in the process of making the gig, so the outer prongs were bent slightly inward, and converted into a two-prong.

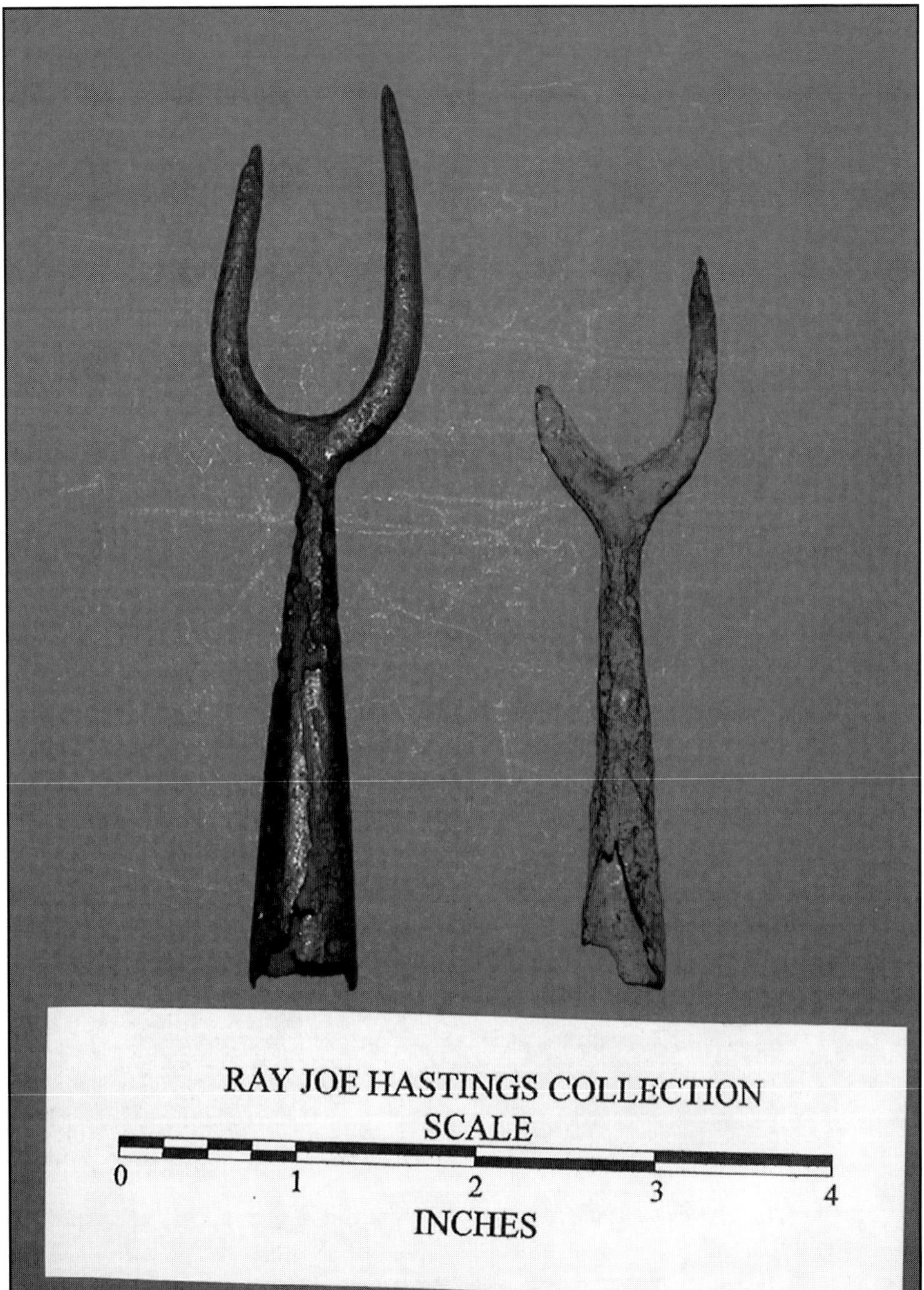

Both spikes are from Ripley County. The two-prong on the left was owned and used by John D. Young, a well-known farmer. Mr. Young farmed land on the Current River, a few miles North of Doniphan, Missouri. It's easy to see it saw extensive use (no beards are visible, and one-prong is worn down shorter than the other). The two-prong on the right must have been lost in the yard for several years, because it is almost rusted away. Nonetheless, it tells a story; it was probably lost while the kids were playing with it. I have heard several stories about how these little spikes were lost or misplaced, some of them never to be found again. Shown actual size.

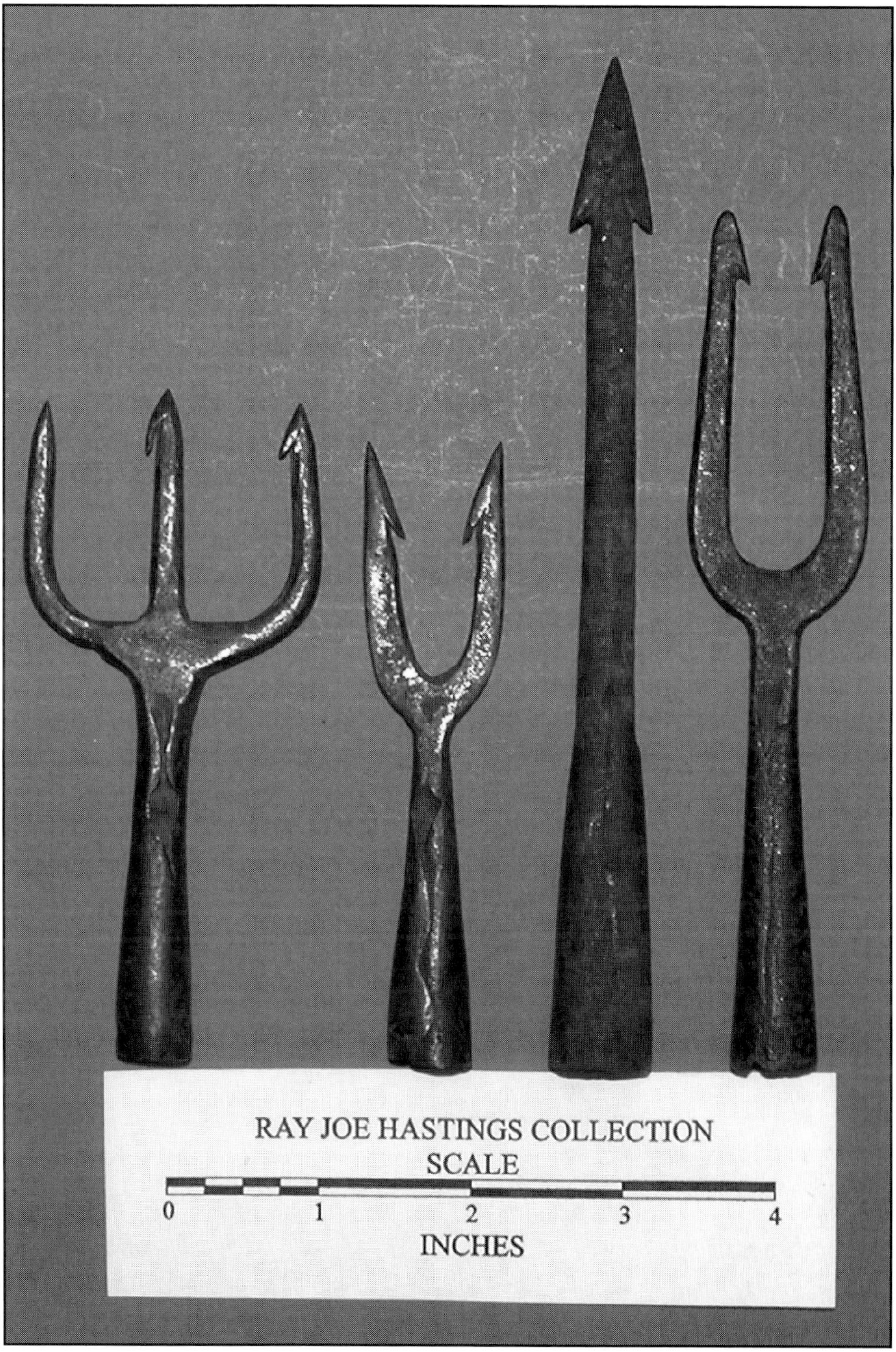

These four spikes came from Iron County, Missouri. The three-prong on the left was bought at a farm sale on Marble Creek. The two-prong that is the second from the left is only 4" long, and was made by Mr. Hardin Eldridge in 1945, or '46, in Des Arc, Missouri. The single spike came from Ironton. The two-prong on the right was made by Mr. Tom Brawley of Des Arc between 1945-1952.

Tacklebox of Stories

The Hillbilly Name and Cartoons "Patched Overhauls, Straw Hats, and Corncob Pipes"

I'm not sure when the label of "Ozark Hillbilly" started, but it may have been after the big sawmills in the southeastern Missouri Ozarks shut down about 1909-1910. The hundreds of men who were without jobs went home to eke out a bare existence any way they could. As stated earlier, before the big mills started up, the people in the Ozarks were, for the most part, a cashless society, and for most of the men, the big mills that started up in the 1880s were the first paying jobs they had ever had. When it was all over, many men had no choice but to return to the "old days" of a cashless society. For many of them, that time period was when men started hunting, trapping, and fishing as a way to provide food for their families. With their patched overhauls, straw hats, and lying on the creek banks fishing, it did not take very long before the cartoonists had a field day depicting the scene on post cards and in the newspapers. Nor did they spare the colorful dialect the Ozark people spoke. In fact, it may have been trampled on even more than the hillbilly drawings. The dialect and the mispronunciation of words is still carried on by some of us who are getting up in age.

The scene of a lazy, laid-back individual on a stream bank fishing, or in the woods hunting has been used thousands of times down through the years. In their defense, most of them were hard-working men and women. Many of the men worked at the big mills, and others cut logs with "ol' gappy" crosscut saws, and then were expected to cut ten thousand board feet of logs each day just to keep their jobs. Then there was the tie-hacker who received ten cents each for the ties he made–a good tie-hacker could make only ten to twelve ties a day–and that was after he had walked a few miles to the woods each morning and back home late in the evening. In defense of the women, most of the Ozark women whom I have ever known have always worked all day long just to cook and do the chores while their husbands were working, and they did it while they were caring for a houseful of "young un's." If the cartoonists had followed those men and women for a day or two as they performed back-breaking jobs and had seen how hard-working those people were, they may have painted an altogether different picture of the Ozark Hillbilly!

Hillbilly Slang

In the past, and even in the present day, the Ozark hill people have had their own colorful dialect or unique way of speaking the American language. In fact, the language is sometimes spoken so differently that people from other parts of the United States who visit this area may have difficulty understanding some of the words that are being said. Admittedly, I am also guilty of butchering the English language quite often.

A funny story that I share with my friends and family is when my grandson Cody Hutcheson, from Arizona, who was about eight years old at the time was visiting us. He and his cousins from Missouri went with me to our cabin in Carter County to pick up some unique rocks and scout for deer. It had been a long day of hiking, and I said, "I am gittin' tard, let's go home." My grandson said, "What, Papa?" I repeated, "I am tard, Cody, don't you know what that is?" Very apologetically, he said, "No, Papa, I don't." I did not believe that he could not understand why a person could not be "tard," but my Missouri grandson, Andrew Smothers, came to the rescue and said, "Cody, he means he is TIRED." Cody said, "Oh, now I understand." And finally, a little ashamedly, I did too!

Now he has moved to West Virginia, and one night he told his mother that he was "tard." She said, "Cody, did you notice what you just said?" He replied, "Oh no, Mom, don't tell Papa." Of course, she couldn't wait to call to tell me. It is amazing how different the regional variety of language is between the states, and what the children grow up listening to is what they learn to speak.

My wife and I have been noticing these differences for a few years, and together we have compiled a list of the pronunciations of various words of the Ozarks and the correct pronunciations of the same words. Dr. James E. Price has also compiled a list, and we are including his along with ours. We have enjoyed putting this list together, and hope you will enjoy it too.

Words of the Ozark Dialect and their Common English Equivalent

Aahr – Hour
Aahrn – Iron
Akeern – Acorn
Afeered – Afraid
Aggervatin – Aggrevating
Aholt – Holding onto
Ain't – Am not or are not
Aigs – Eggs
Alkehol – Alcohol
Allus – Always
An' – And
Arral – Aerial
Arr' – Arrow
Arse – Iris
Backerds – Backwards
Badern – Bad one
Bar're – Borrow
Bile – Boil
Brahr – Briar
Bresh – Brush
Flahr – Flour, flare
Flahr – Flower
Foller – Follow
Ford – Forward
Ford – Forehead
Forsythee – Forsythia
Furry – Furrow
Ganghem – Gingham
Giverment – Government
Good'un – Good one
Hade – Head
Hain't – Is not
Heathern – Heathen
Henspahr – Inspire
Het – Heated
Hisself – Himself
Hit – It
Holler – Hollow
Idee – Idea
Insharance – Insurance
Peench – Pinch
Pint – Point
Pison Ivory – Poison Ivy
Purty – Pretty
Rassle – Wrestle
Rench – Rinse
Rosen'ear – Roasting ear – (Corn on the cob)
Rumatiz – Rheumatism
Sahr – Sour (also sire)
Sallet – Salad
Sceer – Scare
Schoolin' – Education
Seed'em – Saw him
Sheer-croppin' – (Sharecropping)
Shet – Shut
Sich – Such
Sic-e-mor – Sycamore
Skeeter – Mosquito

Bum – Bomb
Cain't – Can't
Chaw – Chew
Cheer – Chair
Clum – Climb
Cole Aahl – Coal Oil
Com'ere – Come here
Cuz – Because
Cost-es – Costs
Crik – Creek
Dinneymite – Dynamite
Divved – Dived
Dudn't – Doesn't
Ellum – Elm
Fahl – File
Fahl – Foil
Fahr – Fire
Feller – Fellow
Fer – Far
Figger – Figure
Fit – Fought
Jine – Join
Jist – Just
Keer – Care
Kilt – Killed
Kin – Can
Kivver – Cover
Knowed – Knew
Lahr – Liar
Larn – Learn
Leastways – At least
Lectrick – Electric or Electricity
Nary – Any or none
Nekked – Naked
Nest-es – Nests
Notchet – Not yet
Nurn – None
Oneasy – Uneasy
Onliest – Only one
Ort – Ought
Ov – Of
Pert near it – Pretty near it (almost)
Sprang Brantch – (Spring Branch)
Summers – Somewhere
Swaller – Swallow
Tahr – Tire
Tard – Tired
Tobaccer or Baccer – (Tobacco)
Tobble – Tolerable
Vahl – Vial
Wahr – Wire
Warsh – Wash
Wasper – Wasp
Wheelbaher – (Wheelbarrow)
Wormern – Woman
Wuz – Was
Y'all – You all
You'uns – You ones

John Counts' Story

I mentioned earlier about a story that was written by Lennis Broadfoot, and published in the book *Pioneers of the Ozarks.* I have permission from the Harlin Museum in West Plains to copy the story for this book. It is written in the dialect of the Ozark hill country, which Mr. Counts spoke at that time.

JOHN SAYS:

"I am three-quarters Indian, an' I'm seventy-four years ol', an a 'bow an' arr fisherman' by profession. My home is jist anywhere in the Ozark hills, but I am a native of Reynolds County, Mo.

"I fish with 'bow an' arr' an' I make 'em myself. They are made ov cedar wood, an' the spikes are made ov ol' worn-out files that I pick up here an' there, take 'em into the shop, an' hammer 'em out into a nice spearhead or spike.

"I am knowed all through the Missouri Ozarks an' parts ov Arkansaw as 'ol' fisherman John Counts.' I know all the streams in the Missouri Ozarks an' North Arkansaw like a book, an' have waded an' fished in about all ov 'em.

"I never use a boat. I wade around kinder slow an scare the fish out frum under rocks, logs, an' ol' tree roots, an' shoot 'em on the run; an', boy, I can git 'em! I can plunk a perch between the eyes fifty feet away!

"I hardly ever miss a shot, an' I've killed a heap ov squirrels an' turkeys with my ol' 'bow an' arr.' My paap wuz an expert with 'bow an' arr,' an' he larned me how to make 'em an' use 'em; an' he killed a heap ov deer; he killed big deer; an' I've killed big turkeys too, an' a whole lot ov squirrels.

John Counts, Reynolds County, Missouri. Illustration by L.L. Broadfoot, 1938.

"I sleep out lots ov nights along the rivers an' creeks in the Ozarks–I sleep under big sycamore trees on white gravel bars, an' watch fer squirrels, an' when I see one runnin' grapevines or jumpin' frum tree to tree, I pick up my 'bow an' arr,' an' I shoot 'im, an' I make a fire an' brile 'im on a stick. If I can, I get a sassafras stick 'cause sassafras gives the meat a better flavor.

"I kill big heaps ov fish an' squirrels an' give 'em to the peepuls along the streams where I go, 'cause they like me-they know 'ol' fisherman John,' an' they are my friends.

"I used to do lots ov fishin' in a little crooked mountain stream called 'Big Creek' in northeast Shannon Co., Mo., fer a man by the name ov Swiney–ol' Judge Jim Swiney ov Rat, Mo., who ran a little country store an' Post Office.

"Judge Swiney would have country picnics an' basket dinners, an' would hire me to come an' kill fish fer 'im.

"He had a son named Ben. He'd say, 'Now, John, I want you to fish fer me today, an' Ben, I want you to go along an' carry the fish fer John, an' actually, I have loaded that boy down with fish till he couldn't walk.

"I'm gettin' purty old, but I still love the sport, an' the Ozarks has been a wonderful home fer me."

No Girls Allowed

To my knowledge, girls did not participate in the sport of "bow and spikin'," and I have not heard of a single instance where they used the bow and spike. However, in the 1950s, my sisters, Shirley, Eunice, and sister-in-law, Corrine Nickell-Hastings went fishing with dad and his cousin, Mr. Fred Faulkner, but they only participated by carrying the lantern. Today it would be a different story as women have become a big part of the outdoor crowd and are very sports-oriented.

I remember a story that one of my sisters, Shirley, and sister-in-law, Corrine Hastings, told of going "bow and spikin'" one night with my dad and older brother Prientus. The girls took turns holding the light, as was always the case when they got to go along. They were in a deep hole of water on Well's Creek when a big snake came swimming along toward the light. That was more than the girls could stand. In a flash they were gone, running down the creek, hollering and screaming and leaving my dad and brother standing in waist deep water watching the snake swim toward them in the fast-fading lantern light. Some tense moments ensued until the girls could be coaxed into returning with the light. Events such as this and the telling and laughing about it later were just part of the fun. This story happened over fifty years ago, but at a family gathering a few days ago, it was told once more, and the laughter was just as loud as right after it first happened.

Using the Bow and Spike from the Creek Bank

One of the ways to fish with the bow and spike was to walk along the creek bank very slowly and quietly, and watch for fish that were floating near the surface. After the fish were spotted, a person had to get as close as possible in order to make sure he could hit the fish. This was not as easy as one might think. The main reason to bow and spike from the bank was that on some of the bigger creeks, the water was too deep to wade and the hole of water might have been thirty to forty feet wide, or more, and since with this method of fishing from the bank the bow was held at a slight cant, which is halfway between the perpendicular and horizontal position.

If the shot was missed, one had to walk only to the shoal at the lower end of the hole and wait to retrieve the arrow as the fast-moving water floated it downstream. If the fish was hit and swam into some brush along the opposite bank, the only other choice was to take off your clothes and swim over and retrieve the spike and fish. If you were lucky and the fish did not get caught in some brush or lily pads, you could go to the shoal at the end of the hole and wait for them to float down. One thing was for sure, when fishing this way a person usually got wet from either accidentally falling in, or having to go into the creek to retrieve the fish. No one really minded getting wet; in fact, it was really expected, and was part of the excitement!

I have already mentioned that the shaft that went into the spikes were most often made of some kind of wood (pine, etc.) or cane from along the creek bank. They would float, that is, the small gig would hang down in the water while the top of the shaft would float on the surface of the water. Sometimes the man fishing with the bow and spike was lucky and would have a youngster with him who could swim out and retrieve the fish. Ronnie Steen and his brother Bob would sometimes swim out and retrieve the fish for Mr. Ted Keel. This took place on the Buffalo Creek in Ripley County, Missouri. According to Steen, Mr. Keel carried three or four spikes with one, two, and three prongs and would use various spikes for different fish.

"Bow and Spikin'" from a Johnboat

Not all fishing with the bow and spike was done by wading the creek or walking along the creek bank. Some was done from a boat like modern-day giggers. Mr. Weaver Braschler of Pratt, Missouri, used this method with the bow and spike. I had several conversations on the subject with Mr. Braschler before he passed away a few

Ray Hastings, who stands 6'6", poses with two set, or push paddles and one pike pole. The longest paddle is 10'4", and was made circa 1940, by Winfield Bell for Louis York of Doniphan, Missouri. Mr. Bell was a Doniphan blacksmith for over fifty years.

The push paddle on the right was made and used by Addis (Monk) Cochran, a well-known hunter, fisherman, trapper, and river guide. Mr. Cochran made quite a few things including the johnboat. He was one of the few men who made, or could make, about anything they needed, such as turkey calls, paddles, and even johnboats. Some are still alive today who are quite capable of this feat, but the two who come to mind are Cecil Murray and Acel Price of Ripley County. I have seen a bow spike or two made by Mr. Price that are of top-notch quality.

The pike pole in the center was made by Dewey Murray for me about 1980, who used it on the Current River for a few years while trapping. It was a very handy tool for pulling the boat to the river bank, and for picking up traps when changing trap locations. It even came in handy to pick up a beaver that had drowned in a trap in deep water.

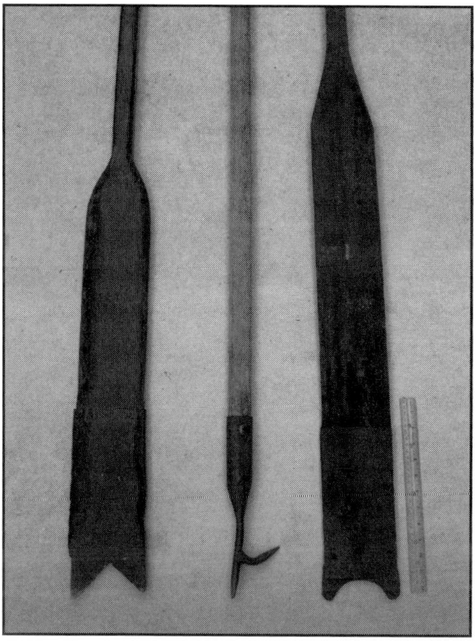

A closer view of the push paddles pictured with Ray Hastings.

years ago. He told me that the man with the bow and spike stood in the front of the boat looking into the clear water of our Ozark rivers until he spotted a fish. The boat was usually moving at a slow pace controlled by the man in the back of the boat, either by using a paddle or a small motor. The bays and cutoffs of the river where this type of gigging was usually done provided plenty of fish.

Another method of fishing from a boat with the bow and spike was with the use of a "foot-bow," as it was sometimes called. Mr. Arnold Braschler of Pratt, Missouri. was one man who sometimes fished this way. He would stand on the front seat, until he spotted a fish. A leather strap was buckled onto the bow and provided a place for his boots to fit into. This was a powerful bow, and a great deal of power was needed to shoot into big fish that were in several feet of water. If the spike hit the fish and did not kill it right away, the fish was followed until it succumbed. The fish was then brought to the surface with the aid of a pike pole, or sometimes a set paddle–or a push paddle, as they were also called–were sometimes used.

These were specially made paddles that had steel tips on narrow blades with the overall length of the paddle and handle being nine to twelve feet long. They were used in the late 1800s to the 1930s by the early tie and log rafters to push their johnboats back upstream, and by river guides who also used them to stop the boat on a shoal, or to back the boat up when a fisherman hung up his lure on a snag. About the only place a person can see a push paddle now is in a museum or in a private collection. They are another piece of the Ozarks history that has come and gone.

Bow-Spikin' with Slingshot and Strips of Inner Tube

Bows were not the only method used to shoot the arrow shaft when "bow and spikin'." The slingshot, which was also called a "bean-shooter" by many Ozarkians, was used by some who either did not have a bow, or simply preferred this method to shoot the fish. The arrow was laid in the fork of the slingshot with the back end of the arrow shaft placed in a piece of leather that was attached to two strips of inner tube that were tied to each fork of the slingshot. When the slingshot was pulled back and released, the results were the same as with a bow. Also, when he was through fishing, the slingshot was more easily carried than the bow, since the fisherman could just

This "bean-shooter" device was used in lieu of the bow to shoot the spike to take fish. It was a unique find.

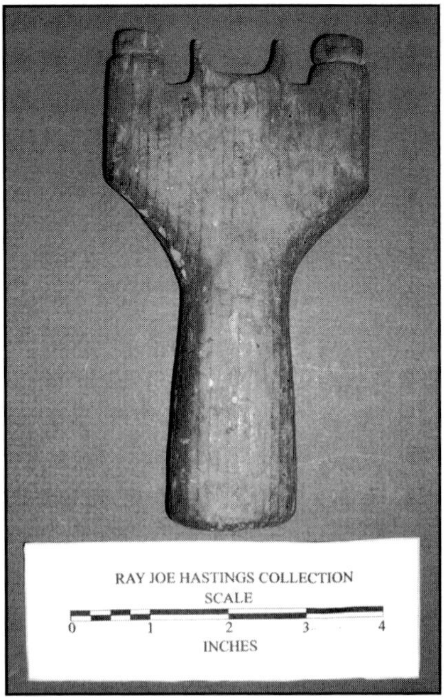

put it in the back pocket of his overalls. It is hard to say how many men and boys used this method to bow and spike fish; the important thing is that it was employed to take rabbits and squirrels as well as fish. The latter two were most often taken with the slingshot and a small rock. Some species of large birds were also taken, such as the yellow hammer (flicker), some hawks, and the pileated woodpecker whenever possible.

Another method employed to shoot the arrow was just a strip of inner tube of less than an inch wide. This would be circular in shape like a rubber band, but much larger. One end of the piece of inner tube would be threaded through the finger of one hand, and the back of the arrow shaft would be placed in the opposite end of the strip of inner tube. When a fish was close enough to shoot, one simply pulled the strip of inner tube back far enough to shoot the spike through the fish–much like the slingshot method above. It served its purpose, but the method was not as popular as fishing with the bow. However, it does show the ingenuity of the Ozark hill people–when they needed something, they "made do" with whatever they had.

Just a few days before going to press with this book, a bean-shooter-like device that replaced the bow for one Ripley County man was discovered. The person who had it asked that his name not be used in this book, but in several conversations about the bow and spike fishing with my friend, he told me the story of how it came about that he started using this device.

As previously stated, the Ozark hill people asked little from the outside world–"making do" with what they had on hand, so it was not all that unusual for someone to come up with this method to shoot the spike. My friend stated the first person he saw using this type of device was a Ripley countian by the name of Charley Decker. He liked this method better than the bow, so he made himself one out of a one by four inch pine board. My friend stated that this new device was easier to use in brushy areas where the bow would hang up on limbs. It must have worked pretty well, as he used it for approximately forty years (from around 1946 to about 1986).

The design of these are very unusual, and they are uniquely made, somewhat on the bean-shooter design, except the forks are shortened down to only one-half inch high; or just high enough to tie on the strip of inner tube that went over it. In the center of the forks there is a raised platform with a deep groove in it to hold the arrow shaft. This groove would keep the arrow from moving around; therefore, better accuracy could be achieved. In this book, there are pictures of how it would look with the strips of inner tube tied on and with the string attached to the strips to place in the back of the spike shaft.

My friend stated that several men used this type of device, preferring it over the bow in the Little Black River area. My thanks to my friend for trading it to me. This device probably started with the bean shooter, and was just a fancy "souped-up version" that someone thought out and converted. However, it did add another page of history to this book and was one more different way someone "thought up" to fish and hunt.

Refraction

The word "refraction" was totally out of place in a young country boy's vocabulary. I don't think my dad had ever heard the word either, since he had never mentioned it; however, in a roundabout way, we knew what it was. My brother Pal and I often marveled at the part of the arrow shaft that was under the water as it–due to refraction–would appear to bend upward, while the part of the arrow shaft above the water would remain straight. We soon learned to take aim under the fish even if it was close to us, and to judge the depth the fish was below the surface in order for the arrow shaft and spike to hit the fish since–due to refraction–the fish was simply not where it appeared to be. This did not come to us immediately, but we learned after a few missed shots, and a trip or two down Briar Creek. We were "onto refraction," although we never actually heard the scientific word until we were grown.

Lights used to Bow and Spike

The only lights available in the 1800s that are known to me were pine torches, and the "coal oil" kerosene ball. Pine torches were used because pine was readily available in the Ozarks. It is known they were used up until as late as the 1940s because Mr. Bill Davis related to me that he had used the pine torches on the north prong of Little Black River in Ripley County from 1938 to 1943 to bow and spike fish. The way to use the pine was to split pieces and bundle them together. They would burn high and give off a good light. The men who were fishing with them would sometimes stash extra pine bundles up and down the creek to use when one torch burned out. They knew from previous experience how far the light would last, and so they would be prepared for their fishing trips.

The "coal oil" or kerosene ball that was used to bow and spike was sometimes used as a light for river gigging. Pieces of cloth were wrapped around an approximate five-feet long limb until it became as large as a small-size hornet's nest. It was then placed in a bucket of kerosene until it was well soaked, and it was taken out when needed and lit on the creek bank as the men started out on their "bow and spikin'" trip. One funny story related to me as I was listening to the men who had used this method to fish, was that when gathering the cloth material for the ball, one had to be very careful not to let the "woman of the house" catch him taking the material, or he was sure to catch the wrath that followed, because the material was very hard to come by and was jealously guarded. Burlap was another material that was used for the cloth for these lights; it too was wrapped around a limb that was five or so feet long, and placed in the kerosene to soak until needed.

Another light was the carbide light. When it became available, it was a big improvement over the two previous methods because the light was attached to the person's cap; thus a bow-spiker could go by himself at night and not have to rely on someone else to hold the light for him. Still later on in the mid 1930s, a gas lantern became available. This required two men; one to hold the lantern, while the other one would bow and spike. I remember the lantern that Dad bought in the late 1940s would burn white gas, as it was called back then, but it would also burn kerosene. Both are written on the side of the lantern, and although the globe is missing, I still have this old lantern (see page 24). We used it quite often back in the late 1940s and early 1950s; it gave off a good light and we took quite a few fish with it.

Fishing with a Hook and Line

On many fishing trips we did not take the bow and spike, choosing instead to fish with a hook and line. After cutting the poles and attaching the line to it, we would need to find the fishing bait. Most of the time, we took a can of worms with us, so we would not have to carry a shovel. Worms were good bait, but sometimes the small creek catfish (bullheads) would prefer small frogs. We would busy ourselves catching them until we had enough, or until darkness came, then we would pick

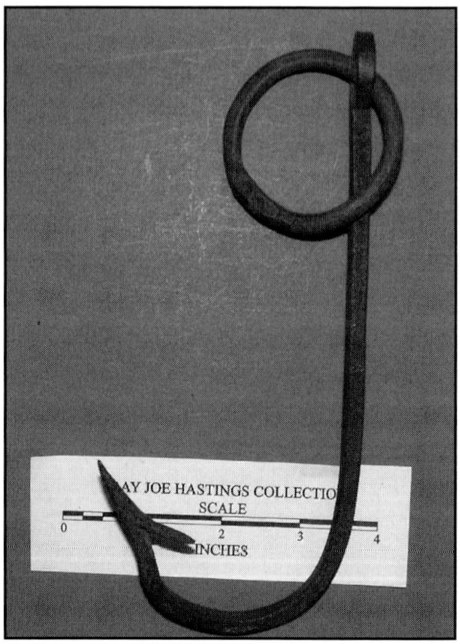

These large fish hooks, pictured right and on the following page, are from the general area, and were used to take large catfish out of logs, and from under banks and large rocks. These are very old, and show that man had many different ways to take fish. All three fish hooks were hand-forged.

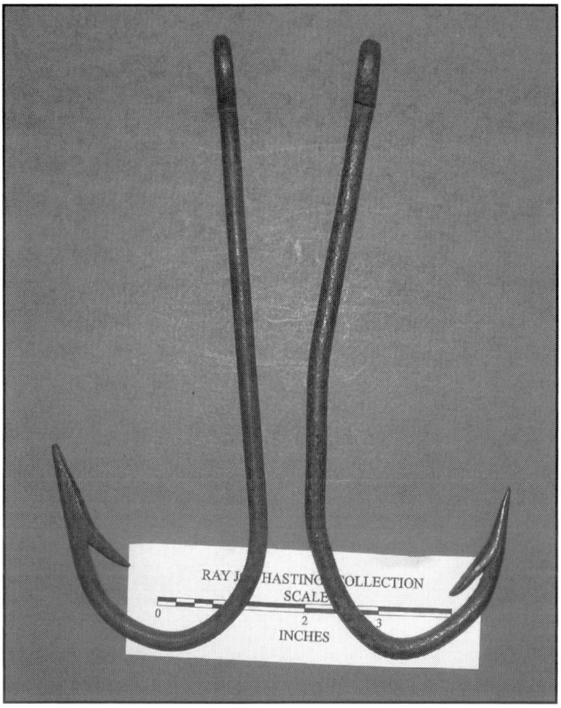

up our poles, put the bait on the hook, and go sit on the creek bank at a spot we had picked out earlier. Sometimes we would catch several bullheads fishing that way.

When the creek was clear, and in the daytime, fishing was more difficult with the hook and line, but when the creek was rolling and muddy during a rise, the fish would feed more. They would also not be able to see us, or feel the vibrations from our feet walking on the ground, and we could often bring back a "big mess of fish," on a tree-limb stringer. Although we considered this nothing but fun, I can now look back and see that it helped provide the nutrients and protein that were needed for the family to survive. Anytime we did not have school or chores to do, we were allowed to go fishing and hunting, and that is exactly what we did!

Hunting Rabbits and Deer with a Bow and Arrow

Deer were scarce in the mid-1900s and were hunted mostly with a rifle or shotgun. Still, a few people used a bow and a special broad head made by a local blacksmith, or by the person using it. The broad heads are not unlike the two-bladed broad heads used a few years ago that had a socket which the arrow shaft went into.

One of the people I remember using a bow and arrow to hunt deer was Mr. Ernest Murray. About 1950, Mr. Murray met a person of Indian descent, and they became good friends. At that time Mr. Murray did not have a hunting bow and his new friend did, so this problem was soon solved. Finding a bodarc (osage orange tree), Mr. Murray cut a section of the tree and rived a bow blank from it. Being one of the best craftsmen in the county–whether it was making johnboats, paddles, or bows and spikes–he set about making as fine a hunting bow as anyone could ever want. With the bow he also made a leather quiver, and an arm guard to go with it, of equally fine craftsmanship. Though they hunted with their bow, no deer were ever taken, because deer were very scarce in the 1950s in the Ripley County Ozarks.

Rabbits, on the other hand, were quite plentiful. Joe Hastings, my dad, talked about hunting rabbits in deep snow with sticks in the 1920s and 1930s. The rabbits were not

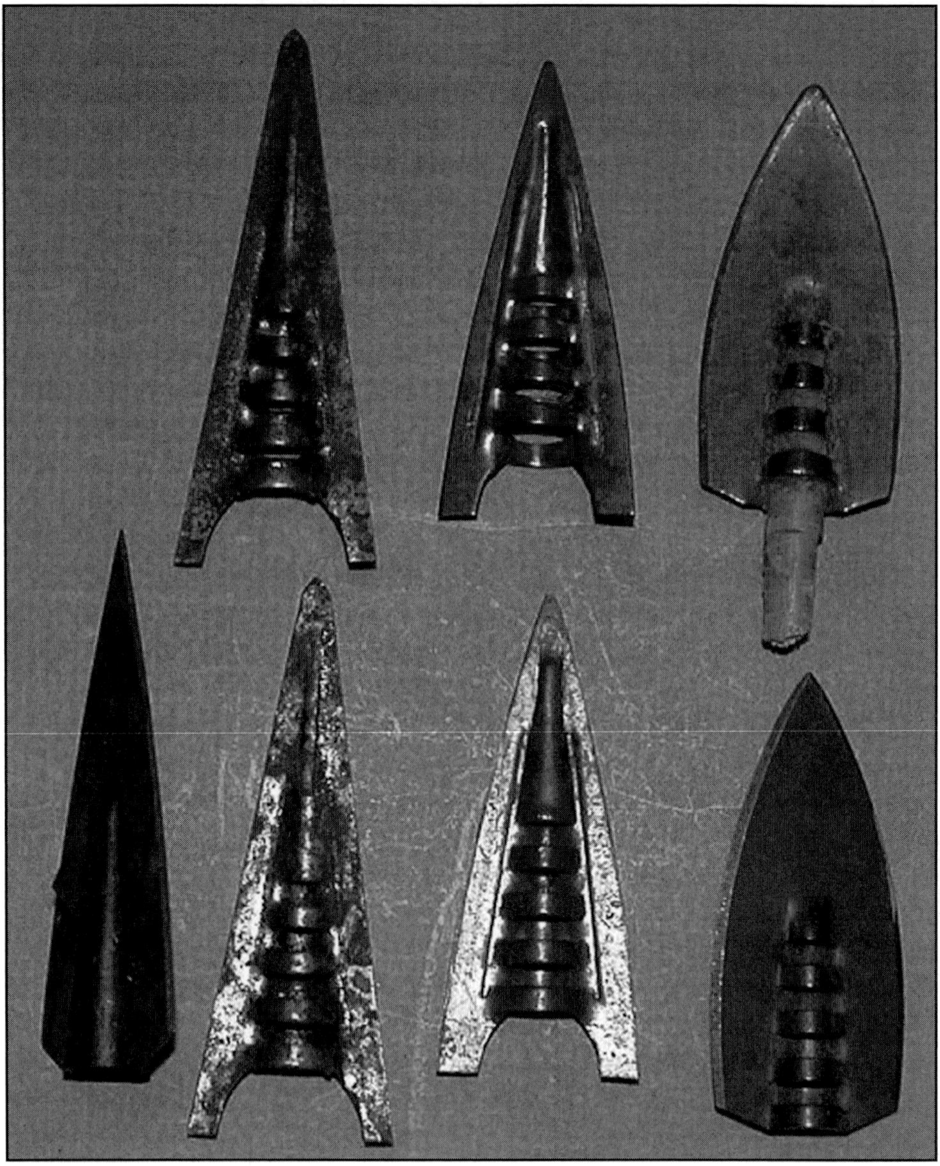

These are a few examples of broad heads in my collection. Some date back several years. I began bow hunting for deer around 1960 when archery was in its infancy here in the Ozarks. There weren't many deer, and taking one with a rifle was quite a feat, much less with a bow and arrow. Nevertheless, I persisted in the sport, and the first time I took a deer with my bow (which was just a metal recurve), was quite a thrill. Even today I find the thrill of the hunt is still with me, and each year when the fall woods beckon, I pick up my modern bow and arrows, and head for the woods. Shown actual size.

able to run in the deep snow and would just sit there when Dad would walk upon them, thus allowing a quick kill with the stick. Although my dad never talked about ever hunting rabbits with a bow, there were other people who did hunt that way.

Two people that I have knowledge of hunted for rabbits with the bow and spike. One was Mr. Charles J. Braschler of Pratt. Mr. Braschler lived along Current River

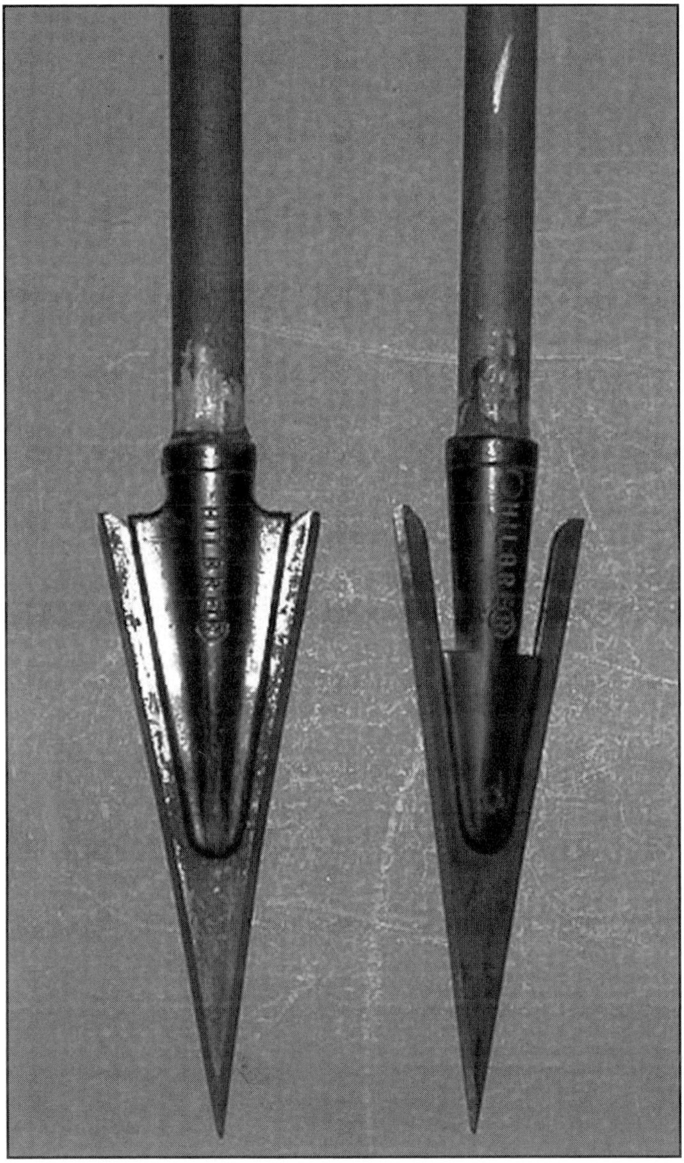

Examples of early factory made broad heads.

where there were many rabbits including swamp rabbits, which are quite large. In one day alone, Mr. Braschler stated he killed five rabbits with the bow and spike. The other person who also hunted rabbits with the bow and spike was Mr. Everett Cole. He lived near Fourche Creek in the late 1940s and 1950s, and possibly longer. Many others who could not afford ammunition, or who saved it for "hard-times"–as the old saying goes–also hunted with the bow and arrow.

Bows, Spikes, and Gigs of Pratt

A very good friend of mine, Eugene Braschler, grew up in the Pratt Community in Ripley County, and he related to me many "bow and spikin'" stories of his younger days when he was growing up, and fishing the creeks of that area. I asked him if he would write about his memories of those experiences so I could include them in this book. He was very kind to do so, and the following is the story that he wrote.

Pratt, Missouri, was a name place as a community for some 40-45 years. It was a thriving and proud community many years previous and after the Pratt name diminished. This needs some explanation. Early Ripley County records reflect land ownership in the community soon after Doniphan began receiving white settlers. In fact, Doniphan's so-called first citizen was an early owner of land in the community. There was a crossing on Current River some six miles below Doniphan and 1 ½ miles from the community later called Pratt. This crossing was first called Gain's Landing, later Gain's Ferry, and still later, the John Ruff Ferry. There was also an Indian ford within 100 yards–this is the same crossing General Price used in his September 1864 return to Missouri during the Civil War. Early references to this place usually just mentioned that it was beyond Gain's Landing or Ferry.

The Pratt name was established when an Alabama family by that name purchased land on the west side of the river. Their daughter, Mary, soon established a school which gave the community its name. Later, a post office was established. By World War II both had become almost nonexistent.

By the turn of the century, the community was settled by Braschlers, Burkes, Rays, Fosters, Eagans, Johnsons, Pierces, Stanleys, and others. The Eagans were of heritage pioneer persuasion. They also owned a good portion of a spring-fed stream which flowed within a few yards of the Pratt school. My family, the B. (Boone) Weaver Braschler family, owned the next quarter-mile stretch of the stream (Eagan Branch). Even though the Eagans and Braschlers were not always on the best of terms, their fishing and hunting activities insured a continued association.

I was born December 11, 1924, and had a brother seven years and one week older. We were closer than most brothers, which gave me an automatic "in" with the big boys. Also, my father was somewhat of a local celebrity. The three of us were often at the center of outdoor activities.

Being as close to Current River as we were, bow fishing, or "bow & spikin'" as we later called it was more for sport and a "learning" pastime while in school than it was as a serious pursuit. With the spring-fed stream so close, we spent a lot of time after "hornyheads" or creek chubs.

Hunting was a different proposition with bow and arrows. Not only did we have plenty of cottontails, but during high water we also had swamp rabbits that would move to higher ground where they were somewhat out of place. We would often find them inclined to "sit" for a shot. They were large, meaty, and when mixed with pork belly, made excellent sausage. This was a sport that put meat on the table and was usually taken seriously. Arrows for rabbits were usually tipped with a spent-center fire cartridge of 38 or larger caliber. This required a head shot up close.

For our use, there was never any doubt that second-growth hickory was the wood of choice for bows. My father had followed an Indian custom of water seasoning wood (hickory and ash) for making bows, handles, arrows, ball bats, and other wood products used around the farm. After sawing blanks for the above uses, he would bundle these together and sink them in a spring for several weeks/months. Once this wood was brought out and air dried for another period, it was ready to work.

The wood had been quarter-sawed, being careful to use sections without knots. I don't recall ever making or seeing a bow that could be called a "long bow." That was a European design that was unknown to the Indians. I believe our design (both my family's and the Eagans') came directly from the American Indians. In fact, the soldiers were surprised at the accuracy of the Indians' bow/arrow shooting during the Trail of Tears March. They were surprised at their accuracy. There has never been doubt that the Indians favored Osage Orange or "Bodarc" for making the best bows. However, this wood is exceedingly hard to tiller, and straight-grained material is almost nonexistent. On the other hand, second-growth hickory is usually straight-grained and easily worked. It was ideally suited for our purpose of close-up fishing and hunting. We usually used ash for arrows, and sometimes we substituted local cane.

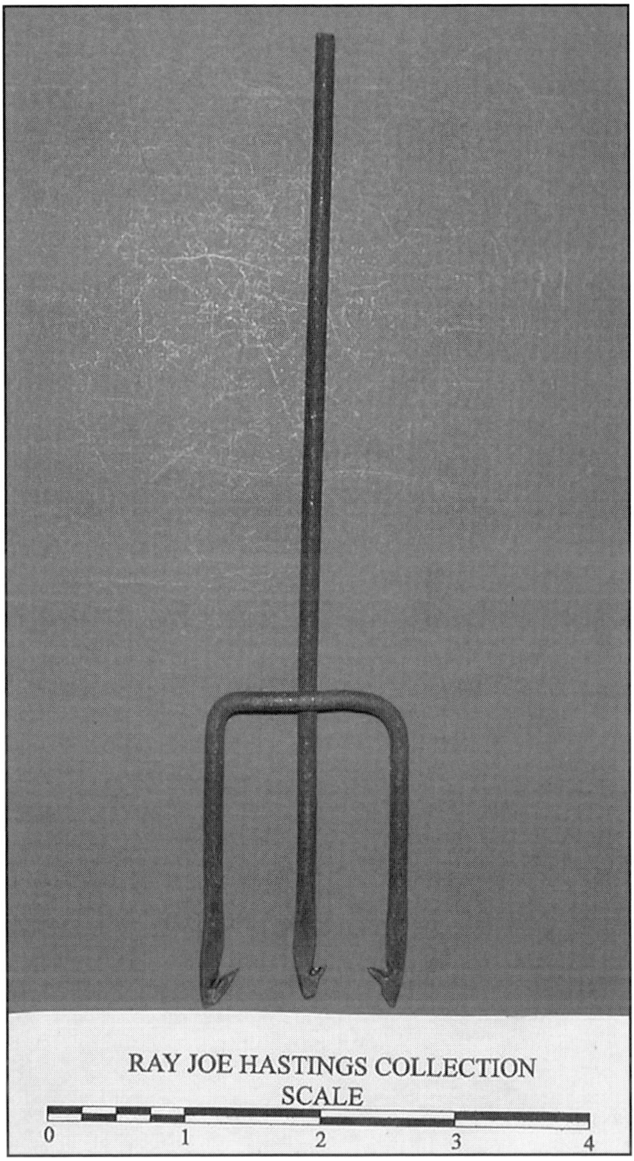

Made by Mr. Eugene Braschler in 2005 to show one kind of bow spike used in the Pratt area in the early 1930s. It is made out of fence wire. Instead of a socket that the shaft went into on the spike, the wooden shaft was partly drilled up into, and the wire on this type was driven into the shaft.

We used pieces of broken glass to shave the wood into the shape we wanted. I believe Indians used both quartz and obsidian. We made handles and other wood items the same way. We would work around the fireplace or stove at night. This left plenty of shavings for kindling the next morning. In recent years, I received a sack of obsidian that was unfit for arrow heads because it didn't chip true. That would have been great (better than either quartz or glass) for shaping wood items. After splitting pieces of ash into arrow lengths, we worked them into arrows the same way. Our arrows were usually about 30 inches long, and occasionally up to 36 inches. The Eagans made theirs somewhat longer.

Our bows were all made in similar fashion. The ends were notched to receive the bow string. The limbs of our bows were somewhat flattened, and the arrow rest was filed or notched for that purpose. Arrows were also notched to receive the bow string. They were filed or shaped to allow the thumb and index finger to draw with some strength. Bow string material was always carefully twisted and waxed with beeswax to keep it strong. Although other items were used, cotton was the normal material. It was usually plentiful.

Perhaps the most exciting innovation was introduced by Ira Eagan. He used welded woven-wire fencing to fashion three-prong gigs. At first, these seemed like nice toys to use in the spring branch on hornyheads. However, after some refinement, they proved lethal for the big boys to play with. We flattened the ends and used a small chisel to split out beards before sharpening the points. We made our own drills to drill out the ends of arrows. The holes were drilled very tight and the shank end of the wire gigs were forced into the arrows. We learned to vary the shoulders for more strength and to make the middle prong slightly longer. Later, we learned that this material was easily heat-welded if we wished to spend more time on the beards.

Hurricane Creek was headed by a nice spring at Poynor and meandered slightly north and mostly east through the Pratt Community. It became a full-fledged tributary as it entered Current River after some six to seven miles. The Pratt road (Highway A) crosses it about the area of change from a clear Ozark spring-fed stream to a low bottom-land river tributary. Fishermen to this day refer to its entrance to Current River as "the mouth of the creek." It is that dominant a landmark. With its oxbows, sloughs and springs, it has always produced an abundance of fish, frogs and Cottonmouth Water Moccasin snakes. I mention this later as my Braschler cousins also used bow fishing as both sport and food. It was not unusual to harvest 10-20 large bullfrogs along this lower stretch of the stream. This may be where the idea of attaching a string to one's arrow began. Certainly, when hunting from a high bank in snake country, a spike with a good beard and a string attached became the weapon of choice as a frog would be retrieved without moving dangerously through heavy cover.

The upper end of Hurricane Creek was a different matter. My mother's family settled part of that area around 1830. It was some 40-45 years later when my father's family moved into the area, beginning at Poynor/Sanky Hall, before actually moving to Pratt. Most all of their bow fishing would have been for sport on the sucker runs, since all fish were legal game during that time. In fact, my family didn't know about scoring suckers then. My mother first learned to pressure them and make fish cakes for breakfast. I can taste them to this day–very good! I believe the term "bow and spikin'" was introduced into the community at a later date. Like old love letters, plenty of evidence yet exists in old tool sheds and where antiques are found.

In summary of this activity, there were three incentives to keep in mind. Number one was that almost all our ingenuity was somehow related to our perception of how the Indians did it. There were many exciting stories about Indians in the community. Most were just that–stories. The one persistent legend was likely true. That concerned the Benge group of 1200 Cherokees that crossed Current River during December of 1838. Before crossing the river, they camped along a trail from Harris Creek, via Popes Chapel Church down to the river near the mouth of Glaze Creek. Although there was little contact with settlers, this observation was made concerning the Indian boy's ability to hunt and fish with improvised weapons–bow and arrows.

Number two was our discovery that the cane growing along the river was made to order for the use of arrows. They were also used for spear and gig handles, as well as fishing poles. Cane works easily when green, and it seasons without warping. Also, we learned that the sections suitable for arrows had very little change in diameter or in length needed for arrows. There were also sections located each six to eight inches that were useful when making arrows. They could be split between sections for inserting fletching without affecting other sections.

The third discovery was the fact that we could shoot arrows with our "bean shooters," i.e. several other names. This was done by resting the point end of the arrow in the fork of the bean shooter, and using the rubber power to propel the arrow forward. About this time, my best friend's father gave us a tube from a large truck. It was very thick, black, and a high grade of rubber. This provided rubber power almost beyond belief. It was obvious that arrows powered by that material could be used on larger fish, frogs, suckers, rabbits, and other small game.

It was about this time that my father made me a "slingshot" handle such as I had never imagined. It was sawed and finished from a regular piece of 1x wide board. It had a carved handle with upright prongs for the strips of rubber and horizontal crossbars for the hen feathers to slide over. I don't recall if the center had a groove or was raised for the arrow rest. However, this contribution from my father, and the heavy rubber tube from my best friend's father completely revolutionized our hunting and fishing potential with arrows.

As told by Eugene Brashler

The Game Wardens

Pictures of men with their bows and spikes and a string of fish may be more rare than articles on the subject. After sixteen years of research, I have not seen or heard of a single picture depicting this scene. However, this may not be too unusual because the only cameras available at that time, at least for most of us, was the old Brownie box camera. Not everyone had one, and the ones that did only took pictures on rare and special occasions. Money was very scarce, and sometimes there was simply not enough money to purchase film. Also, remember it was illegal to take game fish with the bow and spike, so it was sort of like taking a picture of a man and his moonshine still; no one wanted any pictures of evidence lying around.

The game wardens, as they were known back in those days, were very much feared. No one wanted to pay a fine, and we knew we were not supposed to be gigging. On our trips down Briar Creek, we would have to cross a gravel road about half way down to where we were going, and although there were few cars to be seen in the 1940s and 1950s, we always watched for headlights at night when we started back up the creek. More than once I have seen Dad douse the lantern when headlights would suddenly appear. When the car went on up the road, Dad would once again light the lantern and we would resume our gigging.

Although the game wardens never stopped my dad or any of my family, it was a heart-pounding moment of anticipation, wondering if we would be arrested. At the time I did not understand they (the game wardens) were just doing their jobs, which was trying to protect and preserve the wildlife and game for the future generations. As I look back at the work of the conservation agents as we know them today, little did I realize at that time that without the hard work and long hours they put in trying to enforce the law, as well as the time spent educating people on why they should not take game illegally, much of our wildlife would not be around today.

I can remember when deer were very scarce, and turkey were nonexistent in this area. Beaver and raccoon were also two animals that were getting hard to find. Beaver were once again introduced on the Current River and other area rivers about 1960 with hunting and trapping regulations enforced. These animals and many other species that were at one time native to our Ozarks are once again thriving. My hat's off to our conservation agents who are doing a great, never-ending, and sometimes thankless job!

These two broadheads and the two-prong were made and used by Mr. Glen (Buck) Warfel, Carter County, Missouri. The broadhead on the left appears to have been used, and it still retained part of the original shaft. The one on the right appears to be unused. At just under 5" each, there is little question they were made to hunt land animals such as rabbits and deer, and were not made to fish with. The two broadheads help write another chapter in the history of the use of the bow and arrow in the Southeast Missouri Ozarks, as these two are the only broadheads I have found in sixteen years of collecting and researching.

The two-prong was the one used to bow and spike fish, and it is 4 5/16" long. There was also a bow that I believe is made out of Ash that was with these. All are of excellent workmanship. Shown actual size.

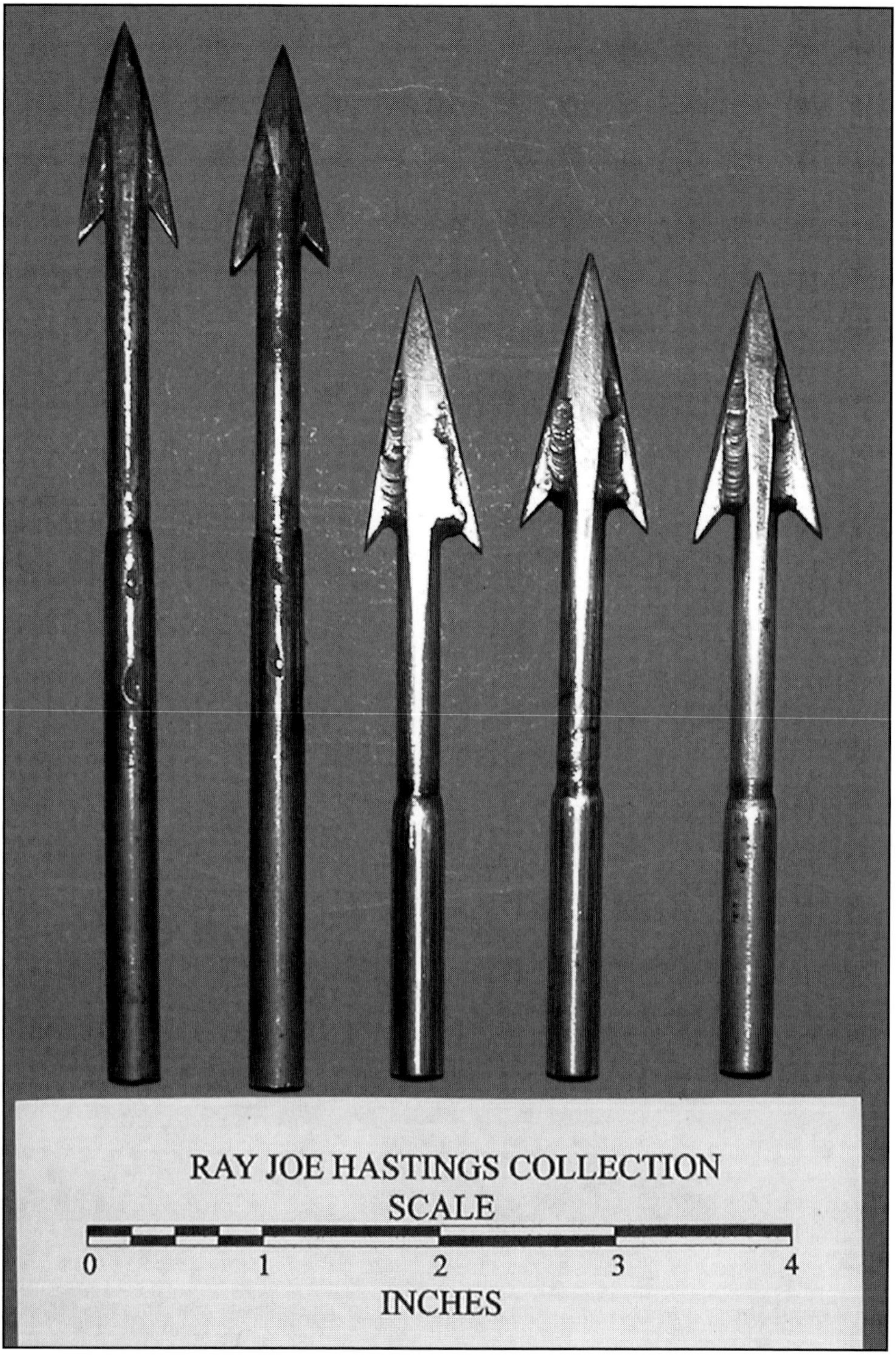

All five spikes were made by Mr. Boyd Kester about 1969. Mr. Kester lives in Van Buren, Missouri, Carter County. These were made to fish the more modern way from a boat. As one can see, he did a very good job on them, and they are a wonderful addition to my collection. My thanks to Mr. Kester for giving them to me. Sadly, Mr. Kester passed away in the spring of 2008. Shown actual size.

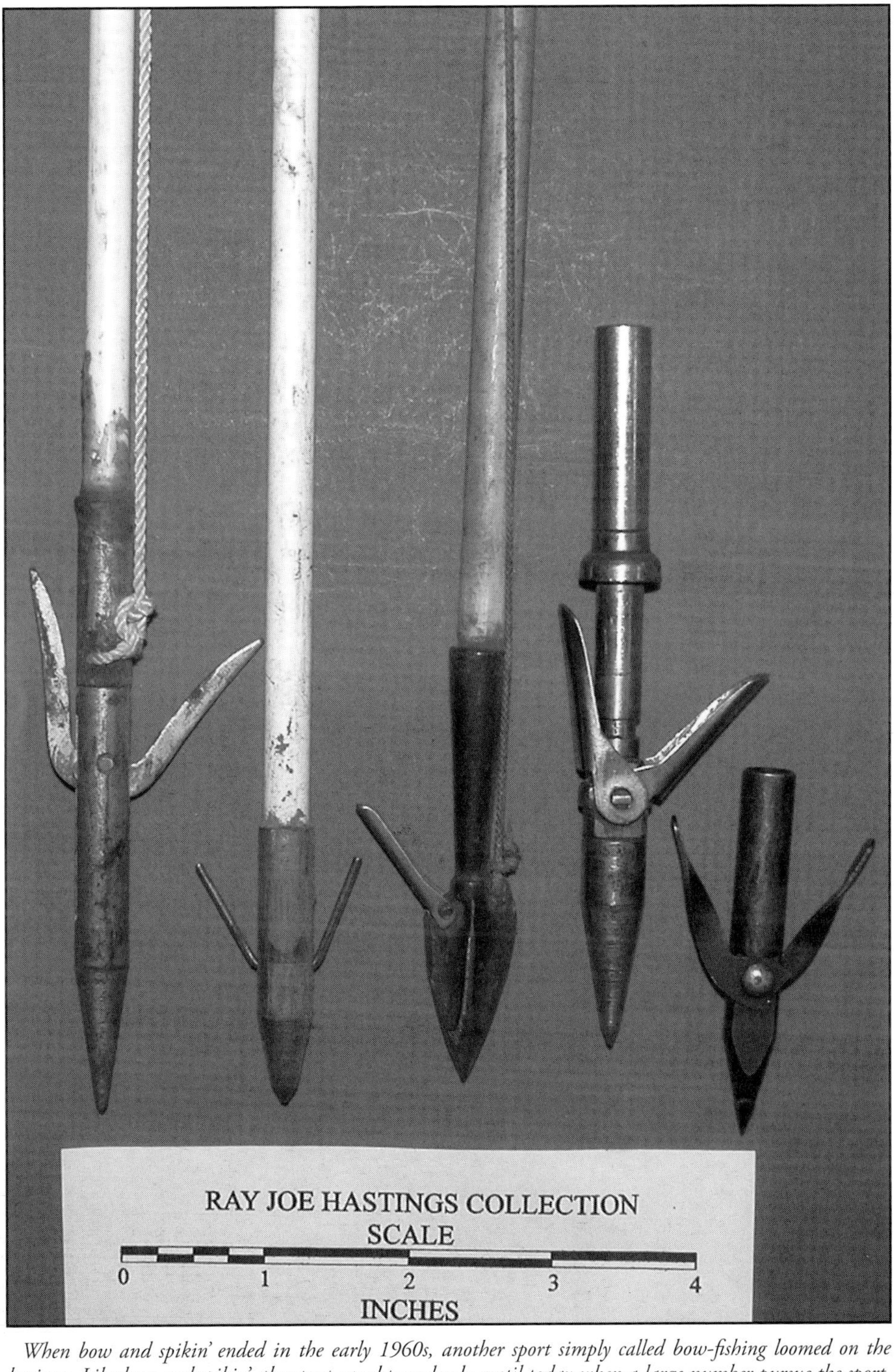

When bow and spikin' ended in the early 1960s, another sport simply called bow-fishing loomed on the horizon. Like bow and spikin', the sport caught on slowly, until today when a large number pursue the sport. Most of today's bow fishing is done standing in a boat on lakes, and large rivers shooting big fish like carp, gar, and buffalo. The picture above shows some of the modern points used in bow fishing. Some are old, and some are newer.

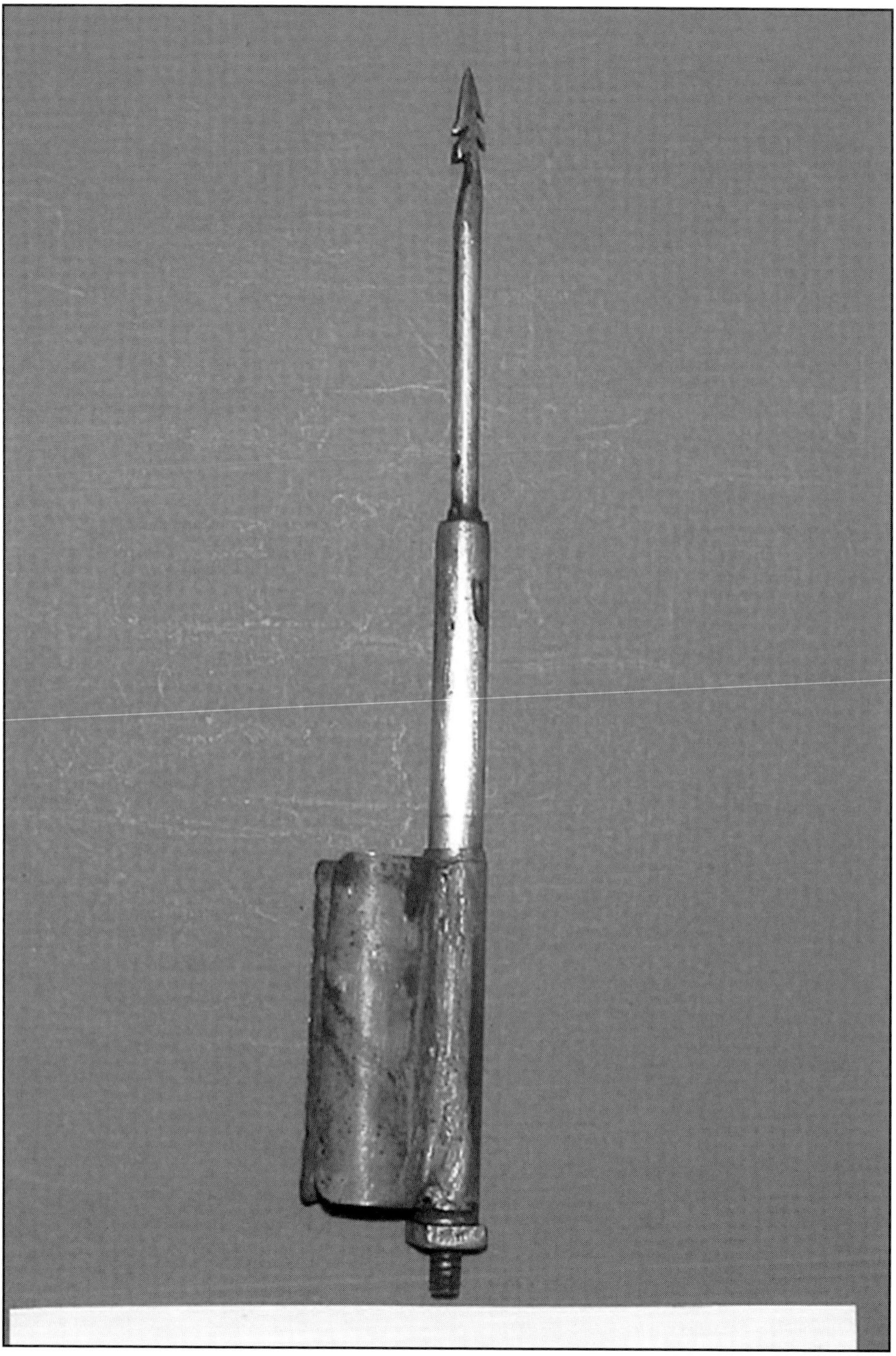

This came from the area where the bow and spike were used. This one took some serious thinking to make. The socket was placed on the side, and there is a spring inside to let the point slide back up the middle section in case a rock was hit. The point has four beards, two on each side. It is well-made, and quite a nice specimen to add to my collection. Shown actual size.

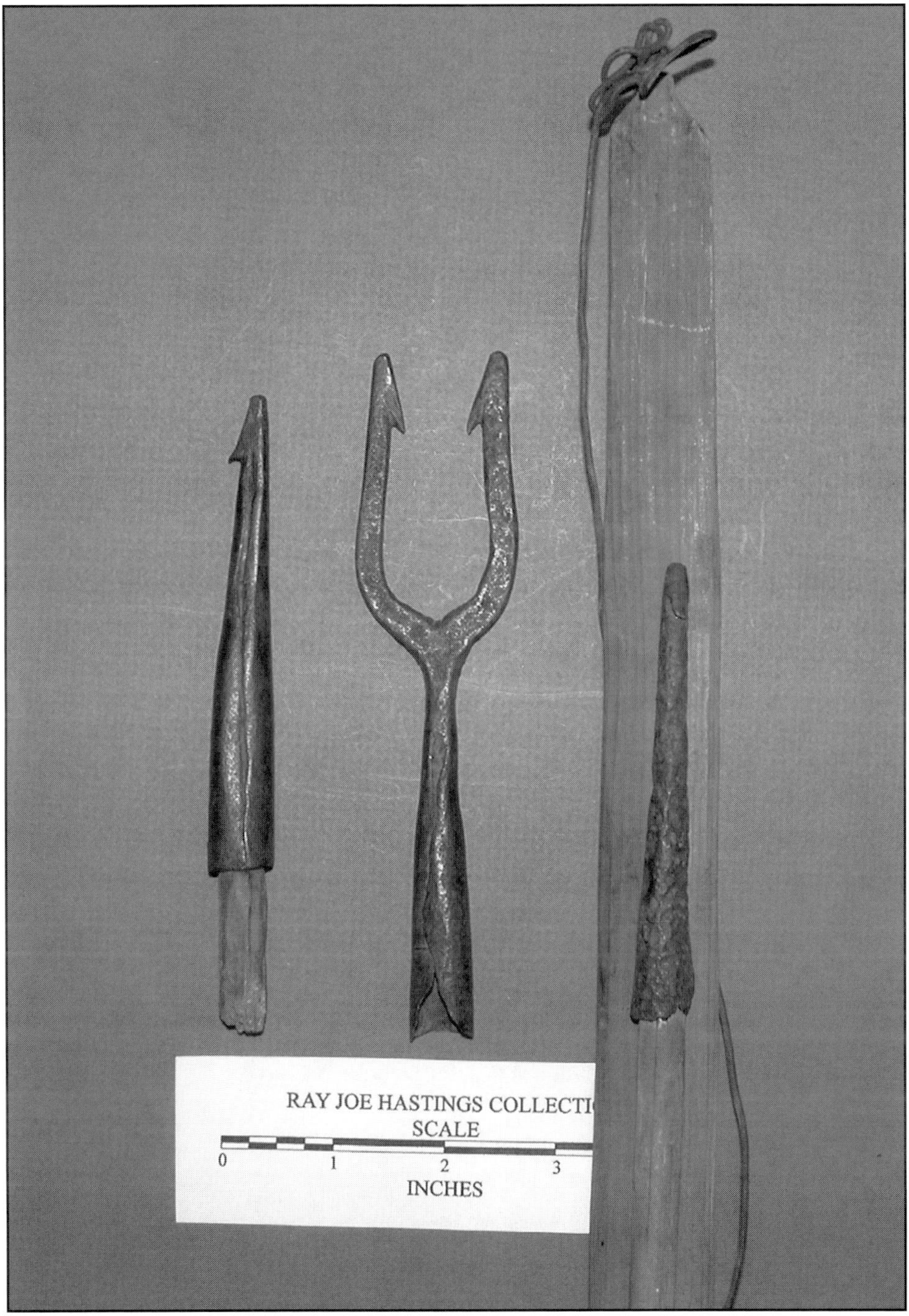

All three spikes are from Ripley County. The single spike on the left was owned and used by the Earl Emmons family. I purchased it at the farm sale a few years after Mr. Emmons was deceased. The two-prong in the center was made and used by Mr. Ron Emmons, Earl Emmons' brother. The bow and single spike attached to the bow was given to me by Earl Emmons' son, Mr. Luther Emmons. All three bow spikes and the bow were made by some member of the Emmons family, and were used mostly in the Little Black River and Flat Creek. All three were probably made in the early 1930s.

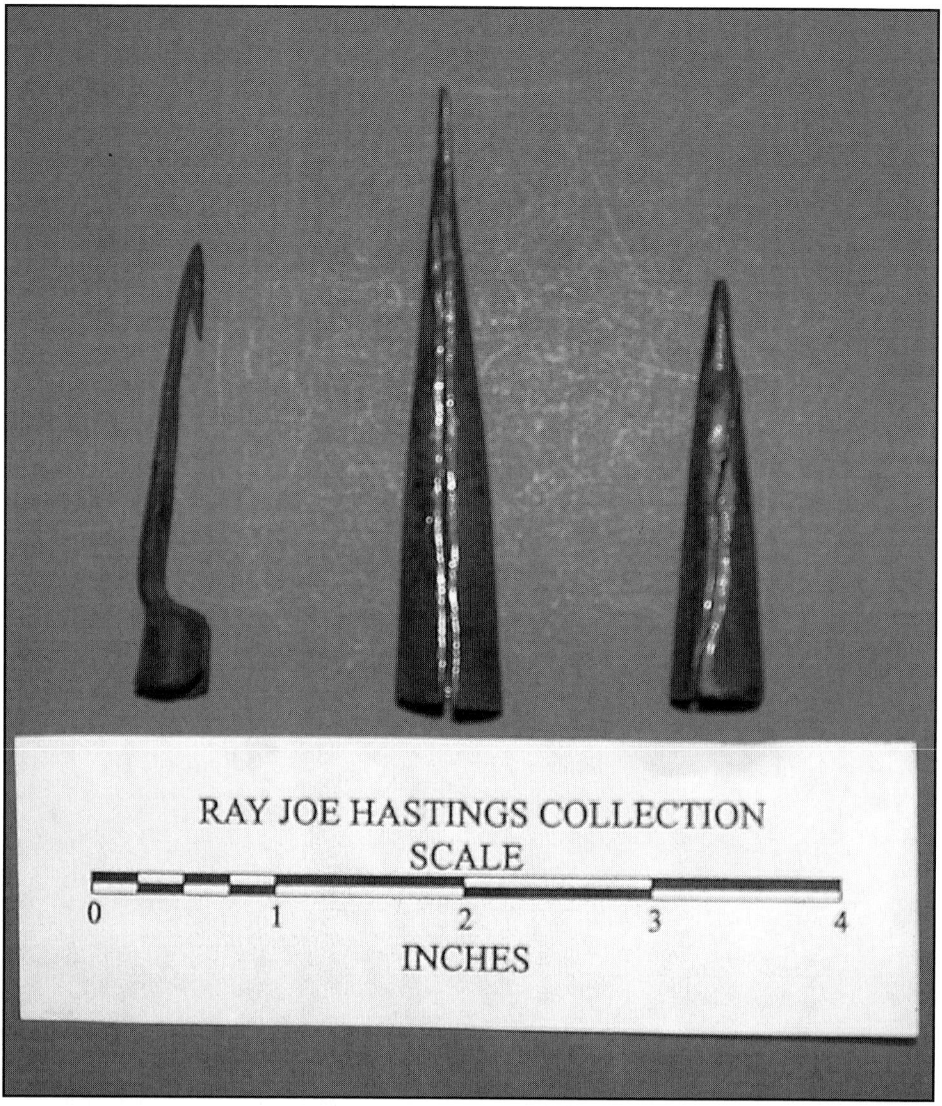

These three points are modern-made. The one on the left is made from a horseshoe nail, and was made like the ones used by a man in Ripley County in his youth. He stated they did not last long when bow and spikin' with them, but they were easily made. I have heard of several other men who also used this type of spike. The other two were made for me by Mr. Acel Price of Pratt. This type has no beards but was sometimes used when needed. Shown actual size.

Right: *From a flea market in Sharp County, Arkansas. This was probably intended to be a straight spike, but for some reason, the maker converted it into a large fish hook. The small socket size is 7⁄16" with no hole for a tack or screw to secure the hook to a pole. This suggests a large catfish might have torn the hook from the pole if it was used this way. The 7⁄16" socket is almost in the middle of the diameter 3⁄8" to 5⁄8" size used on bow spikes. The small beard also suggest it was intended to be a spike. Shown actual size.*

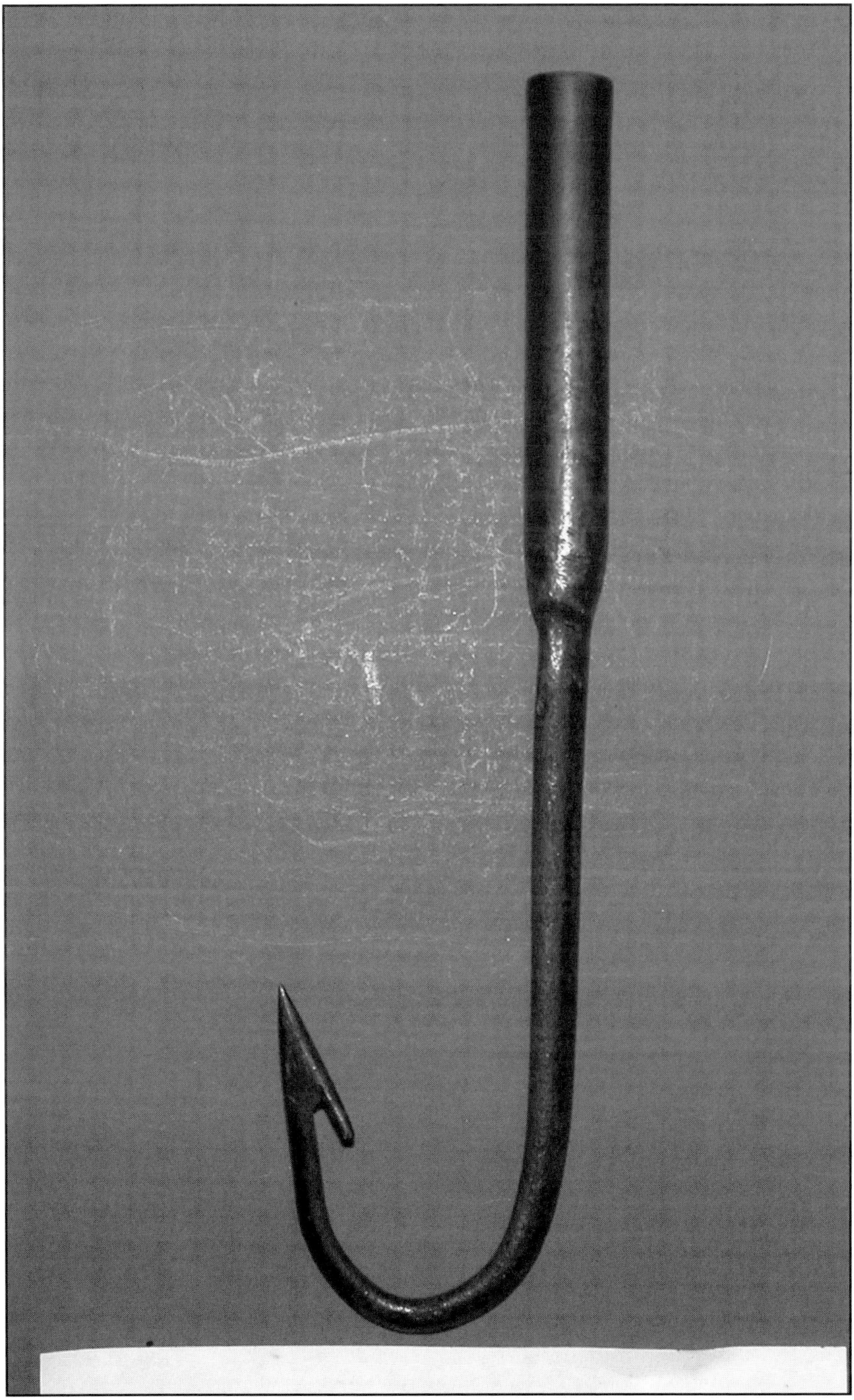

I think these came from Africa, and are only shown to reflect the similarity to the spikes we used here in the Ozarks. Note how far up from the tip the beard is on the one on the right. Shown actual size.

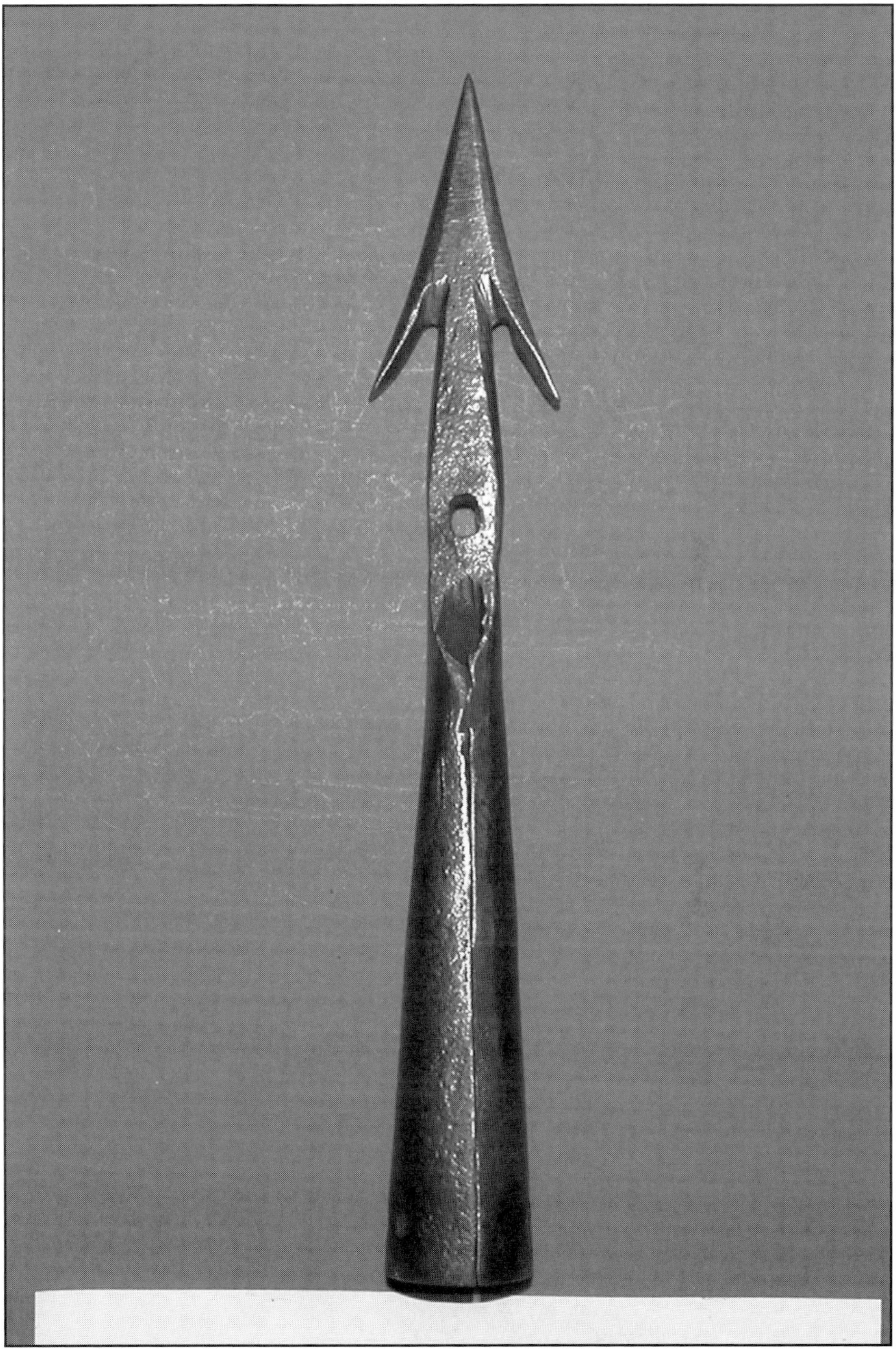

This is supposed to be from Alaska, and was used as a harpoon for seals, or perhaps for whales, walrus, and even fish. Although it doesn't tie in with bow and spikin' in this area, it does show the similarities in the two ways of procuring food for the table. The hole up near the beards was used to attach a line to retrieve the animal harpooned. Shown actual size.

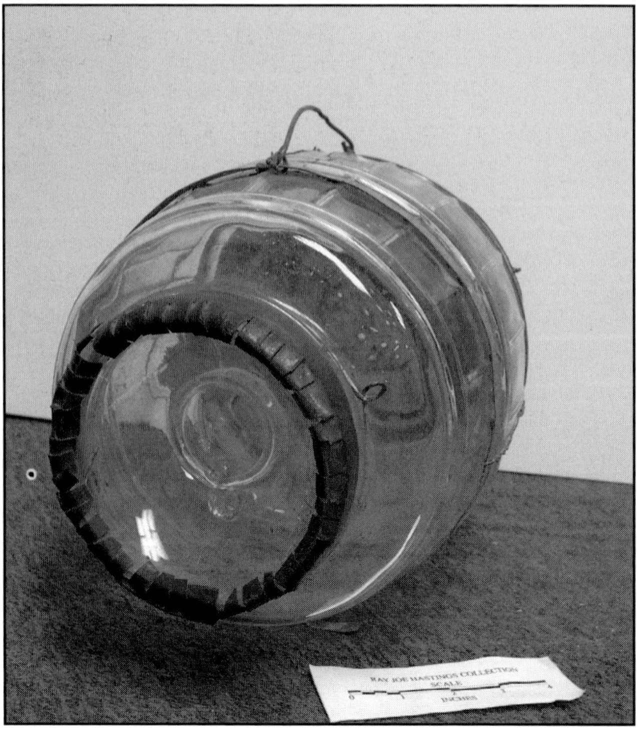

This minnow trap is from the Dave Marek family. It is a rare and uniquely homemade minnow trap that was probably made by Jim Marek, a son of Dave Marek, who not only fished with trot lines, but also with the rod and reel. He also bank fished with a pole, hook and line, and with the bow and spike. The two cedar bows, one three-prong, and three single-prong spikes were also found along with this other fishing gear. To say he was a "fisherman," would be an understatement.

This is a homemade live well and made-up trot line hooks that came from the Dave Marek family. The live well was made from an M.P. Lines railroad can, and was probably made by Jim Marek, one of Dave Marek's sons. Jim was reportedly the "fisherman" of the family. The made-up trot line hooks were inside the live well with a ball of heavy cotton line to stretch across the river to attach the trot-line hooks to. Unfortunately, the ball of twine was thrown away before I purchased these items.

In Conclusion

The Book Condensed

For those of you that may have had trouble following my ramblin' writing style; here it is in a condensed form. The early settlers knew of the bows and arrows the Indians used, but the early 1820 and 1830 spikes seemed to have been an idea born out of necessity by the early settlers. The concept of fishing that way was probably copied from the Indians who were using either a flint or an iron point at that time. The Indians began making the tips for their arrows out of iron as it became available, and the early settlers just improved on the points that the Indians were already using.

Although fishing with the bow and spike had an early start, there is not much in the way of evidence that suggests it caught on and was used in large numbers until after 1910. One thing that needs to be known is that from 1803 until 1860, the Ozarks were very sparsely populated. Then from 1860 to 1864, the Civil War stopped any or all fishing, as almost every young available man was in the war, and it was also very dangerous to be out on the creeks alone. But by the 1880s, the population had increased, which was about the time the big sawmills started up. The mills brought more and more men into the area seeking work. Two of these mills were the King Bee, and the Grandin Mill, but there were many other big mills scattered over several Ozark counties such as Ripley, Carter, Reynolds, and Shannon. However, by 1910, most of the big mills' source of timber had been depleted and they were being shut down and were moving to other areas where timber was more plentiful. The men went home to do whatever they could to just "get by." This is when I believe the use of the bow and spike took off, and by 1920 it was in full use.

Several of my spikes date back to that time period, around the early1920s, and are the earliest ones I have the history of. About 1910 is the oldest bow in my collection, and it was made by Mr. James Talbert Holland, (1-1-1888 to 3-27-1986). Mr. Holland lived on one of the prongs of Fourche Creek in Ripley County, but in the late 1940s he purchased a farm on the east prong of Fourche Creek, which is north of Highway 142 West.

As the use of the bow and spike really took off, the hard times of the depression, 1929-1933, and the later years of World War II ensured its continued use. The use of the bow and spike to take fish as well as land animals peaked in the late 1950s and then started to slowly fade away. Oddly enough, it was still in use by some as late as the 1980s. More than 150 years have passed since its slow beginning (from at least 1820-1830 to 1910-1920, to its peak in 1920-1960) and then to its slow demise in 1960-1990. I am proud to have been a part of this Ozark phenomena, and sad to have seen the end of fishing with the bow and spike here in the southeastern Missouri and northeastern Arkansas Ozarks.

The big-river gig is somewhat harder to put a starting date on, as none have been recovered in a controlled archaeological dig. However, like the spikes, they seem to have had an early start (at least pre-Civil War 1860-1864) judging from the way they were made and the type of material they were made from. I believe that the first heavy

The Griff Emmons family, decendents of Col. Timothy Reeves, with bows and spikes and river gigs.

use of these types of gigs began with the big sawmills that had their beginning in the 1880s. For many years men rafted ties and logs on the rivers here in the southeastern Missouri Ozarks by the tens of thousands. The rivers and creeks became a source of protein for many families from the fish that were taken from these fast-flowing, clear streams. It's no wonder that the gig, as a method for taking fish, "caught on." It was fast and it was "a lot of fun"!

These early gigs were always three-pronged with the two outside prongs made together, and then forge-welded to the middle prong and socket that had previously been made. There are variations of these, but most are made as described. All I have ever seen had sockets except one, and it was made to be inserted up into the gig pole. This early style of gig lasted from its heavy-use days of the 1880s to 1910, and maybe a little later. But judging from the bow spikes that were being cut out and hand-forged by the 1920s, it too probably saw a style change after 1910. Although gigs with from two to six prongs were made by the thousands, from this time on there has been very little change in their style, unless one counts the gigs that many blacksmiths made down through the years by using a garden hoe for a socket and a pitchfork for the tines. This style of gig may change too, as most of the blacksmiths who made gigs have just about all passed away. Only time will tell if the manufactured gig will replace it.

Closing Thoughts

Was the bow and spike an Ozark phenomenon, a localized subsistence tool to take fish and other small game (even though it could take bigger game like deer and turkey by just changing the spike to a broad head, and using it with a hunting bow)? This question remains and begs to be answered. Why wasn't this method employed in other states that have clear creeks and rivers flowing through them? If they were ever used anywhere other than the southeastern Missouri and northeastern Arkansas Ozarks, the information on them remains undiscovered.

Fishing with the bow and spike ended like it began–slowly. After 1960, it was almost completely over. Slowly but surely, like stars winking out in the dawn's early light, one by one, they picked up their bows and spikes, put them overhead in what we referred to as the "smokehouse," and quit. A way of fishing and a way of life for many Ozark hill people that went back to as early as 1820-1830 was over, except for a few isolated pockets that were carried on for a few more years by some die-hard "bow and spikers."

However, saying it ended may be somewhat of a misnomer; it has only ended the way we did it. The winding down of using the bow and spike was followed by a new way of fishing that was looming on the horizon. This new method is simply called "bow fishing." It requires a string on a reel that is attached to the bow and arrow with factory-made points that replaces the hand-forged spikes. It is usually done from a boat on lakes and the bigger rivers, and big fish such as carp, gar, and buffalo are usually shot. It is done mostly for sport. There is an open season on many of these types of fish because of the overabundance of them in the lakes and rivers, which is a hindrance to the well-being of the game fish that are in the waters. However, the way it was done for more than one hundred and fifty years has come to an end. It will more than likely never regain the popularity that it once had throughout all those years with the early settlers and as I remember it during my younger years.

Sometimes my mind wanders back to this more simple way of life. Back to a world of no television, and no video games; back to a time when Mom cooked a meal and then called us to eat, and to a time when we would sit down around the table and listen as the blessing was said before we began our meal. While writing this book, I would often think of the past, and in my mind's eye I could see these things that had happened–a boy waist deep in a hole of water, a well-bent bow, and the clink of a steel spike on a gravel-bottom creek. It was, indeed, a much simpler time, and one that will probably never come this way again.

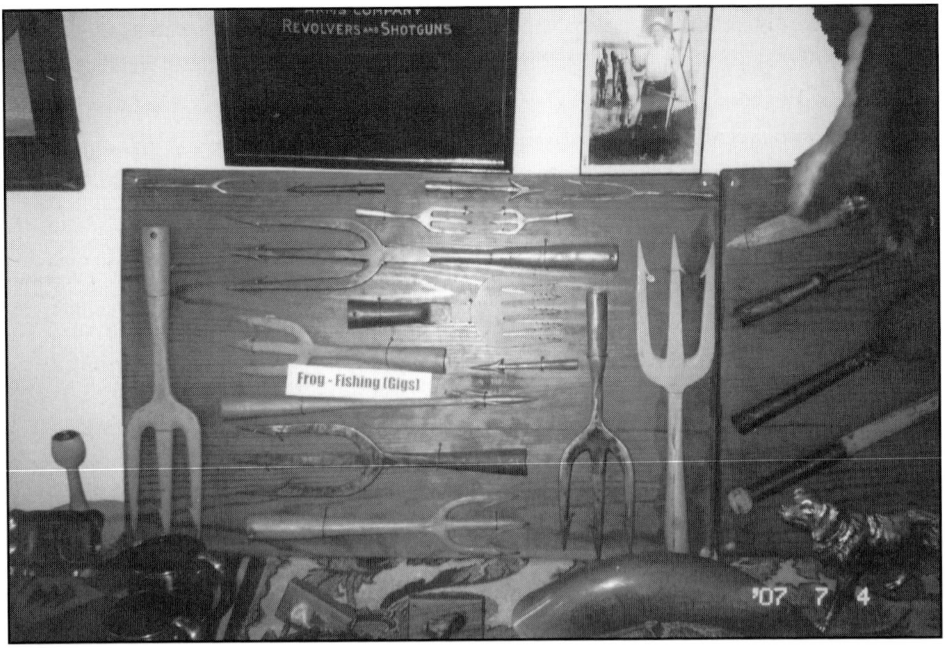

A nice collection of both river gigs and bow spikes located in the town of Berryville, Carroll County, Arkansas, at the Saunder's Gun Museum. I have not personally seen these–just a picture. Most of these river gigs and spikes appear to have been made by the same gig maker and were never used. This fine group of well-made gigs was probably made for the person who collected them by just one, or possibly two different blacksmiths or gig makers. Carroll County, Arkansas is located along the Missouri state line, and is near the two Missouri counties of Christian and Taney, within the area where bow spikes were known to have been used. Although most of the seven–one, two, and three-prong spikes–do not appear to have been used; nevertheless, someone had to have known what they looked like and how to make them.

Although I have no information of spikes from Carroll County, I would venture a guess that this area saw some, if not extensive, use of the bow and spike. There is also one long bow that would have been used mostly, if not entirely, for hunting. It would be nice to know who made the spikes and the bow, and also the area they were used. Perhaps a future reader of this book who has some knowledge about these gigs will contact me with the information.

About the Author

I was born on Sept. 24, 1937, and my earliest memories are of the hard times that my family had to endure. Late in the fall of 1941, Mr. Dewitte Fogle gave my dad permission to build a cabin on some land that Mr. Fogle owned. That piece of ground was on a knoll above the high-water mark on the very headwaters of the east prong of Fourche Creek. Dad and Mom, with the help of some of the older children, built a log cabin there. There were eight children altogether–four boys and four girls–but the two older children were already married, which left six of us at home. Even though there was a need for a larger home, it began as only a two-room cabin with another room added later. I was very small when they built it, but I remember it well because I helped chink the cracks with mud. The rooms had plain board floors with cracks wide enough to sweep dirt through. This was the way of life for us in the early 1940s since we were extremely poor–as were most of the other people we knew in the Ozark hill country.

Ray Joe, Shirley, and Truman Hastings, with mom and dad, Joe and Hazel, and Grandpa John Hastings in the background. Taken about 1945-46 in Ripley County.

The old log cabin we lived in during the early 1940s in Ripley County.

My family lived in the log cabin for only a few years–from late 1941 to 1946–then Dad found a place on the east side of Briar Creek that was only three miles west of Doniphan, and so we moved closer to "civilization." I really liked that place better than where we had previously lived. Of course, being just a young boy, the main reason I liked it more was that Briar Creek was bigger than the creek at our other house. The second reason was the school was a closer walk than the other school, so it did not take as long to get home in the afternoons after school and go to the creek. Although my hunting, fishing, and trapping experiences started at the log cabin when we lived there, our move to the banks of Briar Creek and those many afternoons spent on those banks were where my outdoor skills began to develop.

Ray Joe Hastings back from a night of fishing on Briar Creek in Ripley County. Taken about 1950. The small dog on the left was called Perky. The bigger dog on the right was named Brownie.

Another reason I liked the Briar Creek place better was because there was also a spring where we got our drinking water. It was one-fourth mile from our house, compared to one-half mile at the other house. When a person has to carry water, every quarter of a mile makes quite a bit of difference, especially to a youngster. We also had to use the spring as a refrigerator to keep our milk and butter from spoiling in the warmer weather, so there was a long walk to the spring to retrieve it for Mom when she needed it. Dad finally got around to digging a wet-weather spring in a seepage on our place, but it would go dry in the hot summer months, and then we would have to revert to using the other spring.

During the winter, my brother Pal and I would set out rabbit traps. Dad would make them out of six or eight-inch-wide boards that were one-inch thick. They were about two-feet long with a door at the front and a trigger toward the back of the box trap that would trip the door shut when the rabbit brushed against it as he was going to the food in the back of the trap. Even as young kids, our fishing and trapping helped put food on the table.

Throughout my adult life and after I began my own family (three daughters and one son; two stepsons, one stepdaughter, and a houseful of grandchildren and great-grandchildren), I have enjoyed hunting, fishing, and even trapping when my children were younger in order to supplement my income. I worked on highway construction during the nicer weather, but during the winter I was usually unemployed when construction slowed, so that was a good time to trap, and it also gave me a good opportunity to hunt and fish.

Grandsons Byron Ray St. Laurent, Adam Smothers, Aaron Smothers and Andrew Smothers, learning how to use the bow and spike on Well's Creek, Ripley County, 1995.

Grandson Cordell Hutcheson with a bow and spike on Well's Creek, Ripley County.

Granddaughter Michaela Hutcheson with a bow and spike on Well's Creek, Ripley County.

Grandson Grayson Yates with a bow and spike on Well's Creek, Ripley County.

Grandson Cody Hutcheson demonstrates bow and spike fishing in the Current River, Ripley County.

A historic building, the George Patterson cabin, build about 1865, near Fourche Creek, Ripley County.

This time was also a good occasion to spend many hours roaming the hills and wooded areas of Ripley County as well as surrounding counties as I enjoyed being outdoors hunting and fishing, as well as other sports such as canoe racing. I discovered I had a passion for archaeological discovery, as I would search for arrowheads that were left by Indian people of long ago. Many of the items that I have found are on display at the Current River Heritage Museum in Doniphan, Missouri. My quest led me to many other interests, and throughout the years I have collected old bottles and other artifacts that were left by early settlers.

After I retired from construction, I was the county commissioner for Ripley County for eight years. It was during that time that I became a member and served as president of DNAP (Doniphan Neighborhood Assistance Program), which helps fund different county projects such as the Current River Heritage Museum of Doniphan. While I served as president, we created an area located one block south of the courthouse in Doniphan known as the Pioneer Heritage Homestead where we relocated an old historic log cabin, as well as other types of buildings such as a blacksmith shop, etc. Both the museum and the homestead are very interesting tourist attractions for the city of Doniphan. I enjoy putting on demonstrations of gig making, etc. when we have various activities at the Pioneer Heritage Homestead blacksmith shop. I also put on demonstrations in other communities when they have events that re-create old-fashioned activities.

I am an active member in the Emmanuel Baptist Church, and I was also a member and past president of the Kiwanis Club of Doniphan. It was during the time when I was the county commissioner that I became interested in collecting bows, spikes, and river gigs. As I was fortunate enough to find each item, I carefully documented the provenance of each one, including where it was made, who made it, the year it was made, and the creeks or rivers where it was used. The collection that I have accumulated is what has led me to the writing of this book.

When I first started collecting and gathering information on the bow and spike in 1991, I soon found that printed information on the subject was almost non-existent.

There is not a single book, magazine, or any other type of information that I can find, with two exceptions. The first is the 1938 article by Mr. L.L. Broadfoot, who printed a short story on John Counts, a bow and spike fisherman, who was a native of Reynolds County, Missouri. The story and a portrait of Mr. Counts was originally published in the book *Pioneers of the Ozarks,* and is reprinted in this book with permission from the owners of the copyright, the Harlin Museum of West Plains, Missouri. There is another somewhat lengthier article by Dr. James E. Price titled "Bowin'an Spikin' in Th'Jillikins," which was published in the *Ozarks Watch Magazine,* Vol. 4, No. 3, 1990. Dr. Price's article is very informative with just a touch of humor added, and should be read if one can obtain a copy.

My interest in collecting bows and spikes continued until four years later in 1995, when my interest in how they were made became somewhat of an obsession. One day in a hardware store in Van Buren, Missouri, I noticed a handcrafted gig that was sturdily made and very pleasing to the eye. In the conversation that followed, I discovered that a gentleman by the name of Paul Martin of Bunker, Missouri had made the gig. He was the first person that I had heard of since I had begun collecting, who was still making gigs the old-fashioned way, and I knew right then that I wanted him to show me how to make them.

One day a little later, I drove up to Bunker to visit with him. It just so happened he was in his shop making a gig when I pulled up. After a few minutes of introduction and small talk, I told him of my interest in bows and spikes. Then I told him that I wanted to learn everything I could about how gigs were made–about the forge, the hammers, the chisels; in fact, the whole process–and I asked him if he could teach me! He smiled and invited me to stay and watch him work. That very day he made me a little four-prong spike that is as pretty and well-made as any I have ever seen. He also told me he would have to think about teaching me how to make them, stating age and health reasons. I thanked him for the gig, told him I would stay in touch with him and left, knowing that I had been in the presence of a true master artist.

A historic building, the Camp place, an old hewn log cabin on Buffalo Creek, Ripley County.

Later that summer, I heard about the Missouri

Traditional Arts Apprenticeship Program that is administered by the Missouri Folk Arts Program. This is done through the University of Missouri-Columbia, and is designed to teach the skills of past traditions, or the lost arts, to younger men or women who would like to learn these skills. It is believed that many artistic traditions are being forgotten, and this program was instituted as a way to conserve and preserve their heritage for future generations. I thought Mr. Martin might be interested in the program, so I decided to visit him again to speak to him about it. At that time the master, or teacher, received $1,500 for teaching his or her skill for a period of six months, and the apprentice (me) received mileage for most of his travel expenses. It was the honorarium that finally won him over to teach me how to make gigs.

However, first Mr. Martin and I had to apply and then compete with several others in different fields of artistic tradition in order to be accepted. Out of the many that apply, only a few are chosen each year to complete their respective programs. Thankfully, we were one of those that were chosen, and I began gig-making lessons in the late fall of 1995. Once a week I would drive from Doniphan to Bunker to learn all I could about gig making. I will say once again that Mr. Martin was one of the best gig makers ever, and it was through his teaching that I learned what I know about gig making. It is sad to report that a few years later I lost my good friend, and this area lost a master gig maker and artist when Mr. Paul Martin passed away.

Today things have turned around a bit, and I have been chosen to teach the art of gig making. In the fall of 2006, the opportunity was again presented to me through the Missouri Folk Arts Program to teach the skills that I had learned from Mr. Martin to a new apprentice, Mr. Steve Orchard, who lives close to Van Buren. Steve had some experience in making gigs, which was different from the way I had learned. He is a natural and has already become a fine gig maker in the old-fashioned way. He has not only learned to make the large-river gigs of the three and four-prong style, but also has learned and made several of the one, two and three-prong bow spikes. These are very small and sometimes more tedious to make than big-river gigs. Steve Orchard is becoming a superb gig maker, and anyone wanting one can contact Steve at 573-323-0184. Keep in mind that

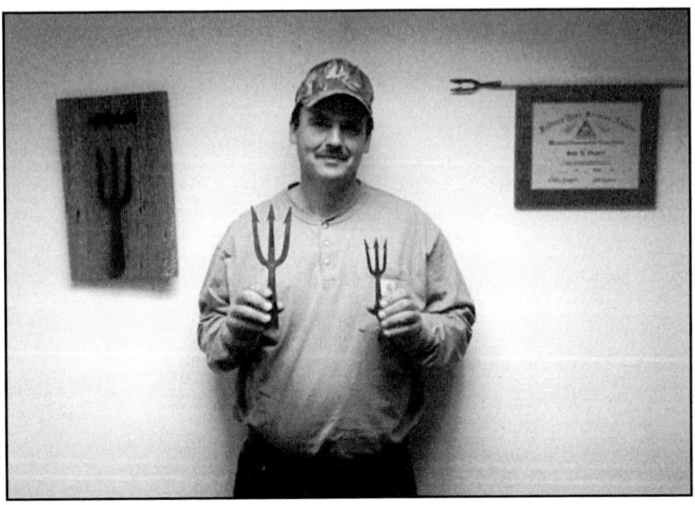

Steve Orchard

a good gig can take all day to make, plus the investment of coal, hammers, chisels, forge, and anvil, so expect to pay one hundred dollars, or more, when buying one of his gigs.

One thing I would like to say is that a good gig is a small investment when compared to a bow, shotgun, or a rifle, and will last for many years if used correctly. I like to ease my gig down into the water until I'm over the fish, and then just punch them, but some people like to throw a gig out to the end of the line that most giggers attach to the poles. When gigging in this manner, it does not matter who made the gig, the prongs are eventually going to spread and may even break.

Ray Joe Hastings

Missouri Department of Conservation Code of State Regulations

Title 3—DEPARTMENT OF CONSERVATION Division 10—Conservation Commission
Chapter 6—Wildlife Code: Sport Fishing: Seasons, Methods, Limits

The following is an excerpt from the Missouri Department of Conservation Code of State Regulations. For complete Missouri state rules and regulations, visit http://www.sos.mo.gov/adrules/csr/current/3csr/3csr.asp. For Arkansas Game & Fish Commission Rules & Regulations, visit http://www.agfc.com/rules%2Dregulations, or visit your local state's conservation website for regulations.

3 CSR 10-6.410 Fishing Methods

PURPOSE: This rule establishes the methods by which fishermen may take fish.

(1) Fish may be taken by the use of pole and line, trotline, throwline, limb line, bank line, jug line, **gig**, **bow**, crossbow, underwater spearfishing, snagging, snaring, grabbing or atlatl, but only as specifically authorized in 3 CSR 10-6.415 through 3 CSR 10-6.550. No person may attempt to take fish by rock or hand fishing, with or without hook. Live bait, mussels, clams, bullfrogs, green frogs, common snapping turtles and soft-shelled turtles may be taken only as specifically authorized in 3 CSR 10-6.605 through 3 CSR 10- 6.620.

(2) Number of Poles and Hooks.

(A) Not more than three (3) unlabeled poles and not more than thirty-three (33) hooks in the aggregate, for any or all methods, may be used by any person at one time.

(B) On the Mississippi River, not more than two (2) unlabeled poles and not more than fifty (50) hooks in the aggregate may be used by any person at one time. While fishing concurrently on the Mississippi River and other Missouri waters, not more than fifty (50) hooks in the aggregate may be used and not more than thirty-three (33) of those hooks may be used in waters other than the Mississippi River.

(C) Trotlines and throwlines of more than one (1) individual may be joined together, but the number of hooks in the aggregate shall not exceed the prescribed number for one (1) individual on the waters that are being fished and the lines must be labeled with each person's full name and address.

(3) Hooks attached to throwlines or trotlines shall be staged not less than two feet (2') apart.

(4) Live bait traps, hooks, trotlines, throwlines, limb lines, bank lines or anchored jug lines (rendered immobile from the location where set) may not be left unattended for more than twenty-four (24) hours or must be completely removed. Unanchored jug lines must be personally attended at all times.

(5) No person may use any explosive, poison, chemical, electrical device or equipment capable of transmitting underwater signals to kill, attempt to kill, or stupefy fish, and no material and equipment may be possessed for those purposes on waters of the state or adjacent banks.

(6) Fish not hooked in the mouth or jaw, except those legally taken by snagging, snaring, grabbing, **gig**, **bow**, crossbow or underwater spearfishing must be returned to the water unharmed immediately.

(7) Fish legally taken by snagging, snaring, grabbing, **gig**, **bow**, crossbow or underwater spearfishing shall be retained by the taker and included in the prescribed daily limit.

(8) Live bait traps, trotlines, throwlines, limb lines, bank lines, jug lines and live boxes shall be plainly labeled on a durable material with the full name and address of the person using the equipment.

(9) Spears propelled by explosive substances may not be used.

(10) Spearguns may not be possessed on unimpounded waters or adjacent banks.

(11) Except as provided in 3 CSR 10-6.605, fish traps, including slat traps and wire traps, may not be possessed on waters of the state or adjacent banks.

(12) As an aid to fishing methods, an artificial light may be used only above the water surface, except that underwater lights may be used to attract fish while fishing by pole and line.

(13) Endangered species and fish included in 3 CSR 10-6.505 through 3 CSR 10-6.545, including their parts and eggs, may not be used for bait.

(14) The director may issue special authorization to properly licensed persons with disabilities to pursue and take fish, mussels and clams, bullfrogs and green frogs, turtles and live bait by methods not prescribed in this chapter and Chapters 11 and 12 if the disability prevents fishing by prescribed methods.

3 CSR 10-6.415 Restricted Zones

PURPOSE: This rule establishes zones, primarily below certain dams, where fishing and fishing methods are restricted.

(1) The following zones are closed to all fishing:

(A) Black River within the wing walls of Clearwater Dam.

(B) Clarence Cannon Reregulation Pool within four hundred feet (400') below Clarence Cannon Dam (the no-boating zone).

(C) Greer Spring Branch as posted upstream from the south boundary of the private reservation.

(D) Lake Taneycomo within seven hundred sixty feet (760') below Table Rock Dam.

(E) Osage River within two hundred twenty-five feet (225') below Bagnell Dam, except that live bait may be taken only by dip net and throw net.

(F) Osage River/Lake of the Ozarks within five hundred twenty-five feet (525') on the left descending bank and nine hundred seventy-seven feet (977') on the right descending bank below

Truman Dam in the U.S. Army Corps of Engineers' restricted zone.

(G) St. Francis River within two hundred twenty-five feet (225') below Wappapello Dam.

(2) Fish may be taken only by pole and line from:

(A) Blue Springs Lake, except that shad also may be taken by dip net and throw net.

(B) Clarence Cannon Reregulation Pool from the posted powerline crossing upstream to the no-boating zone four hundred feet (400') below Clarence Cannon Dam.

(C) Little Platte River between Smithville Dam and U.S. Highway 169.

(D) Longview Lake, except that shad also may be taken by dip net and throw net.

(E) Sac River from below Stockton Dam to Highway 32.

(F) Salt River from below Clarence Cannon Reregulation Pool Dam to Route A except that fish may also be taken by **bow** as prescribed in 3 CSR 10-6.550 from the noboating zone (one thousand one hundred feet (1,100') below the Reregulation Dam) to Route A.

(G) Lake Taneycomo between the closed zone seven hundred sixty feet (760') below Table Rock Dam to the mouth of Fall Creek.

(3) Fish may be taken by all prescribed methods except trotlines, throwlines and limb lines from:

(A) Bull Shoals Lake from below Powersite Dam to Highway 76.

(B) Osage River from the no-fishing zone below Bagnell Dam to U.S. Highway 54. Snagging, snaring and grabbing are also excluded in this zone.

(C) Osage River/Lake of the Ozarks from the no-fishing zone below Truman Dam to U.S. Highway 65. Snagging, snaring, grabbing and use of jug lines are also excluded in this zone.

(D) Black River within seven hundred feet (700') below the spillway walls of Clearwater Dam. **Bowfishing** and **gigging** are also excluded in this zone.

(E) St. Francis River within seven hundred feet (700') below the spillway walls of Wappapello Dam. **Bowfishing** and **gigging** are also excluded in this zone.

(4) Fish may be taken by all prescribed methods except **gig**, atlatl, crossbow and **bow** on the following waters and as further restricted in subsections (5)(A), (B), (C), (D), (F), (H), (J), (K) and (M) of this rule. Fish taken by **gig**, atlatl, crossbow and **bow** may not be possessed on these waters or the banks thereof.

(A) Barren Fork Creek in Shannon County from County Road A-D to its confluence with Sinking Creek.

(B) Blue Springs Creek in Crawford County from Blue Springs to its confluence with Meramec River.

(C) Crane Creek in Stone and Lawrence counties upstream from Quail Spur Crossing on Stone County Road 13-195.

(D) Current River from Montauk State Park to Cedar Grove.

(E) Eleven Point River from its confluence with Greer Spring Branch to Turner Mill.

(F) Little Piney Creek from the Phelps County line in Sections 9 and 16 of T35N, R8W, including Piney Spring Branch and Lane Spring Branch, to Milldam Hollow Access.

(G) Mill Creek in Phelps County from Yelton Spring to its confluence with Little Piney Creek including Wilkins Spring and spring branch.

(H) North Fork of White River in Ozark County from the upper outlet of Rainbow Spring to Patrick Bridge.

(I) Spring Creek in Phelps County from Relfe Spring to its confluence with Big Piney River.

(5) Fish may be taken by all prescribed methods except that only flies and artificial lures may be used when fishing and soft plastic baits and natural and scented baits are specifically prohibited in:

(A) Barren Fork Creek in Shannon County from County Road A-D to its confluence with Sinking Creek.

(B) Blue Springs Creek in Crawford County from Blue Springs to its confluence with Meramec River.

(C) Crane Creek in Stone and Lawrence counties upstream from Quail Spur Crossing on Stone County Road 13-195.

(D) Current River from Montauk State Park to Cedar Grove.

(E) Dry Fork Creek in Crawford and Phelps counties from the elevated cable crossing to its confluence with the Meramec River.

(F) Eleven Point River in Oregon County from its confluence with Greer Spring Branch to Turner Mill.

(G) Hickory Creek in Newton County from the Highway 86 bridge to its confluence with Shoal Creek from November 1 through the last day of February.

(H) Lake Taneycomo in Taney County from the closed zone seven hundred sixty feet (760') below Table Rock Dam to the mouth of Fall Creek.

(I) Little Piney Creek from the Phelps County Line in Sections 9 and 16 of T35N, R8W, including Piney Spring Branch and Lane Spring Branch, to Milldam Hollow Access.

(J) Meramec River in Crawford and Phelps counties from Highway 8 bridge to Scott's Ford.

(K) Mill Creek in Phelps County from Yelton Spring to its confluence with Little Piney Creek including Wilkins Spring and spring branch.

(L) North Fork of White River in Ozark County from the upper outlet of Rainbow Spring to Patrick Bridge.

(M) Roubidoux Creek from the elevated utility cable crossing approximately one-half (1/2) mile below the Business I-44 bridge in Waynesville to its confluence with the Gasconade River.

(N) Spring Creek in Phelps County from Relfe Spring to its confluence with Big Piney River.

Editor's Note: Bow and river giging are unusual and uncommon sports in some areas and some Forest Service personnel may not be familiar with it. It is recommended the reader make a copy of the state regulations and keep it with him/her or in the vehicle when going bow gigging.

Index